D0387772

# SHINING PATH

# SHINING PATH

*Terror and Revolution in Peru*

Simon Strong

TIMES BOOKS

RANDOM HOUSE

All rights reserved under International and Pan-American Copyright Conventions. Published in the United States by Times Books, a division of Random House, Inc., New York. This book was originally published in Great Britain by HarperCollins Publishers, London, in 1992.

Library of Congress Cataloging-in-Publication Data
Strong, Simon.
    Shining path: terror and revolution in Peru/by Simon Strong.—1st ed.
      p.   cm.
    Includes bibliographical references.
    ISBN-0-8129-2180-1
    1. Sendero Luminoso (Guerrilla group)   2. Peru—History—1968–1992
3. Government, Resistance to—Peru—History—20th century.
    I. Title.
F3448.2.S77   1993
985.06'33—dc20                                                    92-27404

BOOK DESIGN BY SUSAN HOOD

Manufactured in the United States of America on acid-free paper
9  8  7  6  5  4  3  2
First U.S. Edition

*For Luciana*

The force of revolutionaries is not in their scholarship; it is in their faith, in their passion, in their will. It is a religious, mystical, spiritual force. It is the force of the Myth.

*José Carlos Mariátegui, 1925*

# Acknowledgments

This book is based on hundreds of interviews carried out between 1988 and 1991, as well as on documents, articles, and books. In particular I should like to acknowledge my debts to Gustavo Gorriti and his excellent book, *Sendero, Historia de la Guerra Milenaria en el Perú* (vol. 1), which mainly covers the years 1980 to 1982, and the late Alberto Flores Galindo, whose classic work, *Buscando Un Inca*, traces the history and spirit of Indian resistance in Peru. John Hemming's *The Conquest of the Incas* was also invaluable.

Among the many people to whom I offer my great thanks for providing me with the benefits of their knowledge and expertise in diverse forms are: Jean-Marie Ansion, Luis Arce, Armando Barreda, Héctor Béjar, Enrique Bernales, Bishop Augusto Beuzeville, Rolando Breña, Manuel Burga, Humberto Campodónico, David Chambers, Edmundo Cruz, Ibán De Rentería, "Elva," "Enrique," Colonel Bob Froude, Father Robert Gloisten, José Gonzalez, Raúl Gonzalez, Manuel Granados, Father Gustavo Gutiérrez, César Hildebrandt, General Adrián Huamán, General Sinesio Jarama, General Héctor Jhon Caro, Michael Kenny, Nelson Manrique, Germán Medina, Caleb Meza, "Miguel," Mario Munive, Enrique Obando, Adolfo Olaechea, Juan Ossio, James Painter, Salvador Palomino, Miguel Angel Rodríguez Rivas, Julio Roldán, Father Michael Smith, Francisco Soberón, Janet Talavera, Carlos Tapia, Alfredo Torres, Jimmy Torres, Bill Tupman, Colonel Christopher Van der Noot, Fernando Yovera, Elvia Zanábria, and Enrique Zileri.

I would also like to express my deep gratitude for their support to the library at *The Independent*, James Blount, Nick Law, Tony Daniels, Bill Hamilton, Sally Bowen, Tony Cavanagh, Jonathan Cavanagh, and my industrious and eternally unflappable assistant, Ana María Díaz.

The Peruvian publications of which I have made abundant use are *Caretas*, *Sí*, *Oiga*, *Que Hacer*, *Expreso*, *El Comercio*, *La República*, and *El Diario*. A full bibliography may be found at the end of this book. Organizations that have provided their assistance include the Association for Human Rights (APRODEH), the National Library in Lima, the Library of Social Sciences at the Catholic University, the Centre of Development Studies and Promotion (DESCO), and the Andean Commission of Jurists.

# Preface

Miguel swung the black Saab Turbo 900 over the arched bridge towards Gamla Stan, the old island city at the heart of watery Stockholm. The Italianate façade of one of the biggest palaces in the world reared up in shadow ahead. "That's the King's house," he said and, nodding with a wrinkling of the nose to the columned bulk on his right, added, "That's Parliament." The disdain was so slight it was almost unconscious. Miguel's fine Latin features and well-groomed mane of dark hair glowed with a cultivated but rather fragile sense of self-assurance. He was bordering thirty yet still a mother's boy; warm, presentable, considerate, and honest, but burdened with a dream that clouded his good-natured gray-tinted eyes.

That dream—in the age of glasnost and perestroika—was Communist revolution, thousands of miles away in Peru. For Miguel, who was committed to the overthrow of not just his own state but of all others as well, Stockholm's statuesque symbols of European monarchy and democracy were quaint relics of history. The worldwide collapse of Communistic regimes was, for him, nothing but a brief interlude in the march of time. They had strayed from the paths of Marx, Lenin, and Mao and thereby brought about their own downfall. The revolution would triumph one day as surely as day followed night, as surely as monkey became man. And the revolutionary flame was now burning in the mountains, coast, and jungles of South

America. The word was being spread by the Communist Party of Peru, nicknamed Shining Path, which was led by one man: the brother-in-law of Miguel, Abimael Guzmán.

I had last seen Miguel four and a half years earlier, when he was visiting Bolivia with his rather earnest but beautiful Swedish girlfriend, Kristina. We met in a Chinese restaurant in Cochabamba during Carnival in February 1986. The two previous days had been spent avoiding water bombs and traveling from Oruro, the heart of a mining zone and host to a magnificent Carnival procession that had ended triumphantly, as everybody said it did every year, in blasts of lightning and a torrential thunderstorm that cleansed the fruits of excess, washed away the old agricultural year, and baptized the new.

Among the multitude of colorful masked and costumed figures were the ragged characters representing contemporary Indian peasant life; draped in dirt-brown sacking, their neck labels read DYING OF HUNGER, WIFE OF THE DEVIL, and TODAY IS LIKE THIS; TOMORROW IS ANOTHER DAY. While the Cochabamba bus weaved among the Andes, an Indian dietitian had lectured on the Tibetan Book of the Dead before discussing parallels between Oriental religion and subatomic physics. Amid the ubiquitous presence of the Far East—there was spirited public concern about plans to let five thousand Chinese families migrate from Hong Kong—a large, white American had boasted in a restaurant called the Gandhi International of how, after he had been soaked by a Carnival water bomb, he had promptly punched the culprit's face in—"His teeth went all over the floor."

The Carnival, the Indians, the poverty, the odd kinship with the Far East, the aggrieved and contemptuous superiority of the North American: It was all a foretaste of Peru. So, too, was Miguel. The first I had read of Shining Path was in a Chilean newspaper article the previous December, and there I was eating wun tun with a man near the heart of the party. Everything I had heard about the revolutionaries had prompted cravings to interview Guzmán, and the fortuitous meeting with Miguel seemed a step in the right direction.

Miguel—a pseudonym I have given him for his protection—spent the evening praising his brother-in-law and justifying the party's cause, eagerly backed up by Kristina, who was younger than he and at that time even more vigorous a defender of the faith than he was: Where he was soft-spoken, she was strident. They outlined how Shining Path received no help from the Soviet Union or China; how it "confiscated" its weapons from the "genocidal" forces of order; how the atrocities it was accused of were mostly committed by the government and that, when there were excesses, they were sacrifices for the greater good—although Miguel did not always agree with them; how farmers tilled their land by day and bombed electricity pylons by night; and how he had lived with Guzmán and his sister, Augusta, for several years. He blasted the popular myth that the rebels trafficked in cocaine; nevertheless, he had some on him and we snorted a little in a dark corner.

Almost inevitably, the violence of the ideology preached by Miguel seemed to spill over into his life as an exile. He and Kristina were holidaying in Brazil and Bolivia and unable to cross into his home country in case Miguel was arrested. As it was, they had suffered problems: They were in a fight when she was nearly raped, and on a separate occasion were detained for a day because they had forgotten to carry their passports. However, their visit was very possibly more for business than pleasure purposes anyway. According to the Peruvian embassy in Stockholm, the passports of several exiles with Shining Path sympathies are laden with stamps for Bolivia and Ecuador. It is presumed that they make contact with the party in order to convey funds and correspondence.

By the time of my next meeting with Miguel, in Stockholm in 1990, I was living in Peru, and Shining Path had dramatically expanded, much as Miguel had foretold. It was autumn and, as the dewy concord between the superpowers of the Eastern and Western blocs was being marked by a joint military march through the city by the Moscow Marine Band and the U.S. Army band, Pershing's Own, Miguel confessed that Kristina, whom he loved deeply, had left him because she had taken against the revolution. "She rejected the violence and felt I dedicated too much time to the party," he said, as he ate apple strudel on the edge of a tiny, cobbled square on the medieval island city of Gamla Stan. He had had to choose between his love for her and the revolution. One woman or the masses. Kristina now lived a couple of hundred kilometers away, and they had last seen each other two years earlier. Possibly torn apart deep down by his own doubts about Shining Path, doubts that were smothered by loyalty and love for his family, he nevertheless insisted it would not be long before he returned to the Andes to join the fight.

Even as he spoke, Kristina stepped into the square, clutching a baby. The color drained from Miguel's face as he recognized her and muttered who it was, his eyes transfixed. I was shocked, too. But for me, their paths would not have crossed, and the last time I had seen Miguel was the last time I had seen her. I remained seated as he made his approach, hoping it would be over fast. It was. Mutually amazed, they greeted each other nervously, she keeping her distance. After a few minutes of strained conversation, during which, at the behest of Miguel, I popped up like a jack-in-the-box before returning to my chair, she backed away, swung her head from his gaze, and vanished down an alley in a swirl of woolen scarves. Miguel returned to the table. "It wasn't her baby, it was her sister's," he murmured, looking down at the empty plate. Personal tragedy would strike him directly a few months later: Shining Path announced that his sister, Augusta, was dead.

She died, childless, on November 14, 1988, according to the Peruvian police, although the death was kept a secret by the party's central committee until the police raided a safe house in Lima in early 1991 and uncovered documents and a video suggesting she died neither in action nor of natural causes. The video showed Guzmán, after asking if the camera angles were right, approaching what was evidently his wife's body and kissing her on the forehead. Augusta La Torre, or Comrade Norah, was covered up except for her face, which bore a serene expression as if she were asleep.

During Guzmán's rambling homage over the corpse, he said: "Her passion, her feelings, and her courage storm against my face. . . . How powerful is the power of the masses, how indispensable the party. With the magnificent Marxist-Leninist-Maoist ideology it is capable of generating beings such as Comrade Norah, who prefer to destroy their life rather than damage the Party. . . . In her lamentable confusion of nervous solitude she preferred to be annihilated, to wipe herself out. . . . That was what she said. . . . Without the comrade I am in a lesser place; but that shows the death of the comrade; because we have to understand that we are or we are not Communists. . . ."

Despite Guzmán's implication that, for some unexplained reason, his wife had committed suicide for the sake of the party, repentant letters allegedly confiscated by the police indicated that one faction of the core leadership originally accused Guzmán of her murder.

Simon Strong
November 1991

# Contents

# SHINING PATH

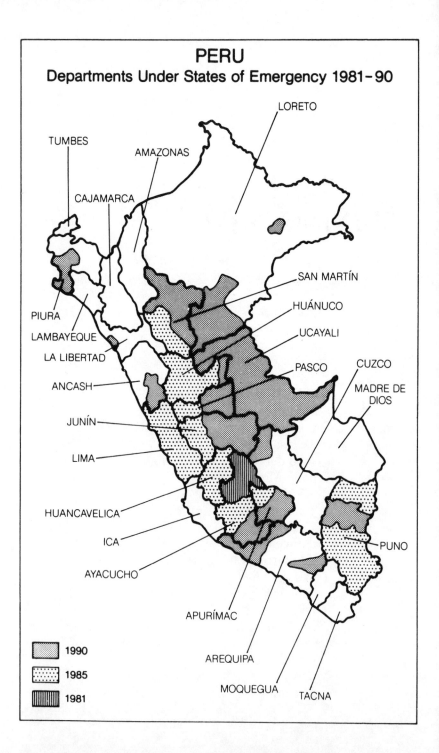

# PERU
## Departments Under States of Emergency 1981-90

LORETO

TUMBES

AMAZONAS

CAJAMARCA

SAN MARTÍN

HUÁNUCO

UCAYALI

PIURA

LAMBAYEQUE

LA LIBERTAD

PASCO

CUZCO

MADRE DE DIOS

ANCASH

JUNÍN

LIMA

HUANCAVELICA

ICA

PUNO

AYACUCHO

APURÍMAC

1990

1985

1981

AREQUIPA

MOQUEGUA    TACNA

# 1

# Rise of the Red Sun

Miguel had left Peru as the guerrilla war heated up in the early 1980s. The direct involvement with Shining Path of his elder sister, Augusta La Torre, who had married Guzmán in 1964, made it impossible for him, his other sister, his five brothers, and his parents to remain. Their names were known to the government and they were likely to be persecuted. They fled to Sweden, having long ago abandoned the family hacienda in the Andes along with its tennis court, swimming pool, and serfs. It was eventually attacked by the rebels; Miguel's uncle, a German-trained dentist, watched it burn. The hacienda had served its purpose. Miguel's father, Carlos, a celebrated lottery winner, bank clerk, and provincial Communist party leader, had allowed it to be used for guerrilla training. Carlos, who had a tendency to name his sons after Soviet leaders—which became awkward once the household spurned the Soviets as "revisionists"—had married off his beautiful daughter Augusta to Abimael Guzmán in what was regarded by some of the latter's peers, albeit with envy, as an adroit piece of social climbing by a semifeudal family on the slide. Despite his nickname, Spartacus, other Communists saw Carlos as a carefree drinker and womanizer, a sly operator who did not take the revolution seriously, preferring to live among the jaded colonial furniture and tatty carpets of his house near the Plaza de Armas in the city of Ayacucho rather than take to the mountains for the

3

armed struggle. The nearest most Communists of his generation expected to get was the hiss and crackle of Moscow Radio.
The family was served by *pongos*, or house servants, excess to
the hacienda's needs. It was there in the city, at The Three
Masks, that Augusta, a teenager, was wooed by the stern, book-
ish lecturer who had mesmerized the university since his arrival
in 1963.

Abimael Guzmán became part of the family, a second father
to Carlos's younger children. He brought Christmas presents,
smoked, drank beer, preached revolution, and was never without a book. He appeared to study almost all the time. The
family adored him. "To know him is such a tremendous pride,"
said Miguel. "To remember him is to make me cry. What luck
I have had! He knew everything; you did not want the time to
pass because he spoke so beautifully, with such wisdom and
logic. I would do anything for him. But Mama would sometimes be mistaken; people would get angry with her and she
would cry. Abimael would then explain everything until she
felt better. He once told her that her problem was that she was
too good. This made her weep all the more. He loves her as a
mother."

The polite, bespectacled lecturer who had taken over the
reins of the philosophy department at the University of San
Cristóbal de Huamanga, in Ayacucho, an isolated, decaying
city eight thousand feet above sea level and populated mainly
by undernourished, poncho-clad Indians, had two doctoral dis-
sertations under his belt: "The Kantian Theory of Space" and
"The Bourgeois Democratic State." They were the beginnings
of an ideological journey that over the next decade would orig-
inate an idiosyncratic form of Maoism given an explosive potency by the Indians' latent, bitter hatred of the state.

Guzmán was born in the village of Tambo near the old
southern port of Mollendo on December 3, 1934, the illegitimate son of a prosperous import wholesaler. His father lived
with another woman above his store in front of the market.
They sold rice and sugar. His mother, Berenice Reynoso,
moved in with her infant down the road in a humble wooden
house boasting two rooms and a yard where they cooked.
When Guzmán was five years old, Berenice died and he was

left to some uncles to care for; eventually, he was sent to live with his father at the Lima port of Callao, where he spent his first year in secondary school. Once more his father moved, this time to the aristocratic, pearl-white southern city of Arequipa, which rests at the foot of the cone-shaped, snow-capped El Misti volcano. Guzmán was now ensconced in a spacious, elegant home in a smart neighborhood; the building has since become a school named the College of the Divine Master.

Remembered as a wealthy young student who had ten times as much pocket money as his classmates, Guzmán excelled at the exclusive La Salle College, run by Jesuit priests. A teacher recalled him showing off his money and spending it lavishly on ice cream. But at the same time, he was aloof and obscure. He was a loner. He never asked questions in class, never attended parties, and never had girlfriends. Instead, he worked. Guzmán was the top pupil in the third year, the third in the fourth year, and the second in the fifth. He consistently won top marks for behavior and tidiness. And he showed a peculiar talent and zest for organizing. In the 1952 school magazine he wrote a report on dividing students into groups to study culture, sports, religion, journalism, and economics: "At the head of each group there will be a leader," he specified. "The group leader will appoint four assistants . . . there will be a central committee made up of nine members."

Aged nineteen, Guzmán went on to study law and philosophy in Arequipa at the National University of San Agustín. It was there that he came under the spell of a formidable logician who provided the backbone of his education. The friendship was so strong that Guzmán dedicated to him the very dissertation that marked their intellectual watershed. He called Miguel Angel Rodríguez Rivas his "dear friend and master." Rivas was his role model. According to his pupils, the philosophy lecturer was a rigorous, even masochistic disciplinarian who was in his office by six o'clock in the morning because he believed too much sleep wasted brain cells. Inflexible and authoritarian, he had a mystical desire for truth. His lectures were theatrical and erudite; they captivated and subjugated. He would sacrifice anything on the sacred altar of reason.

Guzmán was his prize pupil. Rivas, who was alienated from

his earlier Marxism because of his revulsion for Stalin and his admiration of Kant, guided his young disciple through the main German philosophers. He invited him to join an élite group of intellectuals which met in a schoolroom on Friday nights to discuss Peru's future. When the room was closed, they met instead at cafés and drank beer. They argued how an economic system could be organized to increase national production and ensure a fairer distribution of excess profits; how to build an educational system that, said Rivas, "would prepare people to respond to the demands and necessities of society, especially the marginal sectors"; and how to develop "an order of ideas which would permit us to overcome our dependence not only economically and politically, but culturally, on Europe and the United States."

Despite Rivas's influence, the Marxist convictions of Guzmán steadily grew in strength. An article on twentieth-century physics that he wrote for the group's magazine, *Man and World*, in 1955 included a pun on quantum leaps. Guzmán gleefully drew a revolutionary parallel. The following year he was admitted to the Peruvian Philosophy Society. He read avidly but was particularly fond of Dostoevsky and the contemporary socialist Chilean and Peruvian poets, Pablo Neruda and César Vallejo. He liked classical music: Beethoven was his favorite, although he also listened to Bach, Wagner, Brahms, and Mozart. He was intrigued by Rossini and Vivaldi, but dismissed the latter because he found the baroque melodies sentimental and, according to a fellow student, typical of "idiotic palace toadies."

Usually in dark attire, he was never without a jacket and wore it, informally for his time, with his shirt open at the collar. He lived with his father and his stepmother, Isabel Jorquera, who loved him as much as her own children. Her affection was reciprocated and he got on well with his half brothers. Much later, years after the revolution had ignited the land and when any security lapse in communications could cost him his freedom, Guzmán continued to send his stepmother birthday cards. Relations with his father were not so cozy. A student friend, Teresa Lecaros, said, "He held a grudge against his father, who he claimed had discriminated between him and his brother Edgardo by giving Edgardo everything and him not. He complained of being sent to state school in his earlier years." A Peruvian diplomat linked to Guzmán's own family by marriage corroborated the resentment and added: "His father wishes Abimael was dead."

Rivas remembered his student with warmth. "Abimael was an outstanding man and always well informed. He was very kind but dry, a man of few words who communicated only with his friends. He was a good, whole person, always looking to improve institutions he had known or belonged to. He wanted to work for truth and see justice carried out." Colleagues described Guzmán as serious, a man with powerful eyes who commanded respect. "If he were not involved in politics," said one, "he would be a great teacher or a just and brilliant judge." His colleagues went on to be leaders in their fields.

At the same time as he was writing tracts on Pascal's triangle and quantum theory, Guzmán started to play a more militant political role. He came under the influence of a Stalinist painter, Carlos de la Riva, and joined the Peruvian Communist party. He helped Rivas try to modernize the university by founding a school for social science and psychology, separating anthropology from history, and teaching statistics. The reforms failed, partly because there were not enough lecturers able to teach the courses, but not before Guzmán, who had by now graduated, lectured in mathematics. "He was very demanding, more persuasive than Rivas, more of a friend," said a pupil. In 1961, the collapse of the reforms forced Rivas out of the university. The lecturers who supported him were expelled, most of them dispersing to Lima or overseas. Guzmán was kept on in an effort to placate the students.

The blotting out of the university reforms coincided with Guzmán's mounting criticism of the local Communist party as idle, bureaucratic, and lacking in political presence. The frustration in both cases was made all the more poignant by Fidel Castro's victorious revolution in Cuba. "If you are admirers of the Cuban revolution," he told his students, "you have to be like Fidel, because to do the same here it is necessary to work, work, and work."

Inspired, like much of his generation in Latin America, by

Castro's romantic and even relatively bloodless military triumph, Guzmán was also bitterly moved by the poverty he encountered when he helped Rivas carry out a census of the Arequipa population after an earthquake devastated the city in 1960. Hitherto he had lived a comfortable, cloistered intellectual existence without experiencing at first hand the appalling conditions suffered by the poor. The earthquake laid bare the misery of the families in the outlying areas. It stripped the roofs off their homes and razed the mud-brick walls. It exposed the squalor of men, women, and children cramped inside, living on damp earthen floors, crouched around chimney stoves, the houses dark, cold, and airless, with no running water. Guzmán took charge of one hundred pupils taking a census in the west quarter, moving around in army lorries, typing up the information, and organizing it in perforated card files.

Rivas said: "He was very efficient. But what he saw was the fundamental basis for his conversion from a simple ideologue into the active leader of a militant organization. He would say it was one thing to read about poverty and another thing to see it. Once, he remarked on two families who were so poor that not only had they been living in the same room, but whose space was demarcated by a stream that carried the foul-smelling waste from a leather curer next door. Guzmán was horrified."

His two theses were written the following year. In his 178-page "The Kantian Theory of Space," Guzmán argued that Kant was outmoded by the discoveries in modern physics. The thesis was not original but considered by Rivas as "very acceptable" for its time. While respecting Kant for centering philosophy on reason, Guzmán rejected him because of Kant's dependence on Newtonian physics and Euclidean geometry. Guzmán cited relativity theory and stressed that other forms of geometry apart from that of Euclid were equally valid. He perceived Kant as a subjective idealist superseded by the empiric materialism of Einstein. He concluded: "The space-time continuum does not constitute a reference system on the base of which one can build unvarying natural laws."

The philosophy dissertation reflected Guzmán's firm adherence to dialectical materialism and Marxism. It marked his split from Rivas, who a decade earlier had moved in the opposite direction, from Marx to Kant. More than twenty years on, Rivas would be lecturing to the Center of Higher Military Studies as Guzmán ambushed army patrols.

Guzmán's next thesis, for a doctorate in law, was an emotional, uninhibited apologia for revolution. It interpreted history from a Marxist viewpoint and poured scorn on the bourgeoisie's "lyrical affirmations" of liberty and equality, which, he wrote, were useless to the trapped and downtrodden masses. Elections, said Guzmán, were controlled by the manipulation of electoral law and by the economic forces behind the press and media.

He denounced man's exploitation of man. Feudal, semi-feudal, colonialist, capitalist, and imperialist exploitation were "no less cruel and inhuman" than old-fashioned slavery. The Spanish exploitation of Latin America had taken place "without any regard for the interests of these lands and their occupants. . . . [I]t cost, in Potosi [Bolivia] alone, the deaths of five million Indians in two and a half centuries." Guzmán recounted how England had sought to wrest control from Spain of her American colonies in order to establish commercial dominion. He cited the famous words of the English foreign secretary George Canning, who, after the Battle of Ayacucho of 1824, in which the British had helped to rout the Spanish royalists at the last battle for Peruvian independence, wrote in a letter: "The fight has been hard but it is won. The deed is done. The nail is driven in. Spanish America is free and if we do not mismanage our affairs, she is English."

For Guzmán, all oppressed societies had an inalienable right to rebellion. He summoned John Locke and John Milton to his cause. The writer of *Paradise Lost* and *The Tenure of Kings and Magistrates* was cited for endorsing a nation's right to topple a monarch who had abandoned or abused the contractual clauses of his authority. (Milton was writing in defense of the execution of Charles I in 1649.) Thomas Jefferson, who drew up the Declaration of Independence in 1776, was quoted for deeming rebellion "as necessary in the political world as storms in the physical." Voltaire and Rousseau were called upon for further reinforcement.

Guzmán ended on the loose, prophetic, semi-mystical note that would set the tone for the future. "The destiny of peoples resides in the peoples themselves and nobody other than they has the right to order and decide their direction: This is the greatest achievement we owe to the historical era that is now being consummated and knocking at its end. Fresh winds are blowing and stiffening the unbribable soul of the peoples. Humanity shakes before our very eyes and, in its inextinguishable and undefeatable ascending march toward better times, gives birth to new societies."

In the early 1960s, scattered peasant uprisings were beginning to erupt in Peru. Communities organized themselves into labor unions within haciendas. Peasant marches, rallies, and land grabs shook the Sierra. At the same time, in the universities Marxism was displacing the party that had traditionally harnessed leftish sentiment, the American Popular Revolutionary Alliance (APRA), following APRA's electoral collusion with a vicious right-wing former military dictator, Manuel Odría. In Ayacucho, where the University of San Cristóbal de Huamanga had just been reopened with an infusion of international aid intended to revitalize one of the country's most neglected regions, the Marxist rector, Efraín Morote, offered Guzmán the chance of running the philosophy faculty. Initially he refused, apparently unwilling to abandon his native Arequipa. He was finally persuaded by a colleague on the grounds that his hometown, which harbored pockets of considerable wealth founded mainly on the wool industry, was scarcely typical and that he needed to get to know the Sierra.

Ayacucho means Corner of the Dead in Quechua, the main Peruvian Indian language. The city was built by the Spanish as a resting place and military base between Lima and Cuzco in 1539; its original name was San Juan de la Frontera de Huamanga. It was a frontier town from which to fight the rebellious Manco Inca, who had entrenched his troops a few miles north in the ninth-century ruins of the Huari empire. According to the early Peruvian chronicler Cieza de León, it was said that travelers were being captured there by the Inca's warriors, who "tortured them in the presence of their women, avenging themselves for the injuries they had suffered by impaling them with sharp stakes forced into their victims' lower parts until they emerged from their mouths." In 1825, it was renamed Ayacucho in memory of those slain in the last battle for independence.

The city is a model of colonial architecture. It boasts thirty-three churches, several of them with altars decorated in gold leaf. Arches run along the old stone mansions lining the squares. The air is clear and thin but without the bite of higher altitudes; the sunny, temperate climate is prone to torrential rain and sudden wind storms. Its mainly Indian population of about fifty thousand lives mostly off agricultural commerce. The department of Ayacucho is rich in corn, potatoes, and alfalfa. The lower, tropical regions to the east, where the mountains fold into the Amazon jungle, produce coffee and fruit; latterly, they have hosted a booming trade in coca, the raw material for the drug cocaine.

In the bleak, frozen uplands, herds of cattle, sheep, goats, pigs, horses, llamas, and alpacas compete for existence in exhausted pastures. In the jungle, timber merchants see to the gradual deforestation. Gold, silver, copper, and other metals are abundant but the mining potential is largely untapped because of the lack of good roads.

When Abimael Guzmán arrived in Ayacucho, the department's total population was about 450,000. Three quarters of the people scraped out a living by subsistence agriculture. A fifth of the peasants belonged, as serfs, to haciendas. In exchange for every acre and a quarter of land, a peasant would be expected to labor three days a week on the land of the *patrón* and to provide him with a house servant or *pongo* for a couple of months a year. The servants would usually be the peasants' younger sons and daughters, since they were the least useful in the fields. If a girl *pongo* entered the house of the *patrón* as a virgin, she rarely remained so; any subsequent offspring would reside in the cramped, straw-roofed, mud-and-stone huts of their mothers. It would be the child's privilege to have the *patrón* as its godfather and even, if she were a girl, as a lover once more. Feudal relationships ridiculed those of the family.

Those peasant communities that were housed on their own land were still mainly dependent on the haciendas for animal pasture and irrigated, arable fields. Their rent was also paid in labor. When haciendas were divided up and sold, incumbent peasants had no protection. Often perceived as parasitic colonists, they would be evicted by force. Local court rulings in their favor were easily overturned by the landowners' influence over higher courts farther away, beyond the reach of the original plaintiffs. The peasants' homes were then burned down and their harvests trampled on and eaten by the hacienda's cattle. The families would be left to join the steady stream of migrants to the towns and coast. They would arrive in an alien culture, unable to read or write and with just a smattering of Spanish.

With its grinding poverty, its absence of schools and medical posts, its malnutrition and forty-five-year life expectancy, and its contempt of central government, Ayacucho was a rich breeding ground for the Marxist idealists who took the city by storm after the University of San Cristóbal de Huamanga was reopened in 1959. Ayacucho was also a region whose indigenous Huari population had stubbornly defied the expansion of the Inca empire before being militarized under the Spanish; it was the site of the last battle against Spanish rule; a strategic base for repelling the Chilean invasion during the War of the Pacific in 1879–1883; and, of late, it had nurtured sporadic peasant uprisings in protest over illegal land seizures. No other part of Peru had such a warlike tradition.

San Cristóbal de Huamanga is one of Latin America's oldest universities. It was founded in 1677 by a bishop, won the approval of Charles II of Spain, and received a papal edict from Pope Innocent XI. However, the project initially floundered because it was thought the school would be unable to compete with the attractions of the richly endowed National University of San Marcos in Lima. It opened the following century but was closed down in the 1800s for being considered, once again, minor and unimportant. It resumed its activities as part of an ambitious drive to end the city's isolation. Foreign lecturers were hired, and high salaries were paid to attract a good staff.

Ayacucho's isolation had engendered conservatism and an intense religious life. Catholicism was heavily entrenched in the department. Twice a day, when the church bell of San Francisco de Asís tolled, passersby would cross themselves, kneel down, bow their heads, and pray in the street. Long lines waited outside the confessional boxes. The colorful, emotional religious festivals were attended by thousands and were famous throughout Peru. The church offered hope and diversion to an isolated, depressed, and suffering population. Saying the rosary and going to mass also broke the boredom of a virtually pre-electric age, when television and video had as yet failed to materialize, when the only secular attractions were the dilapidated cinema and the occasional visit of a traveling circus.

The reopening of the university in Ayacucho marked the decline of the church. To the fury of their parents and grandparents, young people slowly stopped attending mass. Not only did the university absorb its students' time and devotion, but its authorities introduced a compulsory first-year lecture course called the *ciclo básico* that was deemed to teach students the "scientific concept" of society. Abimael Guzmán became one of the course's main lecturers. The Darwinian evolution of man was preached in such a way as to overturn Catholicism and, in the same breath, led students toward historical materialism. Marxism was carefully not mentioned; it was left until later. Students were taught that societies created gods out of ignorance and underdevelopment. They would learn that religion was "the sigh of the oppressed creature, the heart of a heartless world, just as it is the spirit of spiritless conditions"—that religion was "the opium of the people." The teachings were used as the cornerstone for the rest of the Marxist creed.

So powerful was the effect of the *ciclo básico* that a second university was opened in the city to combat the anti-Catholicism. However, the Catholic University of Ayacucho, as it was called, was swamped by the tide. Its administration was taken over by Marxists, and theology studies were replaced by courses in historical materialism. The university was eventually closed down and absorbed into San Cristóbal de Huamanga. The church was impotent in its anger: Livid priests were reduced to stopping outside the university in the middle of festival processions and shouting that Communists were people of the devil.

Guzmán, who joined the local branch of the Communist party, used the name Alvaro as his first nom de guerre. But he was affectionately nicknamed Shampoo because, said one of his former students in the early 1960s "he washed your brains, he cleaned your thoughts when confused; he clarified problems, he had an answer for everything." Most of his students doted on him. "He was serious and occasionally amiable," said the student, "always very correct and baronial, but very, very dry. He cultivated uncertainty and mystery around him. For his supporters, whatever he said was the last word on any subject. He made them so optimistic, so self-confident. That self-confidence is what I remember most about a friend who was later killed in the jungle by the army."

Another student, who attended a Guzmán lecture while on a visit from Lima, described the packed classroom scene: "Everybody was in awe of him but concentrating totally. It was as if he had a halo around him. He lectured using a blackboard, speaking with a cold, intellectual passion which was academic rather than political. He was relating ideas to the social conditions which bore them. It was not so much the things he said but the way he said them—he was captivatingly dynamic." A fellow Marxist lecturer and future congressman said Guzmán's speeches were reiterative and boring to read but delivered with chilling charisma: "He was a fanatic who had the power to fanaticize others." Guzmán's slightly bowed head and alert, curved poise won him the nickname of El Tigre—"The Tiger."

Guzmán stood out as an intellect within the Communist party. He lent freely from his voluminous library, knew more than anyone else, and directed everyone's reading. Party rivals said his sense of humor was confined to the ironic pleasure he took in other people's political or doctrinal mistakes. While giving the appearance of listening to other points of view, he was purported to be completely intolerant of them. He never debated in public. He was described as a pope among bishops. It was Guzmán's academic guise that misled many into believing he would never take to the "armed struggle" hitherto associated with fiery street rebels who whipped up protest rallies and clashed with police and troops.

Personal relations were subordinated to party politics and the revolution. He told a friend: "The only thing which interests me in life is to bring about the revolution in Peru." He preferred to walk unaccompanied in the street; his wife, Augusta, followed a short distance behind. Even in small, private parties they were rarely seen holding hands. Those parties, at which he was still never seen without a jacket, were like a continuation of the Arequipa study groups except that Guzmán was "like a pastor talking with his flock about the Virgin Mary," said a former colleague. Doubting Thomases were expelled. The chosen few drank beer, danced to waltzes and Carnival music played on the guitar, and sang Indian *huaynos* with Communist lyrics, as well as songs from the Spanish Civil War. "Alvaro" drank but never danced. "I only once saw him totally drunk, everyone was," said a close acquaintance later to be damned as a revisionist. "I helped him to the bathroom where he was sick."

Guzmán encountered the Peruvian Communist party in total disarray. Founded in 1930 out of the Socialist party created by José Carlos Mariátegui, who died young after a bone disease crippled one leg and caused the other to be amputated, the Communist party had followed a pro-Moscow line and failed to harness significant popular support. Its leadership was stale and bureaucratic and by the time of the Sino-Soviet split in 1963 it had explicitly opted for peaceful revolution from within the state rather than for armed rebellion. In 1964, the party fragmented as the Maoists and Muscovites mutually expelled each other. The national rupture was provoked by that in Ayacucho, where Guzmán demanded the party take a Stalinist turn. He formed an alliance with the leader of the Peking "Red Flag" faction, led by a dim-witted lawyer, Saturnino Paredes, who would later be cast out and his group swallowed up.

The philosophy lecturer set about his revolutionary preparations stealthily. Already reasonably knowledgeable of German, French, and English, he began to learn Quechua. He went from house to house in the poorer districts, collecting socioeconomic information and building up contacts with families and especially with students. His assiduous extracurricular philanthropy at the university was rewarded when he was made director of the *ciclo básico* course. He formed a school for practical studies in the countryside, whereby students in the education faculty disseminated communism in illiterate peasant communities under the guise of teaching practice. These students were to be the backbone of Guzmán's organization once they graduated and took up their posts as teachers.

Guzmán's first political success was to organize a student protest against the presence of the United States Peace Corps. David Scott Palmer, a U.S. lecturer, was expelled. "He was an admirer of Castro," said Palmer. "I remember that sometimes I lacked a pupil for four days in a row in class and I would ask what had become of him. The students would sing me a Cuban *bolero* and then say, 'You should ask Guzmán.'" Guzmán later dubbed Castro a "revisionist" and his lieutenant and doomed guerrilla leader in Bolivia, Che Guevara, a "chorus girl."

His opening clash with the police followed soon after. Guzmán was arrested briefly after he organized a university rally, which the police scattered on the grounds that it was stirring up the peasantry. Next Guzmán coordinated a peasants' congress and founded the Revolutionary Student Front; the latter formed the base of the future Popular Student Movement, which in turn would work to create the District Federation of Ayacucho. Augusta, who joined the party using the alias "Betty," was entrusted with the People's Feminine Movement. The interweaving web of grass-roots, popular organizations had begun.

After a spell in China in 1965, on the eve of Mao Zedong's Cultural Revolution—when he is said to have met Che Guevara—and with the approval of the peasants' congress, Guzmán joined Red Flag's regional committee in Ayacucho. His fame continued to spread as he built up the party cells; he was soon made secretary general. After her own trip to China, Augusta joined him on the committee and was assigned the job of organizing the departmental committee of Cajamarca in northern Peru. Her alias was changed to "Sara." Meanwhile, Guzmán's closest supporters set about forming the military committee in Ayacucho. The start of the "armed struggle" was still more than a decade away.

Years later, after reminiscing about how the Second World War impressed on him as a child the "transforming capacity of war," and noting his admiration for Stalin, Guzmán described how his eyes lit up during a Chinese explosives class: "When we were finishing the course, they told us anything could be used for an explosion, and then, in the final part, we picked up our pens and they blew up, and we sat down and our seats blew up. It was like fireworks everywhere, perfectly measured to show us that anything could be blown up if one had the ingenuity. I believe that school was essential in my formation and my beginning to value Chairman Mao Zedong."

Guzman's ascendancy within Red Flag won him a place on the national political committee. He was given the key job of party organization and instantly invited to take part in a conspiracy to topple Saturnino Paredes. The plotters, Rolando Breña (alias Eco, Latino, and Zapata) and Jorge Hurtado (alias Yoveraqué, Barea, and Ludovico), were spurned by Guzmán, who used the opportunity to clear out of his way people who promised to be troublesome party opponents. He stuck to Paredes, and the others were expelled. Breña and Hurtado were later elected to the Peruvian Congress.

While Guzmán consolidated his grip on Red Flag's Ayacucho regional committee and embarked on a vigorous campaign of research and peasant organization in the countryside, his star rose further within the university. Guzmán, already on the university's executive council, directed a seminar on university reform, which led to his appointment as head of planning and, a little later, head of university personnel, where he exerted total control over staff appointments. He fired rivals and hired supporters. At this point, he ceased to be a lecturer, although he became a leader of the Ayacucho branch of the teachers' union.

In 1969, the first time bomb exploded. The left-wing military dictatorship, which under General Juan Valesco had taken power in a coup d'état the previous year, plucking president Fernando Belaúnde out of the presidential palace while still in his pajamas, passed a law restricting free high school education. It touched the rawest of nerves. Putting them through school is perceived as the most precious gift the Peruvian poor can bestow on their children. Education is seen as the road to freedom, the means to escape deception and exploitation. Amid nationwide protests, Guzmán's umbrella group of popular organizations, the Defense Front of the People of Ayacucho, accused the government of abolishing free education because it knew "that when the sons of workers and peasants open their eyes it endangers their power and wealth."

Guzmán's work in the university and countryside had galvanized students' and peasants' yearning and respect for education into something greater still. Now it not only offered personal advancement in traditional terms, whether learning to read or becoming an engineer, but its Marxist context had given it a new, concrete force in their lives. Education actually seemed to articulate their aspirations. To bar them from it was, for them, to remove a guiding hand, to confirm the thrust of the Marxist message; it was tantamount to an act of war.

Thousands of people rioted in Ayacucho and the town of Huanta. Protest marches and strikes by students, teachers, and workers were broken up with tear gas and truncheons. Arrests were made and the crowds grew more violent. Police were hit by gasoline bombs. Two children were shot dead for slinging stones; a third was killed by stray bullets, and when her body was carried to Ayacucho's police station the bearers were machine-gunned. Roads were blocked, telephone lines brought down, and bridges destroyed. A police prefect was taken hostage. In Huanta, waves of peasants came down from the mountains to join a march. An old peasant woman at the head of the crowd was promptly killed by police machine-gun fire. Amid further carnage, the inflamed crowd firebombed the police station and forced the police to retreat. Just as the crowd was about to take over the Plaza de Armas, police reinforcements arrived and fired randomly into the human mass. At least fourteen people were killed and fifty-five injured.

The army moved in and established a curfew; air force jets and helicopters buzzed the area; and the new education law was repealed. Guzmán was jailed for a few months in Lima under the accusation of inciting the attacks. While the pro-Moscow Peruvian Communist party and the government blamed the events largely on the CIA—which was claimed to be intent on destabilizing the regime by trying to sabotage agrarian reform—the Catholic church in Ayacucho won few friends by making the military chief the guest of honor at a banquet for the archbishop.

The rampage followed an assembly that Guzmán had organized of delegates from peasant communities in Ayacucho. He succeeded in splitting the powerful Peruvian Peasant Confederation and creating a new departmental organization that formed the basis of yet another national popular organization, the Poor Peasants Movement. The move struck at the heart of Red Flag. The PPC was among the handful of organizations that it still dominated.

In a packed meeting of the university faculty after the Huanta riots, an emissary of Red Flag, Aracelio Castillo, asked to speak. The lecturers slowly realized he was indirectly criticizing Guzmán. Obviously nervous, Castillo tried to suggest with inept and hesitant sarcasm that there were lecturers who, although they spoke much about defending the university's interests against government budget cuts, did little to help. While he was speaking, Guzmán did not deign to look at him. His eyes were shut and he appeared to be asleep. When Castillo finished, however, he asked to speak. Into the rigid silence he remarked, "Rector, excuse me, I've some family affairs I must attend to," and left. Shortly after, Castillo was kicked out of the university by student demand.

A desperate Paredes, increasingly isolated and taken aback by Guzmán's militancy within and outside Red Flag, counterattacked by attempting to freeze Guzmán's party control and brand him a "liquidationist." It appears that Paredes made his move while Guzmán was on his second visit to China following his release from jail in late 1969, forcing Guzmán to cut short his trip. In the face of Paredes's constant refusals to call a national meeting and hold a debate with Guzmán, the Machiavellian lecturer applied the coup de grâce in February 1970. Guzmán staged his own meeting of Red Flag's central committee in which political officers and regional and youth leaders expelled the absent Paredes (whose faction was left with almost nobody, but a few months later "expelled" Guzmán nevertheless).

That was the moment Shining Path was born. Its full name became "The Communist Party of Peru by the Shining Path of José Carlos Mariátegui"—". . . and Marxism, Leninism, Maoism, and the Thoughts of Chairman Gonzalo" would be added later, via another transmutation when Maoism was simply Mao Zedong Thought and there was no mention of Chairman "Gonzalo." If referring to itself in a shortened form, the party came to avoid the words "Shining Path" (in Spanish, "Sendero Luminoso") and to stick to "Communist Party of Peru," which became its official, everyday title. A mere nicety of grammar distinguished it from the pro-Moscow Peruvian Communist party. The reference to Mariátegui was eventually dropped. Meanwhile, "Gonzalo" became Guzmán's nom de guerre. "Gonzalo" is a name of German extraction and means "strife." It was also the name of the brother of the Spanish conquistador, Francisco Pizarro, who on the one hand rebelled against the Spanish crown and on the other mercilessly caused hundreds of Indian porters to die carrying his artillery from Cuzco to Lima. In years to come, using Indians as cannon fodder against the state would be a charge regularly made of his namesake.

Guzmán was left with Red Flag's most committed revolutionaries. Apart from his own bastion of cells and popular organizations in the department of Ayacucho, he acquired some cells in Lima's shantytowns and in several universities and groups in the teachers' union in the capital and the towns of Chiclayo and Huancavelica. Little by little, Guzmán set about building an élite, authoritarian, vertical party which, he said in the pro–Shining Path newspaper, El Diario, had to impose its will on the masses by "showing them overwhelming actions to drive home the ideas" so that the masses would "serve" the party.

At the same time as he was founding several more national popular organizations, sucking in the powerful peasants' federation in the department of Apurímac, Ayacucho's neighbor, and fortifying the alliance between the most radical secondary-school students, university students, and peasants in Ayacucho, Guzmán had hired a posse of like-thinking lecturers at San Cristóbal de Huamanga. It was they and some students who formed Shining Path's intellectual nucleus, devoting themselves to the study of the works of Mariátegui. Shining Path was the only significant left-wing party not to waver in its hostility to General Velasco's dictatorship, which had embarked on an ambitious and long overdue, if disastrous, program of agrarian reform—not that Shining Path had yet been heard of by almost anyone in Peru beyond Ayacucho. But in Maoist orthodoxy and Mariátegui's dreams of Indian revindication, it found a revolutionary identity as all around were losing theirs.

Ayacucho, meanwhile, was changing. By the early 1970s the military dictatorship, labeled fascist by Shining Path, had expanded governmental presence in the city, and private banks had followed in its wake. A better electricity network was installed, telephones and television arrived, and the airport was given a proper runway. Modernization brought with it outsiders. Guzmán's hegemony over the university started to weaken, but he still maintained control over the faculty of education, which continued to send students out into the countryside, researching peasant communities and cultivating political cells. Even as the 150th anniversary celebrations of the Battle of Ayacucho were under way in 1974, Guzmán was stepping up his preparations for revolutionary warfare. "People's schools" were opened, and militants were now asked to give their lives over to the "armed struggle." Political cells became bases; students and lecturers, including Guzmán, started to withdraw from the university; and Comrade Gonzalo (his chairman's status came later) adopted a lower profile as he prepared to go underground.

He switched his base to Lima. The number of cells he had inherited from Red Flag had swollen to such an extent that Shining Path now dominated the staff and student bodies at several state universities. Rallies and protests broke out in the capital. Near Huanta, the atmosphere was charged with tension. The peasant community of Jarhua-Urán clashed with police, leaving fifteen peasants dead; most of the victims were teenagers. During a public memorial paying homage to Mao Zedong at the National University of San Marcos, Latin America's oldest university, a student announced that the party was preparing to initiate the "People's War." At a convention in the National University of Engineering against "the corporatization of Peruvian universities" a student called on his peers to go and fight alongside peasants in the mountains. The decision to launch the war was made at a central-committee meeting in 1979; those opposed were labeled revisionists and expelled from the party. Students were being sent by Guzmán to the jungle for shooting practice. Naval intelligence reported that groups of Shining Path members went off with rifles to remote parts of Ayacucho and the department of Cuzco on the pretext of hunting wild animals. Others were practicing, without bullets, in sand dunes north of Lima. Army intelligence concluded that the blowing up of bridges in the Cangallo district of Ayacucho might form part of an explosives training course. Police intelligence reported that about five hundred "people's schools" were said to be operating in Lima alone.

In Ayacucho, police were being expelled from villages by popular demand. A "liberated zone" was noticed in the department of Apurímac, where political authorities had been ejected. In the department of Andahuaylas, forty army conscripts deserted with their weapons and ammunition. Guerrillas armed with automatic rifles threatened a hacienda. Dynamite was being stolen. In April 1980, police intelligence reported that Shining Path would launch its revolution the following month. It duly did. On May 17, the day before the general elections that marked the return of democracy and with it that of Fernando Belaúnde, five hooded figures walked into the office of the registrar in the Ayacucho village of Chuschi, tied him up, and burned the registry book and ballot boxes.

Guzmán had embarked on the biggest rebellion in Peru since Manco Inca's revolt against the Spanish in 1536, without the state bothering to lift a finger. Shining Path's general fanfare was ignored because it was an embarrassment to all concerned. On the one hand its existence made a mockery of twelve years of military rule, while its public acknowledgment might look as if the military were trying to prolong its stay in power. On the other, Shining Path's advance demonstrated the relative failure of the other left-wing parties to capture the aspirations of the poor. They refused to recognize its strength. Just as the rest of the left was throwing in the revolutionary towel, linking hands, and switching to the democratic arena, Guzmán was doing what they had never dared. To blow the whistle on Shining Path was almost to betray their guilt and to concede ideological and political weakness. There were also fears it might give the military an excuse to postpone elections (in which the legal left fared disastrously). Among the hard left, there was even a sneaking admiration.

Abimael Guzmán was last seen by the government in the flesh and bone when he shared a jail cell with at least two future congressmen in January 1979, after being falsely accused of helping to organize a general strike. But the dominating image of him for more than a decade was a police mug shot taken ten years earlier, when his prison companions included a future presidential candidate, Alfonso Barrantes. The smoldering black eyes, thick stubble, and swept-back hair glowered into the camera.

Guzmán has achieved a status in Peru far greater than that of a mere guerrilla leader. Dubbed everything from horseman of the apocalypse to philosopher-king, the man whose war has cost the lives of twenty thousand people, mostly poor people, in the crusade for a Communist utopia, is remembered with warmth by old friends outside his political and intellectual orbit. They attest to his honesty, good manners, and kindness.

A former student and friend from San Agustín said: "He was a real gentleman, he had respect for others and did them favors. He was not a rebel at all. I cannot believe it is the same person." For her, the lasting impression was of a slim, well-shaven man with a mop of gleaming, sleekly combed hair, who walked with a slightly knock-kneed gait and was never to be seen without a book under his arm. He had a rather hawk-shaped nose and square-rimmed glasses, and he tilted his head toward the ground as he walked slowly but purposefully between the philosophy faculty and the library.

Books are the cornerstone of his universe. A voracious reader in his youth, Guzmán has such respect for the written word that he all but eschews personal experience. With the delight of a philosopher and mathematician, he encounters in Marxism-Leninism, and especially in Maoism, a set of laws that satisfies his quest for scientific truth and his hunger for social justice. Former friends and colleagues describe the blazing reverence in which he holds orthodox Communist literature. "He gave Marx, Lenin, and Mao the sanctity of the Bible," said a former senator and Red Flag colleague, Rolando Breña. "What was written there could never be disputed."

Such sanctity, however, was not inviolate when Guzmán needed to plug an ideological hole. Carlos Tapia, a former comrade who eventually also committed the cardinal sin of participating in "parliamentary cretinism"—that is, running for Congress—was hauled over the coals by Augusta when he dared to suggest that El Doctor might have misinterpreted Lenin. The point was crucial to Guzmán's support of Mariátegui and revolved around the word "semi-colonial." "The Lenin paragraph plainly did not say what Guzmán claimed," said Tapia. "The pope was lying to his priests. In his absence, Augusta—a beautiful girl whom I liked a lot and who reminded me of Sophia Loren—intimated that my edition was revisionist and untrustworthy, that it was a false Bible. The matter was to go before another meeting with El Doctor." But Tapia was not invited again.

Guzmán's pursuit of Marxist orthodoxy, given the occasional twist for immediate purposes despite his reputation among old friends for impeccable personal honesty, dominates his party's internal ideological struggles. Everything has to be done by the book. Dissidents are condemned as revisionists and subjected to humiliating sessions of self-criticism. Guzmán is often depicted with a book instead of a weapon in Shining Path's rough, hagiographic posters of gun-toting peasant hordes. In his other hand, he carries the hammer-and-sickle flag. "To wage war it is necessary to be a philosopher. Comrade Gonzalo's battle plans are political, not technical," notes one party pamphlet.

Book in hand, he makes ideology the backbone of his every move. "Each plan has an overall political line that guides it," says another document. Elsewhere it adds the Maoist corollary: "Our principle is that the party commands the gun." Guzmán himself, in an interview with *El Diario*, said: "The strength of the party's militants is undeniably sustained by their ideological and political formation." He endeavors to create men in his own image.

Invoking the authority of the written word may seem odd in

a country where the ruling language, Spanish, has historically been used to subjugate the Quechua-speaking Indians. An illiterate or non-Spanish-speaking person is hard pressed to take his case to a judge. But, conversely, literacy in Spanish is looked to as a means of self-improvement, opening the gates to the modern world. Books are keenly valued because they are perceived to be the source of life-changing knowledge. Citing them confers on the speaker an automatic and unusually powerful aura of authority. Accordingly, Guzmán's doctrinal dogmatism and book-waving are accompanied by a strategic use of quotations from other kinds of international literature to back him up at crucial moments inside the party.

On the eve of the revolution, when Guzmán was confronted by a faction that had serious doubts about actually going through with it, he first cited Mao on the "leap from rational knowledge to revolutionary practice" and on the "unity of opposites" which was "a fundamental universal law . . . in nature and society as well as in man's thinking . . . which propelled the movement of things and their change." As the opposition crystallized, Guzmán manipulated the agenda and proceeded to pluck some passages out of William Shakespeare's *Julius Caesar*. The aim was to illustrate how conspiracies took shape.

Next to be hauled onstage to add grist to the mill before the central committee was Washington Irving, whose book *Muhammad and His Successes* was selectively quoted for its inspirational qualities in showing how men acted when they were united under a common cause and took up arms to achieve a new order. Guzmán then switched to Shakespeare's *Macbeth* to expound further on the theme of betrayal and its development in the mind and gestures of the protagonist. Finally, he recited parts of Aeschylus' *Prometheus Bound* to prove the power of rebellion and the importance of the involvement of the masses. Guzmán won the committee's unanimous support —once he had purged any recalcitrants who remained.

His own rhetoric reveals a millenarian streak, which at times is breathtaking in its apocalyptic violence. Guzmán's most consummate performance was at the closing of the party's first formal military school on April 19, 1980: "We are the beginning. . . . The revolution will make its home in our native land. . . . We are entering the strategic offensive of the world revolution; the next fifty years will be the sweeping away of the power of imperialism and all exploiters. . . . The popular war will grow every day until it overturns the old order. . . . The vertex is beginning, the invincible flames of the revolution will grow, turning into lead, into steel, and from the roar of battle with its unquenchable fire, light will emerge, from the blackness, brightness, and there will be a new world. . . . The reactionary forces have dreams of blood and hyenas; worried dreams shake their dark nights, their hearts plot evil butchery; they arm themselves to the teeth but they will not triumph, their destiny is weighed and measured. . . . The people are rearing up, arming themselves and rising up in rebellion, putting nooses around the neck of imperialism and the reactionaries, taking them by the throat, squeezing them and, by necessity, they will strangle them. Reactionary flesh will be stripped and shredded, and those black scraps of offal will be buried in the mire; what is left will be burned and the ashes scattered to the ends of the earth. . . . The trumpets begin to sound. . . . We will convert the black fire into red fire and the red into light. . . . We are the beginning. We begin saying we are the beginning. We end saying we are the beginning. . . ."

For a gentle-mannered bookworm who would not harm a fly, Guzmán had become remarkably unsqueamish. And the apocalyptic note, which is struck elsewhere in the speech—"the beast will finally be brought to bay, and as has been shown to us, the thunder of our armed voices will make it shiver with terror"—is perhaps entirely deliberate. Guzmán, a fanatical reader, educated in a religious school and said to be gifted with an elephantine memory, would doubtless have been as aware of the biblical Apocalypse as of the opening verses of the Gospel according to St. John echoed by the speech's conclusion: "In the beginning was the Word, and the Word was with God, and the Word was God. The same was in the beginning . . ." He wears the mantle of the Apocalypse well. Chapter six of the Book of Revelation features the red horse of war (*The Red Horse* was also the name of a Peruvian Communist magazine). According to the Bible, its horseman had "the power to bring war on the earth so that men should kill each other. He was given a large sword." Among Guzmán's plethora of labels, which include "Red Sun" (translated into Quechua as "Puka Inti"), the party calls him the "Fourth Sword of World Revolution" after Marx, Lenin, and Mao. In the course of his studies he may even have discovered that the Hebrew meaning of his name is "My father is God."

Guzmán's former political colleagues assert that El Maestro ("The Master," another of his nicknames) was a cold, calculating thinker and strategist whose heart was swallowed up by his mind. Some are baffled that Guzmán actually took to arms at all. "He is not a man of action; he is more of an organizer of political penetration. I think it was his wife who goaded him into it," said Breña. "She preferred action to theory; she was very emotional, flipping between anger and happiness from one moment to the next." According to Tapia, Augusta could be reduced to such a paralytic fury that her mouth would quiver and she would be unable to utter a word. In the *El Diario* interview, Guzmán proudly confesses to having comrades rather than friends. He talks of how ideological strength banishes fear; how trusting in the masses, in the party, and in history makes fear fade away. He speaks of a soul at the service of politics.

An early nonpolitical colleague, Armando Barreda, who knew Guzmán in both Arequipa and Ayacucho, remembers him as a humane, likable, and caring man, adored by Barreda's children. "I am sure there are many decisions he has had to make despite the fact that his character has been repelled by them," he said. "As a politician, once the decision to wage war is made, different rules apply. It is his capacity as a military leader that should be judged rather than his personality. As for whether he is right or not, he has obviously struck a chord among people who see his alternative as their only escape or road to a juster society. While the social gap is so huge, such a phenomenon will exist."

On April 3, 1983, Shining Path guerrillas entered the Ayacucho villages of Santiago de Lucanamarca and Huanca-Sanacos. After rounding up the communities and staging "people's trials," they killed seventy peasants for refusing to cooperate. Guzmán admitted to *El Diario* that the action was excessive:

"Neither they nor we will forget it . . . but everything in life has two sides to it. . . . The main thing is that we dealt them a crushing blow and reined them back, and they realized they were up against another kind of people's warrior, that we were not the same people they had fought previously; the excess is the negative aspect. If we understand war, rely on what Lenin says, and bear Clausewitz* in mind, in a war the masses can burst and go overboard in the shock, expressing all their hatred and repudiation. . . . Excesses may be committed; the problem is reaching a point and not passing it because if you exceed it you go off course; it is like an angle, it has until a certain grade of opening and no more."

While in the eyes of his enemies Guzmán suffers from unassailable egotism, Chairman Gonzalo (as he became known in July 1983), considers himself merely a product of historical accident and inevitable social necessity. He attributes his leadership to a fateful juggling of the relationships between masses, classes, party, and leaders. "Every revolution is like that," he says in *El Diario*, "we could not be an exception, it is just a matter of the fulfillment of laws." What makes him more equal than others is the party's adoption of Gonzalo's Guiding Thought, which although technically the product of himself and the central committee nevertheless assumes the name of his alias. "There is no leadership that is not sustained by a Thought," he says, invoking Lenin in the same breath: "The cult of personality is a revisionist position." Gonzalo's Guiding Thought is the application by Guzmán and his colleagues of selected principles of Marxism-Leninism-Maoism to Peru.

Despite the cold-hearted mathematical calculations of a military strategist with a single goal in mind—"the party was prepared to pay up to thirty comrades," he said dryly when rebels were sprung from jail—the warmth generated by Guzmán's character cannot be ignored. Another of his nicknames was "El Tio," or "Uncle." Not only do old, close friends—as opposed to university political foes, whom he dealt with in cavalier fashion—have fond memories of him, but he is also reported to have been very attractive to women. In Arequipa, according to

* Karl von Clausewitz, author of *On War* (1833), a staple military textbook.

Barreda, "women used to fight among themselves to be near him." Although Guzmán initially appears not to have taken advantage, his misgivings dissolved later on. A daughter was reportedly left adrift by a brief liaison before Augusta and, in Augusta's absence, Guzmán was said to have indulged his freedom. It was reported in left-wing circles in Lima that, after receiving a secretive message about a Shining Path rendezvous, girls were liable to arrive to find themselves alone with Comrade Gonzalo, and more than just politics on the agenda. Nevertheless, the last time Barreda saw the couple in the capital, in 1979, they were strolling along with her hand affectionately under his arm. It was said they never had children because they felt it would have distracted them from the revolution. Barreda's glimpse of the pair, near Lima's military hospital, came a few months after Guzmán's release from jail in 1978.

Guzmán had been arrested on a Sunday evening at the home of the La Torre family in Avenida Pershing, Lima. His young brother-in-law, Miguel, almost enabled him to escape. "I helped him out of the bathroom window to reach the roof terrace, but I was too small to help him climb onto the house next door. It was there on the terrace that the police found us." Miguel La Torre need not have worried. Thanks to three generals and a rear admiral whose influences were secured on the pretext that Guzmán was just a harmless, middle-class university lecturer with some batty political ideas, he was released almost immediately. "Except power, all is illusion," as Guzmán would say.

Grim reaper or utopian visionary, Guzmán has proved himself an expert strategist who has outwitted the state for more than a decade. What he may lack in intellectual originality he makes up for in tenacious and methodical hard work, in a ruthless sacrifice to the god of reason. The lumbering, heavy-handed, and apocalyptic rhetoric of his set speeches compares to the rather dry, although equally repetitive, style of his impromptu answers in the *El Diario* interview. For all their blood and thunder, his set speeches come from the head and not the gut. The Guzmán who measures the excess of a massacre with the precision of a geometrist is more authentic than the one who waxes bombastic about turning his opponents into black scraps of offal and burying them in the mire. The apocalyptic rhetoric is merely to light the fire, to inflame his columns of peasants, students, and workers to sacrifice everything to create "the radical and definitive new society toward which fifteen billion years of matter in motion—that part of eternal matter which we know—has been inevitably and irresistibly heading." For Guzmán, it is all just a matter of scientific truths. And time.

Abimael Guzmán was for a long while rumored to be dead. Medical records show that apart from an unimportant skin disease, psoriasis, which caused him to scratch himself and always wear a jacket, he also suffered from polycythemia, a blood disease, which during the 1970s increasingly prevented him from staying for prolonged periods in the mountains at high altitude. However, although the blood disease could be aggravated by stress, reasonable precautions would keep him out of danger. Family sources also say he had kidney problems. Innumerable tales of his demise in a clash with the police or armed forces have swept the media but have never been proved. Early on, a minister of interior, José Gagliardi, claimed erroneously that Guzmán was "agonizing in a local clinic but we are not taking him prisoner because our Christian spirit does not permit us to do so." The idea was for Guzmán to turn himself in and be given asylum; but he was nowhere to be seen.

The nearest Guzmán appears to have been to capture was in June 1990, when police raided a modern house a few hundred yards from the Ministry of Defense in Lima. Four tons of propaganda, newspaper archives, plans, maps, reports, committee minutes, and identity papers were uncovered, as well as war-memorial trophies such as trays, textiles, and ceramic hammer-and-sickles inscribed with the dates of guerrilla actions. There was a bust of Guzmán in the style of Beethoven. His writing was found on books and in party documents. In an upstairs bedroom a pair of his spectacles was found on a desk. Two wrinkled brown-suede boots stood near a simple wooden bed. On the headboard there hung the skin of a puma. And upon a bedside chair rested a woman's dark wig. The horseman of the apocalypse had turned into a master of disguise; it was believed he had escaped before the police's eyes dressed as a gardener.

Clumsy wishful thinking by the security forces, together with a succession of alleged close shaves has served only to enhance the mythical status Abimael Guzmán has cultivated by preserving an extraordinarily effective clandestineness while at the same time running an organically complex and expanding national movement. His mythical status has further benefited from Indian legends in the Sierra. He has lived for too long to be forgotten and has taken his own place in the Indians' magical world. For the man with less than $14,000 on his head (in July 1991), who is responsible for more than $20 billion of economic destruction, has appeared to be both invisible and ubiquitous. In jungle areas the Indians reportedly say he escapes by transforming himself into a bird and flying out of harm's way; or into a snake, which vanishes into the bush. In the southern Andes he is said to fool his hunters by turning himself into a stone. Elsewhere he is thought to have a double, and, in the mountains of the department of Libertad, the peasants believe he comes and goes like a spirit. There is little doubt that the myth of Chairman Gonzalo would survive him. Whether Shining Path would continue to prosper as a political movement is another matter.

# 2

# Down the Inca Trail

With the Bible in one hand and the sword in the other, the Spanish conquistadores ripped apart the Inca empire, and with it one of the world's great civilizations. At its zenith, its territory stretched for more than three thousand miles, from Colombia to southern Chile. The Andean empire was crisscrossed by an intricate network of stone roads, bridges, and tunnels at breathtaking altitudes; its towns, forts, and temples were often architectural marvels built on mountain saddles and spurs or in lush agricultural valleys. The Inca dynasty ruled with a rod of iron from the top of a tight, decimal-tiered, pyramidal system of government. Agricultural tribute or public labor was demanded in return for protection, both secular and divine. Food that was not needed by the army was redistributed and stored for times of need. Land was collectively owned in such a way as to ensure that natural resources, especially water, were shared and used rationally. Communal property ownership was reinforced by the tradition of communal labor. Even the three basic laws against theft, laziness, and deceit were conceived primarily as protecting the state; punishments were brutal, but people knew where they stood, and by its own terms the empire was just and free of corruption. Instead of writing, complex systems of knots were used to record everything from tribal rights to work distribution; taxes were linked to age grades and work capacity.

In effect, the Inca empire was a sophisticated, well-nourished, and rigidly efficient war machine at the service of the Inca and his nobles, who lived luxuriously as their subjects toiled. The sacred dynasty traced its roots to the world's highest inland lake, Lake Titicaca. Its emperors were identified with the sun and deified. For all their might, the Incas held sway for little more than ninety years; before that, they were just another tribe. When Francisco Pizarro launched the Spanish conquest in 1532, the Inca empire of Tahuantinsuyo was already overextended and embroiled in civil war. Its destruction eventually helped finance the Industrial Revolution in Britain: Once the Spanish empire in turn fell into decline, the gold and silver stolen from the Incas and extracted by slave labor in Peru and Bolivia left the grasp of its plunderers and loaded the bullion accounts of Dutch bankers instead.

The rape, pillage, and murder that disarticulated the empire and decimated the Indian population—in Peru alone its numbers were reduced from about nine million to 600,000 by 1620 —began in the very moments that the Inca Atahualpa was treacherously captured in the town of Cajamarca in northern Peru in November 1532. According to the early chroniclers, the beautiful holy women who were being prepared either to worship at the temples of the sun or to be concubines of the Inca were promptly grabbed by the Spanish soldiers. Gold and silver effigies, jugs, basins, drinking vessels, and emeralds beyond the conquistadores' wildest dreams were carried off from the Inca's military camp. And Pizarro's band of 150 infantry, artillery, and cavalry men slaughtered up to seven thousand of the Inca's troops as they stood in a state of shock after walking into the Spaniard's trap. To meet Pizarro, Atahualpa had arrived ceremoniously in a litter decorated with parrot feathers and shining with gold, his troops only lightly armed. As cannon were fired and the cavalry charged, the Spaniards fell upon the litter. The hands of the Inca's litter-bearers were cut off by swords; they died one by one until the litter at last was heaved onto its side. Atahualpa was escorted from the carnage.

The sheer nerve of the Spaniards effectively turned the tables on the Inca empire in one day. If the Indian warriors, who were undone by their innocent self-assurance and sense of invulnerability in the presence of a handful of foreigners, were traumatized by the attack, they were devastated by Atahualpa's capture. They were left like a body without a head. Records indicate that Atahualpa was so sure of himself that he had already been planning what to do with the Spaniards' horses—which were what had impressed him most about the strangers—and had been thinking vaguely about sacrificing some of the Spaniards to the sun while castrating others with a view to appointing them guardians of his household women. Atahualpa's confidence was not just that of a man who symbolized the empire he ruled; it was that of a semi-deified monarch who was perceived to embody his empire in a metaphysical sense as well. For the Inca's subjects, his capture was an unimaginable spiritual shock. Their world was suddenly inverted.

Atahualpa's capture was provoked by his rejection of the Catholic missal. It was presented to him by a Dominican priest in the square minutes before the ambush while the rest of the Spaniards lay hidden in the surrounding buildings. The priest approached the Inca between the rows of troops and, through an interpreter, explained that he represented the Christian religion and had been sent to reveal to Atahualpa the message of God. The message, said the priest, was inside the book he was holding. The Inca asked for it to be handed over. At first he was unable to open the missal's clasp; when he finally did, he was baffled by the writing (the Incas were nonliterate). After leafing through its pages he hurled it in fury to the ground. The priest, livid with rage, ran off weeping and crying that Atahualpa was an overproud dog, a Lucifer. He called on Pizarro to march out against him. After the cannon shots into the Inca's massed troops and amid battle cries of "Santiago!" ("St. James!"), the butchery began.

Seven months later, Atahualpa was publicly garrotted. Although the Inca was initially promised his freedom in return for a room full of gold, which he provided, Pizarro worried that he was summoning armies to his aid. Atahualpa, who meanwhile had learned chess and impressed the Spaniards with his intelligence, his fierce, lordly charm, and the mystique in which his subjects held him, was killed once the numbers of Spanish troops were doubled by the arrival of reinforcements. Atahualpa would have been burned at the stake save for his extraordinary last-minute conversion to Christianity. He was baptized and garrotted instead, after repenting his "sins." The Inca's corpse was left in the square overnight, and the following day received a sumptuous Christian funeral.

Although the Inca empire was itself despotic and imposed its own culture on other tribes, its era is still looked to as a golden age by many, if not most, Peruvians, excepting those of strong European descent who dominate the country politically and economically. Since losing their giant haciendas and political stranglehold following the agrarian reform carried out by General Juan Velasco's left-wing military regime, the descendants of the old colonial families have retreated mainly to Lima. Few value the country's pre-Columbian past other than for the textiles, gold artifacts, and pots it yields via gravediggers. The objects were ignored until it was discovered there was a huge foreign market awaiting them; they came to be appreciated more for their financial value than for their artistic or cultural merit. But although pre-Columbian objects are part of the typical trappings of a well-to-do household, colonial art is prized much more highly. The hearts of the rich lie elsewhere: in the United States, Spain, and England, anywhere but the Andes, which are identified either nostalgically with the tranquil comforts of the feudal past or as a source of mining wealth. Latterly, however, the mountains have become associated with the swarm of Shining Path guerrillas, with what Abimael Guzmán describes as "the thunder of armed voices" making the reactionary beast "shiver with terror."

The tension between Western and Indian culture is at the heart of Peru's post-conquest history. The dominating classes have always depended on the Bible and the sword, the Catholic church and the armed forces, to maintain their control over the Indian population. In recent times, the racial division has faded as intermarriage and greater political and economic freedoms, accompanied by improved transport and communications, have produced a burgeoning middle class of mestizos; this has coincided with white emigration. Nevertheless, mestizos as well as Indians are liable to be disdainfully dubbed *cholos* by the remaining upper-class whites, who meanwhile are finding it increasingly difficult to marry others of their own skin color at home. In imitation of the ruling classes—who have cut the umbilical cord with Europe only to attach another one to the United States—the mestizos are afflicted by a similar cultural and racial fixation in line with the modish requirements of upward mobility. In the slavish pursuit of all-American Disney, apple pie, and Coca-Cola culture, an overly deep suntan can be an embarrassment, and an ancient Indian pot in the house a sign of neither wealth nor artistic appreciation, just an uncomfortable reminder of ethnic roots. Material success and social climbing in Peru entail a corresponding denial of everything Indian.

Pizarro's execution of Atahualpa marked the true founding of the Peruvian state. The gulf between them has never been bridged, the guilt never assuaged, and the resentment never vanquished. The dominating classes as a whole may be darker than they used to be, but the cultural and economic abyss between them and the poorer Indian majority is just the same. It is a gulf sanctified in Andean rituals. The historic conflict is relived every year, usually around Independence Day in July, in a fiesta in which the encounter between Atahualpa and Pizarro is represented as a fight between the Inca and a figure called the Captain. The manner in which it is played out depends on the sympathies of the participants. Traditionally, the week-long sessions of animal sacrifices, feasts, Catholic masses, heavy drinking, processions, and dancing ends with the death of the Inca, followed by a bullfight—real or symbolic—in clear homage to the Spanish triumph. But often the bull is mocked and baited, as if the victory is hollow. The Captain, who foots the bill, is usually a rich and influential leader of the community; the Inca is normally somebody of lesser means.

Where the scene ends with the Inca's capture and ransom followed by an embrace between him and the Captain and a reconciliating dance, symbolizing a union of the two cultures, the community has usually come under the sway of middle-class merchants. Where the Inca is still decapitated or has his throat slit, or an animal is slaughtered in his place, it is more likely to be the opposite: The peasants are running the show and faithful to Atahualpa's memory. Any reconciliation would for them be a façade and a cover-up of the truth. The ritual is a dynamic enactment of actual power struggles within a community using as its overall narrative the very confrontation from which they stem.

Occasionally, the pot boils over. In the town of Chiquián in the department of Ancash in 1984, the owners of the former haciendas—broken up, as elsewhere, under agrarian reform—had returned from Lima to their old, empty mansions in order to take part in and take charge of the annual fiesta in honor of Santa Rosa, a Dominican nun canonized in 1670 and Peru's foremost female saint. But times had changed at Chiquián, a small town in the province of Bolognesi, 12,700 feet high among snow-crested mountains. The economic decline that set in after the hacienda owners departed had worsened year by year. The people left were poorer and their resentment nearer the surface; the balance had turned against those seen as the envoys of the state.

During the fiesta, in which the Indians and the Inca were not accorded the same privileges as the Captain and his more aristocratic entourage of *blancos* and mestizos, the mock fight between the two principal characters provoked a real one. While boiled sweets were flung and blows rained down on him and his men, the Captain, as he approached the Inca on horseback, used the Peruvian flag to defend himself and jabbed at his attackers. When the Captain tried to speed up the ritual and "capture" the Inca more quickly than he was supposed to, that was the final straw. The Inca refused to attend the reconciliation feast. (A few years later, Shining Path penetrated Bolognesi. Rebels blew up Chiquián's electricity station, killing four policemen. Then, in 1990, a guerrilla column dynamited the National Bank, telephone exchange, hydroelectric plant, and government offices before killing two policemen and the former mayor. A state of emergency was declared, bringing the province under control of the armed forces.)

Atahualpa and other heroes of Indian resistance have become confused in the Andean popular memory. Atahualpa has been depicted in paintings and drawings having his throat cut or head cut off when in fact it was the last Inca, Túpac Amaru I, who was decapitated by the Spaniards in 1572 after he was flushed out of his jungle refuge. Like his uncle, the last Inca also asked to be baptized before having his head slashed off with a cutlass in Cuzco. He was given full Christian funereal honors, and his head was stuck on a post—although the Spaniards quickly removed it because it came to be worshiped by thousands of grief-stricken Indians.

The military conquest was over but there now began the campaign to conquer souls. During the next 150 years, the domination of the Indians was spearheaded by the church. Evangelization brought with it political control exerted through the church hierarchy. The Indians' "idols," such as ceramic figures of the sun, moon, and animals, were destroyed, their religious sites desecrated, and their holy men jailed and banished. The Christian calendar was imposed, partially displacing the Indian one that was based on the four seasons, and whose festival dates were used for baptisms and marriages. The Indians were enjoined to produce wheat and grapes for Mass and rather less corn, guinea pigs, and llamas. Corn was used by the Indians to make beer, which was spilled in homage to the earth, and the animals were sacrificed in religious rituals.

To avoid the repression, the Indian communities hid their beliefs under the Catholic cloak. Pre-Columbian divinities were worshiped simultaneously during a feast in honor of the Virgin Mary; sacrificial mounds were discovered behind Christian altars; and the dead were removed at night from churches to be reburied in the Indians' sacred sites. At the same time, however, there was a degree of assimilation: The Indians' polytheistic culture was tolerant of other gods. But the Spanish priests were often bitterly resented for their rough inquisitions in the Indian communities. Threats of divine punishment trapped the peasants between two fires: Betrayal of their own gods entailed equivalent penalties.

The servile religious deceit required for personal survival contributed to the foundation of an entire social attitude toward the outsiders. Indian leaders practiced Christianity in order to protect their political power and secure tax exemptions. But they were excluded from becoming priests or monks, a hierarchical privilege nevertheless allowed to mestizos. Under the Christian onslaught, the Inca empire took on the sheen of a golden age. The figure of the Inca himself became associated by the Indians with the Christian devil, in accordance with the time-honored logic that one's enemy's enemy was one's friend. History was mythologically reworked to explain the Andean cataclysm in terms that provided hope for the future. The image of the Inca came to embrace not only Atahualpa and Túpac Amaru I but also their legendary ancestors, including Pachacútec, who ruled in the empire's heyday and was famed as its great architect. The idea of the return of the Inca became linked to the emergence of a future utopia.

Nevertheless, the relationship with Christianity remained ambiguous. Its god, Jesus Christ, and the saints were perceived to be powerful by the Indians because it was believed they must have vanquished the Indians' gods for the Spaniards to have defeated them. The first messianic movement advocating a rejection of Catholicism—Taqui Onqoy, meaning Disease of the Dance—was spearheaded by a shadowy figure in Ayacucho called Juan Chocne and two women called Santa María and Santa María Magdalena, whose names were evidently part of an attempt to expropriate Christian power and turn it against their aggressors. The movement is believed to have initiated the *pishtaco* myth that the whites extracted Indian grease. Its followers danced and fell into trances in which they were supposedly possessed by their old gods maddened with jealousy by their rejection. They preached a return to an amended native religion and an expulsion of the Europeans.

By 1565 the movement had spread widely and was adopted by the Inca Tutu Cusi, who was still running a pocket state in the region of Vilcabamba and who sought to turn Taqui Onqoy to political advantage. However, the Spaniards nipped it in the bud and the participants were whipped or fined or had their heads shaved. According to anthropologists, the movement represented the beginning of an ideological tradition under which the conquered Indians sought a savior embodying both the Inca and Jesus Christ in order to deliver them from the chaos created by the conquest and to restore the natural order.

In 1663, an Indian uprising invoking the Inca was quickly stamped out north of the colonial capital in Churín. But in 1742 an obscure rebel leader who emerged in the jungle after the rainy season fared rather better. Juan Santos Atahualpa, who was believed to come from Cuzco and was said by Franciscan missionaries to have traveled to Europe and Africa and have a criminal past, sparked off an Indian rebellion that lasted a decade and survived five military expeditions until Atahualpa disappeared and it fizzled out. Juan Santos Atahualpa's name was probably an assumed one and born from both Christian and Andean traditions; he called on the Indians in the name of the Incas to overturn Spanish rule. He also adopted a mystical, messianic role.

Historians write that, according to his followers, "the Inca" allowed nobody to touch his food or walk in his tracks. He claimed to possess divine powers and, like the legendary founders of the Inca empire, to have lived in a house of stone and be one of four brothers. "The earth will tremble at his command, because he is sent from heaven to establish the Incas and expel the Spaniards," one supporter is reported to have told officials. Sure enough, it did. In 1746 South America's worst earthquake of the century flattened Lima, leaving only twenty-five houses standing. The cathedral's towers collapsed and the viceroy's palace was rendered uninhabitable.

While the earthquake triggered alarm because it seemed to bear out prophesies attributed to Santa Rosa, according to which Lima was condemned to disappear because of natural disaster, and Peru to be returned to its legitimate owners, Atahualpa's cause had been bolstered by another prediction: A monk had prophesied that in 1742 "an abominable beast" would rise up and gloriously crown himself king of the "New World of Peru." The self-styled Inca, at the head of hundreds of Indian archers gathered from jungle tribes as well as Indian and mestizo migrants from the highlands, destroyed timber yards in the district of Tarma and occupied the small town of Andamarca in the central Andes. Amid colonial panic and speculation that the uprising was being instigated by the English, there were both clashes with the viceroy's soldiers and, later, increasingly vicious rebel attacks on the Franciscan missions. The Franciscans' arrival in the jungle, whence they attempted to herd the semi-nomadic Indians into mission centers, had brought epidemics of smallpox, measles, malaria, and typhoid, which devastated the Indian population.

Even before the revolt of Juan Santos Atahualpa, missionaries were being killed. Asked by one missionary why they were going to murder him, an Indian leader was reported to have replied: "Because you and your kind are killing us every day with your sermons, taking away our freedom." When two Franciscans were rejected by Atahualpa's jungle Indians after they tried to return to recoup their missions, one drowned in a river and the other was pierced with arrows before being finished off with clubs. The revolt, which succeeded in expelling the missionaries, melted away after failing to take root in the highlands.

Nationalist movements invoking a return to Inca rule swept Peru throughout the eighteenth century, culminating in the particularly bloody rebellion of José Gabriel Túpac Amaru II in 1780. The revolts were led by the Indian nobles, who were used by the Spaniards as provincial administrators and resented being forced to impoverish and exploit their own kind by imposing illicit taxes, unfair prices, and slave labor. Their power was enshrined by the conservation of the Inca empire's political structure underneath the Spaniards'. The nobles' nationalist sentiment was fueled further by the circulation of a book on the empire's history written by an Inca, Garcilaso de la Vega, which idealized the empire and in one edition accompanied what seemed to be a prophecy cited by Sir Walter Raleigh to the effect that the Inca empire would be restored by the English.

The Indian nobles were split between the moderates, who simply sought reforms to restore greater power to them and respect for their people, and the radicals, who wanted the restoration of the Inca dynasty. Since the Indian nobles had been educated by the Jesuits, they were not against the church; rather, they wanted greater access to its hierarchy. Historians have uncovered at least a hundred revolts against the Spaniards during the eighteenth century, most of them minor ones directed against abuses committed by the provincial Spanish administrators. The Indian nobles' flirtation with the church was their undoing in 1750, when a conspiracy was leaked to the viceroy by a Spanish priest who had been informed of it under the secrecy of the confessional box. Six Indian nobles were hanged, and further executions followed after a wave of connected uprisings near Lima and elsewhere.

The rebellion under José Gabriel Túpac Amaru II was the most serious threat to Spanish rule. The noble's determination to legalize his dubious claim to direct descent from the last Inca emperor illustrated his recognition of the tenacious power that the Inca tradition held over the Indian mind. Túpac Amaru, who had inherited land in the province of Tinta in the department of Cuzco, took Indian support for granted and worked to build an alliance with the mestizos and even with some criollos (descendants of the Spanish). Despite the lesson of the 1750 Lima conspiracy, like Juan Santos Atahualpa he was not initially opposed to the church. Along with the abolition of forced labor and the dismantling of the big haciendas and the system by which Indians were effectively obliged to buy goods from the haciendas against their will, Túpac Amaru II sought a revival of monarchic Inca rule.

Songs testified to the messianic conviction he aroused: "Long live Our Inca Gabriel, let us swear him in as King, because it is coming to be in law." Túpac Amaru turned to revolution after the frustration of his attempts to secure reforms legally. He launched it to coincide with the birthday celebrations for King Charles III of Spain, jailing a corrupt criollo administrator and later hanging him after a trial by a people's tribunal. The revolt was politically well prepared and spread like wildfire through the mountains of southern Peru and Bolivia—where the rebels, who initiated their rebellion at Carnival time, took La Paz. As Túpac Amaru marched from village to village with his army of Indians, reputedly equipped with a handful of cannon and blunderbusses although most were armed with spears, knives, and slings, revolts broke out simultaneously elsewhere. Túpac Amaru set up his own political authorities and went as far as to impose taxes in the areas cleared of colonial influence.

In the Indian mind, the rebellion was what they term a *pachacuti*: Time and space were being inverted as a new world was born, just as it had been by the Spanish conquerors. Túpac Amaru's opponents perceived it in similar terms. A government news sheet reporting the war said:

*Either the world is in reverse*
*or it is off its hinges,*
*because the judge was substituted,*
*the criminal becoming judge.*
*What is at the foot becomes the head,*
*the vile slave, Señor,*
*the thief, legislator,*
*the wretch, person.*

In the ensuing clashes with troops loyal to the Spanish crown, tens of thousands of people were killed in what one historian, with the typical contempt of the white upper classes and their blindness to the depth of the Indians' resentment, dismissed as "the isolated cry of Tinta."

Túpac Amaru's revolution failed mainly because of his military errors and the abandonment and treachery of rival Indian nobles, criollos, and mestizos, which cost him the capture of the city of Cuzco. The revolt turned increasingly into a savage backlash against all things colonial as the pent-up hatred of the browbeaten peasants boiled over into a murderous orgy. Anybody with a vestige of Spanish blood or culture was slaughtered. There was no neutral ground; people were on either one side or the other. Entire families were killed, young and old alike. The ferocity of the killings and the denigration of the victims—in the village of Calca, a woman's murdered corpse was raped in a church—was for the Indians both a form of ethnic revenge and a ritualistic show of domination.

The ethnic bloodlust and aggression against the church were out of Túpac Amaru's control. Priests were killed—sometimes thrown from church towers—and all kinds of torture and bodily mutilations inflicted. One rebel leader wrote: "The Sovereign Inca king orders that all criollos, women, children of both sexes, and everyone who is or looks Spanish, or is dressed in imitation of the Spanish, should be knifed. And if this species of people are given refuge in a holy place, and some priest or anybody impedes or defends them from having their throats cut, they will also be trampled underfoot, the priests knifed and the churches burned." The Spanish were conceived of as barely human. Written evidence shows that they were often seen by the rebels as *pishtacos*, living Dracula-like off the sweat and blood of the Indians. *Pishtacos* had to be killed and mutilated according to certain rituals in order to ensure that they remained dead. Historical traditions of ritual fighting and human sacrifice for the sake of fertility may help further to explain the ferocious cruelty.

Massacre followed massacre: The Spaniards were equally ruthless and random in their revenge. They made indulgent use of their superior firepower and swelled their battle ranks with peasants forced into fighting by those Indian nobles who had remained loyal to the crown, as well as by priests and Spanish administrators. Unable to tell which peasants were rebels, the loyalists also slaughtered entire families and communities. After Túpac Amaru was captured through betrayal, his tongue was cut out and his body attached to four horses, which were spurred in different directions in Cuzco's central square. Still alive, he was decapitated.

The revolt died away shortly after. Its main consequence was the destruction of the power of the Indian nobles by a shocked Spanish crown. Attempts were made to stamp out the trappings of Inca culture, and the Indians were left without obvious leaders. But in the battles for independence from Spain, which culminated in 1824 at Ayacucho, the provincial criollo élite nevertheless took advantage of the Inca tradition to win over Indian support. Republican groups fought in the name of the Inca and under Santa Rosa, among whose legendary prophesies was a return to Inca rule. Later on, criollo art even stole the Inca tradition to bestow legitimacy on the architect of independence, Simón Bolívar, who in making Spanish the official language of the new republic effectively banned the native ones (mainly Quechua and Aymara).

Independence, which was helped financially and militarily by England in a bid for commercial expansion, left Lima's white aristocracy in control. Freed from the constraints of the Spanish crown and much more keenly aware and fearful of the danger Indian nationalism posed to its interests, it strove, pathetically, on the one hand to absorb it by utilizing Inca-related images on its coins and official seals, as well as in hymns, and on the other to cripple it by letting the provincial criollo landowners fill the vacuum of power left by the Indian nobles and impose feudalistic regimes that were even more enslaving than before. Bereft of the colonial bureaucracy, the state's influence was severely reduced and the country fragmented. The ensuing political turbulence, revolts, and presidential coups, which saw the rise of military power—Indians, mestizos, blacks, and Chinese were press-ganged into the ranks—were primarily a white affair and revolved around tensions between the old colonial aristocracy and the upper-middle-class, more merchant-minded criollos.

As the whites enriched themselves exporting guano (bird droppings rich in nitrates), gold, and silver, the Indian peasants and miners were subjected to hunger, the whip, and the stocks amid an increasingly concerted ethnic debasement. Daily resistance, such as by refusing to work at their hardest, was perceived as laziness; this was taken to be a racial flaw. The lost War of the Pacific against Chile was partly blamed on the Indians' supposed cowardice. A servant's murder of his master was seen as evidence of their innate criminality. Meanwhile, lowland Indians were slaughtered like animals as the army spearheaded the colonization of the Amazon rainforest.

The animal simile was explicit: Sebastian Lorente, a historian writing in the late nineteenth century, dubbed the Indians "llamas that talk." By the century's close, the people who had produced the culture briefly hailed by the whites as their own inheritance were considered, as the writer Clemente Palma said, nothing but "an old and degenerate branch of the ethnic trunk from which all the inferior races emerged." At that time the pure-blooded Indians still formed about sixty percent of the population. Since they neither spoke nor wrote Spanish, none was allowed to vote.

The whites' unmuzzled racism would have been more genocidal had it not been for the fact they needed the Indians to work for them. The racism was founded on the whites' guilt and fear. Guilt aroused paternalism, and fear provoked hatred. The structure of the state was so weak that the government in Lima was forced to rely on landowning petty tyrants to control the Indian population any way they chose. With rebel leaders still being identified with the Inca by the Indians in the southern Andes, the whites themselves began to view the conflict as a race war in which, instead of trying to reconcile the two cultures, the Indians had to be ruthlessly browbeaten and absorbed into theirs.

But by the 1920s, it was too late. The scores of Indian revolts, unleashed mainly because of the hacienda owners' land grabs, coincided with the beginnings of an indigenous consciousness among white intellectuals. Also, missionaries of the Seventh-Day Adventist church had made inroads into the bleak altiplano in the Puno department. Unlike the Catholic diocesan priests, the Adventists' ministers worked closely with the Indians, set up schools, and told them that they, too, had rights as citizens. It was the first challenge to the hegemony of the Catholic church.

Just as the landowners were using the Indians' utopian desire for a revival of Inca rule to justify their expropriations, arguing that the Indians did not wish to be part of the republic, the criollo writer José Carlos Mariátegui set the cat among the pigeons by declaring the Inca empire to have been a primitive form of communism. Fresh from his travels in Europe under the shadow of the bolsheviks, he wrote: "Indigenous aspiration is absolutely revolutionary. The same myth, the same idea, are decisive agents in awaking other ancient nations, other old races in decline: Hindus, Chinese, etc. Why does the Inca nation, which built the most developed and harmonious Communist system, have to be the only one indifferent to external experience?"

The potentially explosive combination of the socialist and Inca utopias was initially snuffed out by decades of political repression interspersed with military coups and dictatorships. Mariátegui died in 1930, shortly after founding what became the Peruvian Communist party, which was promptly proscribed and went underground; it adopted a fossilized pro-Soviet line with no time for local nuances. But the Inca myth, smoldering away as ever in the Andean mind, had adopted a more livid place on the political stage. The Inca empire's name, Tahuantinsuyo, had already been adopted by a national Indian congress, an event that was evidence of a greater political consciousness among the Indians themselves. However, the power of the myth was also recognized by Víctor Haya de la Torre, the founder of the party that has since dominated Peru's twentieth-century political life, the American Popular Revolutionary Alliance (APRA). Forced into clandestineness, Haya de la Torre adopted the name of the Inca Pachacútec as his pseudonym. He accepted the mantle of the messianic savior, too. One poem dedicated to him ran: "You are the light that shines on the path / before so dark. . . ." Already looming on the horizon was a movement whose name would be abbreviated to Shining Path.

Mariátegui, who in his youth was said to be deeply religious, perceived socialist revolution itself in mythological and religious terms. He wrote: "The force of revolutionaries is not in their scholarship; it is in their faith, in their passion, in their will. It is a religious, mystical, spiritual force. It is the force of the Myth." In linking racial with economic and political vindication under the banner of spiritually fired communism, Mariátegui laid the fuse for the explosion of Shining Path half a century later.

From 1920 to 1960 the Peruvian population more than doubled, placing increasing strains on the petty fiefdoms of the landlords, whose dependent peasants were beginning to be starved of usable land. At the same time, the peasants began to organize themselves into unions and to initiate formal community land claims against the landlords and the Catholic church. Since the land claims were often expensive and futile in the face of corrupted judiciaries, they turned into waves of land seizures instead. The Indians, who formed about half the population, were still mostly illiterate because Quechua was not officially recognized and therefore not taught in schools. Hence, they were still unable to vote. A shortage of schools ensured that at the start of the 1960s only forty percent of children attended school anyway. And a mere three percent of Peruvians owned more than eighty percent of the available arable or pastoral land.

The land squeeze not only sparked off an increased migration to the towns and the coast, where the Indians found themselves culturally alienated and marginalized from the relative urban prosperity. But in doing so, it also put a bitter and receptive peasantry more in reach of the predominantly middle-class mestizo revolutionary intellectual leaders inspired by Fidel Castro's success in Cuba in 1959. Nevertheless, Abimael Guzmán must have watched attentively from Ayacucho as revolt after revolt ended pathetically, cruelly, in disaster. Messy and unprepared, for him they were thereby aborting and delaying the true revolution. The fundamental reason for the rebellions' failure to survive very long against the security forces was the lack of the peasants' commitment. Although the guerrilla leaders enjoyed the Indians' support, they failed to develop deep grass-roots political contact with them. Furthermore, the peasants were successfully terrorized by the tactics of the police and soldiers; the guerrillas were unable either to defend them or to help them defend themselves. Napalm provided by the United States was reportedly used in the saturation bombing of villages in the department of Junín. Haphazard attempts at agrarian reform also helped to take some of the steam out of the peasants' resolve.

Once again, the revolutionary leaders adopted the Inca image. But it was skin-deep: Years later, Hugo Blanco, a Congress deputy, was said to be observed by other first-class air passengers switching from his sandals and jeans into a suit once aboard flights bound for Stockholm to visit his Swedish wife. Nevertheless, Blanco, the bearded, mestizo son of a lawyer, was the first rebel to embody both the Marxist and Andean traditions. A Trotskyite, he swapped his Western clothes for a poncho and went to till the fields in the valley of La Convención in the department of Cuzco.

Blanco organized the peasants, who were still living in semifeudal conditions, into unions, which in turn organized strikes and land seizures. The peasants are reported immediately to have identified him with the Incas. The revolt broke up after it was let down by the international Trotskyites, found itself unarmed and isolated nationally, and was crushed by the security forces. Blanco was jailed after killing a policeman while trying to help a peasant whose wife and daughter had been raped by a landowner. He was saved from the implementation of the death penalty partly because of an international campaign.

For Blanco, the Indians' oppression was not just economic but racial. He wrote: "Although the wall separating the Indians from the mestizos and the whites is not as solid as in the case of the Afro-Americans and the whites in the United States, their humiliation and oppression are worse. Their language, their music, their manner of dress, their tastes, and their customs are ridiculed, suppressed, and denigrated." No doubt conscious of the ambiguous nature of his own color—never mind the agony of his name—and striving to legitimize himself as an indigenous leader, he was keen to emphasize that there were " 'Indians' of Indian language, Indian dress, Indian customs, who are white by birth." Elsewhere, he switched to the first person: "They destroy our culture, our Quechua, our Aymara, our Guaraní, our *yaraví*, our aesthetic values. They spit on us. . . ." (The Guaraní are an Indian people in Paraguay; *yaraví* is a form of Indian music.)

Blanco's immediate revolutionary successors in 1965 assumed Inca names for their guerrilla groups, such as Túpac Amaru and Pachacútec. Their leaders—the most notable being Luis de la Puente, a myopic, middle-aged lawyer—were variously shot in captivity or thrown out of a helicopter. The last to move into action, Héctor Béjar, called for an alliance invoking "the vast majority of the Peruvian people who make up our most glorious traditions, handed down to us by the Incas, and those who gave up their lives for their country, like Manco Inca, Juan Santos, Túpac Amaru . . ."

In historic imitation of Túpac Amaru II, whose execution of a local administrator heralded the start of the rebellion, Béjar launched his guerrilla movement in the department of Ayacucho by hanging two landowners notorious for rape, torture, and murder. The revolt was eventually suppressed by army patrols, and most of its members were killed. Béjar said shortly afterward that the peasants "quickly understood the need for revolution" but that "political work" was needed "to make them understand that the revolution does not end with driving out the landlord." He added: "The Peruvian Revolution will not take months, but years. But when it comes it will be one of the most profound and beautiful in America. . . . Our tactics should be to adapt ourselves to the psychology of the Peruvian peasant."

The agrarian reform carried out by General Juan Velasco after the expulsion of President Francisco Belaúnde—whose right-wing populist party had claimed an element of Incaic inspiration—broke up estates larger than thirty to fifty hectares. It swept the carpet from underneath the left-wing parties, furthering their fragmentation as they bickered about "reformism." While Guzmán stuck to his guns and, almost unnoticed, developed deeper and deeper links with the Indian peasantry in Ayacucho, studying the local anthropology and sending out his students to teach in the countryside, the other sectors of the radical left began to abandon their rural work and to concentrate more on the towns and their traditional stronghold, the mines. This reflected migration patterns and Peru's shift away from agriculture. The left also joined forces with the other political parties in making a return to democracy, with free and open elections, their major platform.

Guzmán turned in the diametrically opposite direction just when the Indian peasantry was suffering from the chaos caused by the agrarian reform. The state failed to fill the vacuum of power left by the removal of the big landowners who had wielded such a viselike control. Its agricultural cooperatives were a disaster: corrupt, poorly conceived, and badly run. With agriculture in decline, it was not long before the hopes raised by agrarian reform and wider educational opportunities were dashed, especially in the poorer southern Andes. And, slowly, those sons and daughters of peasants who had dreamed of a better life through the previously forbidden fruits of education found only disappointment and frustration in the absence of sufficient economic growth to incorporate their labor. The incipient racial anger was present not only in Andean fiestas but, perhaps more menacingly, in the *huayno* songs. In the lyrics of one *huayno* recorded in 1979, there ran the words:

> *We have gone around lost for a long time*
> *but it will not be for ever. . . .*
> *The rich will come face to face with the poor*
> *and between all the poor*
> *we will bring you to bay*
> *as if you were the thieving fox;*
> *wait, just wait,*
> *you who starve my people to death,*
> *I will kill you.*

Peruvian society is still racist to its very core. For all the inter-marriage, the economic scale from riches to rags can be corre-lated directly with skin color; the whites are the richest and the Indians are the poorest. Among the whites and the not-quite-so-whites, racism in Peru is understood only to refer to the treatment of the black descendants of the African slaves im-ported to work in the Andean mines in the late sixteenth cen-tury, and who later, after they perished like flies because of the altitude and inhumane conditions, labored on the huge sugar plantations along the coast, where they died of malaria instead. "Racism" is also considered a valid term for the treatment of the Chinese, who were imported in turn under slavelike con-ditions in the nineteenth century in order to shore up the labor forces on the haciendas, and for the extraction of guano, once the African slaves had been freed.

The idea that the vast majority of the population—the In-dian peasants, small merchants, miners, industrial workers, and wandering street vendors—is discriminated against racially is not even entertained. Yet their poverty, which stems from a history of economic stifling and exploitation by the whites, is dismissed as inevitable and their plight next to hopeless on the grounds of their race. The fact that the poverty is blamed on some kind of racial flaw is not conceived of as being racist. Racism is perceived as something that is physically aggressive, something enshrined in the law and constitution. But in Peru, neither of the latter counts for much. To condemn Indians as lazy thieves is viewed as a somber statement of truth; it may occasionally be accompanied by a patronizing, reconciliating call for charity. Dark skin is seen by the whites as ugly and worthless: National beauty contests exclude overly dark girls almost by definition. The scandal in Britain of the House of Commons call girl Pamela Bordes was greeted with bafflement by a prestigious Lima magazine; it could not understand why the MP should involve himself with a girl from India, much less what all the fuss was about.

The Indians are perceived to be an inferior race, the Achilles heel of the nation. The whites fail to recognize that the sullen inefficiency and deceit they encounter in the Indians and mes-tizos are everyday forms of preserving personal dignity, assert-ing independence, and getting their own back. They widely attribute the more successful and sophisticated economies of Chile and Argentina to their governments' extermination of almost all their indigenous peoples.

Indians' relationships with whites in Peru are on an almost exclusively servile footing. They and the poorer mestizos are forced to work for a pittance in order to survive because of chronic unemployment and underemployment. They are the house servants of the urban rich, the army of street vendors who hawk everything from plastic coat hangers to smuggled wine and Amazon monkeys. They are the tiny, dirty, bare-footed boys who jump onto car hoods to wipe the windshield at traffic lights; who sell their places in cinema queues; who beg as mercilessly as their benefactors off-load last year's worthless banknotes. They are those who form endless lines for buses that never come or buses that are already packed, their passengers bursting out through the oily, broken windows to inhale Lima's humid and smog-laden fumes of fish meal, garbage, and urine. The wounded shock of those such as the rare, well-to-do Indian, probably on a short visit to the capital and turned out smartly for the occasion, after being pushed off a minibus in an upper-class district because of the jealous snobbery of a mestizo conductor, can only turn to rage.

The Andean and Amazon Indians are valued as tourist curios and little else. Before Shining Path's recent advances, tourism had become one of Peru's biggest foreign-currency earners, after cocaine paste and copper. Otherwise, for the dominating white oligarchy, which tends to secure contracts and monopolies by the bribery and corruption of government and judiciary officials, driving up prices to produce profit margins three times as high as those in the average European country and closing down companies when faced with reducing them in times of recession, the Indians are seen as "dumb animals." The words were those of an imports dealer who claimed to know them inside out. His studies must have taught him something: He never went anywhere without his Smith & Wesson gun. Fear grips the white élite. In the middle of the bloodiest and most radical challenge to their authority, most prefer to build sentry boxes and high walls around their houses and factories, to shift their investments abroad, and to arm themselves, instead of concentrating on attempting to bring about a fairer, more open, and genuinely democratic society which might endanger their historic grip.

In 1979 all Indians were finally able to vote: The Spanish-literacy requirement was dropped. The peasants and poorer sectors voted strongly for the left-wing parties in the assembly that paved the way for the general election, but in the general election itself the left's divisions contributed to its collapse against Francisco Belaúnde, whom the poorer sectors favored for the road-building and public works of his earlier government. Nevertheless, if the nonregistered are taken into account, only about half the people technically eligible to vote did so. When Alan García swept to power with APRA in 1985, more than one fifth of the registered voters failed to show up, spoiled their votes, or left them blank. And when Alberto Fujimori, whose parents are Japanese immigrants, won a landslide victory over the writer Mario Vargas Llosa in 1990, that figure had increased to almost one third. The lack of electoral interest, fueled by an unfathomable mixture of terror and support of Shining Path, is further underlined by the fact that voting in Peru is compulsory and failure to do so punishable by a heavy fine.

President Fujimori's victory was based mainly on his color. He was runner-up in the first round by playing on his Japanese ancestry while at the same time canvassing from farm tractors, depending on the Protestant churches' formidable organizational support, and cashing in on people's revulsion for the millions of dollars spent by the traditional parties on television propaganda. He had neither a proper party nor a government program, just a notebook, which from time to time he flourished reassuringly to the multitudes. His success provoked a racist backlash by the right-wing, upper-class white élite behind Vargas Llosa, much to the author's own disgust. Anti-Japanese chants were screamed out hysterically in front of Vargas Llosa's house and people of Japanese and Chinese background were roughed up in the street and kicked out of restaurants in the smarter neighborhoods of Lima.

The racism was instantly identified by the overwhelming majority of poor Indians and mestizos with that suffered by them.

Fujimori took advantage and ran a racist campaign in which he stirred up their resentment with sarcastic antiwhite remarks. These, together with Fujimori's lying promise that he would not apply a "shock" austerity program to revive the bankrupt and hyperinflationary economy, ensured that Vargas Llosa never really had a chance. It was the white minority against the colored masses, the rich against the poor.

Salvador Palomino, of the Council of South American Indians, said: "All our governments since independence have consisted of European criollos. The whites were scared and angry at seeing their hegemony threatened. Orientals are physiologically, philosophically, and religiously closer to us—many of us are only superficially Catholic, we use it as a façade, a defense mechanism. The criollos think that we are not wise, but Fujimori attracted the Indian vote because Vargas Llosa was backed by the traditional, rich, oppressive parties, while the left fails to represent Indian culture. Fujimori does not have a party, he is not bureaucratic. His entry into government means that any Indian can one day be in power; it paves the way."

Of the other main player in the general elections, Shining Path, who embarked on a savage attempt to sabotage the elections wherever they could by bombings, intimidation, and assassinations, Palomino added: "Our people are caught between two fires, the military and the subversive groups. The right-wing parties join in the repression and the left-wing parties just allow it to happen. Unfortunately, Shining Path provides, on a personal level, an opportunity for revenge against the whites."

While Guzmán led his rebels, literally, by the book, Fujimori waved his in the air, and Vargas Llosa campaigned under the banner of a world-famous novelist—he has been mentioned as a possible winner of the Nobel Prize for Literature—there was another candidate brandishing his own preferred tome, the Bible. Ezequiel Ataucusi, a former sacristan whose education was cut short at primary school after his father left home, tapped the messianic, millenarian utopian tradition by preaching "agriculture power" and flying the rainbow flag of the Incas. He promised worldly salvation for the chosen people, namely his sect, which is prevalent in all the poor districts of Lima but also found in the jungle around the river Pachitea in the Amazon department of Ucayali. Ataucusi and his followers sacrifice a cow each Saturday and, apart from the men's peaked caps, try to imitate the dress of the ancient Israelites. The men have long beards and never cut their hair; the women wear blue veils. Ataucusi's senatorial list secured more votes than that of the banking community, whose candidates' election banner read "Somo Libres" (meaning "We Are Free"), despite the fortune spent on the bankers' campaign. And 70,015 people voted for Ataucusi as president.

Ataucusi's nighttime closing rally beside the Lima Sheraton was attended by thousands of people, all waving fish in the air: wooden fish, papier-mâché fish, plastic fish, tissue-paper fish, fish with twin fishlets, two-men, eighteen-foot fish with chomping red mouths, glittery fish . . . and up on the podium Ataucusi shook a large silvery fish the shape of a barracuda. Enraptured cheers of "Ezequiel!" were accompanied by music combining white electric noise and video-game blips with the occasional electronic organ chord and the thump of a bass drum. A felt picture of Machu Picchu in burning neon colors was draped from the podium itself; women dressed as Inca concubines in gold paper crowns danced beneath it.

When asked where he had come from for the rally, one supporter said: "The City of God." He was originally from the department of Arequipa, but had followed Ezequiel for two years because Ezequiel was "sent by God, taught the word of God, and cared for 'us' like children." Four cows walked by, yoked together for plowing. How did he know Ezequiel was sent by God? "It is in the Bible." There was a feverish flicking of pages to Deuteronomy, chapter 17, verse 15. He ran his finger along the words: "Be sure to appoint over you the king the Lord your God chooses. He must be from among your own brothers. Do not place a foreigner over you, one who is not a brother Israelite." But how did he know it was Ezequiel? He flicked to Ezekiel, chapter 24, verse 24: "Ezequiel will be assigned to you. You will do just as he has done. When this happens you will know that I am the Sovereign Lord." But still, how did he know it referred to Ezequiel Ataucusi? "The scriptures are clear," he exclaimed. "Ezequiel picked us from the jungle and the coast!"

More flicking and quoting. This time from Isaiah, chapter

43, verse 5: "Do not be afraid for I am with you. I will bring you children from the east and gather you from the west." And why the fish? Over to Jeremiah 16, verse 16: "But now I will send for many fishermen, says the Lord, and they will catch them [the lost Israelites]. After that I will send for many hunters and they will hunt them down on every mountain and hill and from the crevices of the rocks." In a passage prior to the quotation, the Israelites are chastised for abandoning their gods and adopting strange ones. They are then promised they will return to the land of their forefathers.

Ataucusi has won a following by tapping the search for identity by a section of the poorest of the Indians and mestizos, either recent urban immigrants or settlers in the jungle, who feel alienated not just from the U.S.–European culture of official Peru but also from their own Andean roots. Ataucusi creates a bridge for the two cultures by which each fortifies the other. He grants hope based on a mystical mixture of both traditions by invoking the Bible and the Incas. The utopian nature of the Inca myth is reinforced by a utopian interpretation of the Bible. Furthermore, he uses the written word of the Bible to confer legitimacy on himself and his followers. Ataucusi falls in the tradition of Taqui Onqoy, Juan Santos Atahualpa, Túpac Amaru II, and a host of other messianic Peruvian rebels who have in some way tried to mold the traditions together, often in an apocalyptic fashion, to throw off the colonial yoke and its modern heritage, to free their people. Like the Israelites, they are a people in search of a home.

The leaders' own determination to prove their legitimacy—by Inca ancestry, by biblical prophecy—directly reflects their followers' own quest for an identity. The most poetic expression of this search was the life of the important mestizo novelist and anthropologist, José María Arguedas. Arguedas, whose widow is in jail accused of being a member of Shining Path, shot himself because he was unable to reconcile his sense of split cultural roots. His mother died in his infancy; he was brought up in the mountains by Indian servants in the absence of his father. Eventually, his father remarried and Arguedas became deeply attached to his second wife. "I am the son of my stepmother," he said.

Arguedas's feelings of being an orphan and being torn between the Quechua and Spanish worlds mutually reinforced each other. Feelings of illegitimacy—and rejection—were truer still to José Carlos Mariátegui, whose heady mix of socialism and Indian nationalism has been one of the pillars of twentieth-century Peruvian politics: He was born out of wedlock to an élite family, which refused to recognize him. Abimael Guzmán suffers from a similar sense of paternal alienation (and is said to have been bitterly unhappy when treated like a provincial outcast while at secondary school in Lima). Like Arguedas, he is deeply fond of his stepmother and holds, as did Mao himself, a deep grudge against his father.

Guzmán's fundamentalist attitude to the classic Communist scriptures radiates with the search for personal as well as political legitimacy. Learning and repetition of selected parts of the texts is at the heart of Shining Path indoctrination. Respect for the word is sacred. And not only does Guzmán forcefully assert that Mao was the true ideological descendant of Marx and Lenin, but he goes to considerable lengths to show that he, Guzmán, has donned the mantle in turn. This conforms not only to his political and psychological needs as a leader but also to the aspirations of those, like Ataucusi's followers, seeking a legitimacy, identity, and purpose in a country which does not feel their own.

Abimael Guzmán and the other leading members of Shining Path—the central committee—have contrived to use the Andean mythical traditions not because they believe in the goals implied but because they serve their purposes tactically. Spanish would be the official language. Nowhere in Shining Path's official documents is it stated that the movement is seeking Indian ethnic or cultural restoration. For Shining Path, that would be nationalistic. It sees the revolution in international and class rather than racial terms. However, racial and cultural resentment is a formidable political tool. It is what has given Shining Path its force and it is largely responsible for the cruel and ferocious nature of the violence.

More than 450 years after Pizarro launched the Spanish conquest, white repression of the indigenous races is as unabated and unforgiven as ever. On a social and work level, the hostility toward whites reveals itself every day in the street. In many areas of the capital—which accounts for a third of the population—as well as in cities, towns, and villages up and down the coast, in the Andes and in the Amazon basin, a white person is liable to be treated with suspicion or contempt. He is often eyed mistrustfully or ignored, and may be hissed at as a gringo or even spat upon. Where there is a chance of squeezing money out of him, he is likely either to be begged from, robbed, or assiduously courted with false bonhomie in the hope of a gift, favor, or purchase. Extreme poverty reinforces the latent hatred: Putting one over on a gringo is a way of exacting vengeance. Sullenness, dishonesty, and laziness in Indians' dealings with whites are forms of asserting and preserving individuality in a country that squashes and strangles them. Indians are hanging on to their souls like a prostitute who sells everything except for a kiss.

The racial resentment is integral to Indian myths and fiestas. In a country where nearly forty percent of children under six years old suffer from chronic malnutrition, and one in nine die by the age of five, the myth of the *pishtaco* who extracts human grease for profit is a nightmarish metaphor for how the Indians see themselves exploited and oppressed. The *pishtaco* is seen as an outsider, mostly white or mestizo, and often a businessman, government representative, or priest. In the past he was often a landowner.

His victims' grease is said to be used either to make products, such as soap, for sale in the towns; or to make church bells ring louder so they can be heard from farther away—and thus summon more people to church; or to be sold to the government for export. Occasionally it is said that the flesh is sold off and eaten in Lima restaurants or the grease used to lubricate machines. In some cases the image of the exploited worker is explicit: The *pishtacos* simply feed people to the ore grinders in the mines. The myth moves with the times: the *pishtacos*, who are perceived as human, not supernatural, beings, are also believed to sell off the peasants' blood to blood banks, and the oil or grease to oil companies in a bid to pay off Peru's national debt.

In the same way that the Pizarro-Atahualpa scene in the annual fiesta in honor of Santa Rosa varies according to the barometer of local political feeling, so too does the representation of the *pishtaco*. During the Santa Rosa fiesta in the town of Puquio in the department of Ayacucho, the *pishtaco*s, who are there called by their other name, *nakaq*s, are no longer depicted as whites but as blacks. "In the fiesta, it is as if the people are not scared of the *nakaq*s anymore," said an engineer who works in Puquio. "They have become laughingstocks, they have been conquered. If the *nakaq*s had stayed white it would have meant that they were still dangerous." In the same fiesta, Indians and mestizos dressed in exaggeratedly ragged peasant clothing strut about in mimicry of gringos, whipping the ground and speaking gibberish in imitation of a foreign language. Any object that represents modernity and comes from the outside world, even if just a motorbike, is theatrically abused.

Shining Path has surfaced in the town. It had been known for a while that the rebels came back and forth through Puquio, in the province of Lucanas, on their way between the coast and the mountains. Suddenly, a few months after Shining Path slogans and posters appeared, two tourists from Australia and New Zealand were brutally killed nearby while traveling by bus from Ayacucho. Notices found beside the corpses were said to claim they were agents of the CIA. The guerrillas cut their throats and, among other mutilations, replaced one of the girl's eyes with a cork. The vengeful, ritualistic style of the killings was typical of Shining Path, and the girl's mutilation corresponded to mythical traditions surrounding *pishtaco*s. The following year, in 1990, the rebels visited each of the surrounding villages in turn. They forced everyone to attend meetings at which they demanded the resignations of the police and of judicial and elected authorities. The demand was explicitly accompanied by the threat of violence. As elsewhere, the villages acquiesced. In August 1991 complementary local elections had to be convoked in each of the twenty-one districts of Lucanas to fill the vacancies. For lack of applicants, the elections were canceled in nearly half of them.

Andean fiestas, music, and art are permeated by the refusal to accept the domination of the whites. The world is symbolically split between those "from above" and those "from below": between those from the valleys or the coast and those from the mountains, between the *mistis*—the whites and Westernized mestizos—and the *runas*—the Indians. In the departments of Apurímac and Ayacucho, and even in the outskirts of Lima, the clash between the foreign and indigenous cultures is still played out, illegally, in bullfights during which a condor is attached to the bull's neck in order to aggravate its agony and rage. In the valley of the river Mantaro in the department of Junín, the mockery of foreign culture assumes a more ludicrous form: Ducks, which were introduced by the Europeans, are hung upside down for horseback riders to take their turn in galloping up and grabbing them away by the neck.

Shining Path rebels are mainly young Quechua-speaking Indians in a country where their language is considered a sign of inferiority. They are those whose communities have been little exposed to the market economy and who have never had the benefit of education. For the young, Shining Path offers an escape, a chance of change, modernity, a challenge to their own elders, and a stab at ethnic revenge. But the movement also attracts those who have been able to acquire an education and have fought to learn Spanish in an attempt to escape their linguistic and economic domination.

So unquenchable is the thirst for learning that it is as if the poorest sectors of Peruvian society seek to use the tools of the status quo against itself. Not only do the parents make every possible sacrifice for their children's education, but the children themselves take their studies very seriously. The schools and state universities are packed day and night with poor students of all ages. The frustration on discovering that the official Peru has no place for them, and continues to discriminate against them via its racism and impenetrable bureaucracy, makes them easy recruits for Shining Path. For all the disillusioned and racially and culturally alienated, the movement offers hope, identity, and self-advancement as well as a chance to unleash historic ethnic and social vengeance.

The same is true for the millions of poor Indians who have emigrated not just to the provincial towns and cities in the Andes and upper jungle regions but to the coast, especially Lima, where the surrounding desert has been engulfed by wave after wave of shantytowns in the wake of the agrarian reform. The migration was also prompted by the collapse in the demand for Andean wheat. The crop that was originally forced on the peasants by the Spaniards in order to feed those who were made to work in the mines, disrupting the Indians' own agriculture, was no longer profitable in the face of cheaper foreign imports. The immigrants form the great mass of street vendors; more than two million of them are without plumbing or regular electricity. Pigs are herded on the rubbish heaps by the port of Callao; garbage cans are scoured for food; and tuberculosis, gastroenteritis, and pneumonia are rife. Cheap, clandestine cemeteries in the desert, where the burials are unblessed and unregistered, stretch for as far as the eye can see.

To the east, however, over the Andes, a red sun dawns for the desperate. Shining Path thrives not only on the social and economic crisis that racks Peru, but also, more than its predecessors, on Indian myth and ideology. Abimael Guzmán benefits from a strange dovetailing of Marxist and Maoist thought with Andean traditions. Perhaps in the light of past rebellions whose leaders' aims have been undermined and their discipline and organization diminished by the uncontrollable fury of antiwhite feeling once released, Guzmán's scrupulously delicate manipulation of Andean traditions is implied rather than explicit. However, his followers and sympathizers are in no doubt at all of the synthesis. As one poet saw the "people's war":

> *Thousands of Indians and mestizos*
> *descend to the town*
> *like a red avalanche,*
> *with muscles of steel*
> *and voices of thunder, shouting "Freedom!"*
> *because they know that the days of Pachacútec*
> *and the Inkarri have arrived.*

Pachacútec was the legendary architect of the Inca empire. According to the myth of the Inkarri, Atahualpa's head vanished after he was "decapitated" by Pizarro; when the head has finished growing its body below the earth, the Inkarri will return again to rule in Tahuantinsuyo.

The Inkarri myth, which emerged with the Taqui Onqoy movement soon after the conquest, sought to explain the turning upside down of the Indian world. Rather like the Israelites',

the Indians' original myth blamed their plight on the abandonment of their old, pre-Inca gods. But the Inkarri became a
composite kingly figure representing the spirit of the Incas; he
is seen as a builder who made stones move and brought order
to chaos. He is said to have been vanquished by Jesus Christ,
who was all-powerful in the sky, and to have gone underground, taking the world of order—as well as gold and silver—
with him. One of his forms is a snake, appropriately the Gene-
sis form of the Christian devil. José Santos Atahualpa claimed
to come from a house of stone and to have stores of silver and
gold hidden away. Túpac Amaru II's name was significant not
just for being that of the last Inca, who himself adopted it: The
words mean "Royal Snake" in Quechua. The name of his lieutenant in southern Peru and Bolivia meant the same in the
Aymara language.

Christian and Andean traditions are yoked together in the
myth. Christ and the Inkarri are perceived as warring brothers.
The Taqui Onqoy movement included Santa María and Santa
María Magdalena. In the same manner, drawing on both traditions, José Santos Atahualpa and Túpac Amaru II claimed to
be sent from heaven; the latter promised that all those who died
in the war would be resurrected when it was over and would
bask in an earthly paradise. The opposition between the Inkarri
and Christ is perceived to be that of the sun and moon, day
and night. Each is seen as an essential part of the other's existence in an endless battle in which one or the other has the
upper hand. The post-European age is seen as that of darkness
and chaos; but the myth bears the hope and promise of another
golden age. In one version of the Inkarri myth collected by an
anthropologist, a peasant says: "The blood of Inkarri is alive at
the bottom of our Mother Earth. It is said that he will arrive on
the day that his head, his blood, his body come together. That
day will dawn in the dusk, reptiles will fly." For his Indian
followers, Abimael Guzmán is the Red Sun and the snake that
vanishes in the grass. He is the messiah of the conquered who
will lead them in another *pachacuti*, when time and space are
inverted; he will reverse the present order and give his people
back their land.

# 3

# In the Flare of the Chinese Lantern

December 26, 1980, held a surreal but grisly surprise in store for the bleary-eyed early-morning risers in the center of Lima. The corpses of various painted dogs were hanging from lampposts with signs saying "Deng Xiaoping, son of a bitch." For a group of Shining Path sympathizers, it was a way of showing their distaste for the Chinese leader who had betrayed the revolutionary policies of Mao Zedong. For most of the passersby, it meant nothing at all; the image seemed simply to sum up the demented nature of some Communist fanatics who had sprung out of a particularly backward corner of the Andes.

Ironically, the ritualistic violence was innately Andean. Not only were dog killings a feature of Chinese culture and of the Gang of Four's crusade in 1976 against the "revisionism" of Deng Xiaoping, a renowned dog-eater, they are also a part of Andean culture: Dogs are sacrificed in traditional Indian funeral rites. Although one Shining Path participant, who said they had been obliged to paint the dogs because they were unable to find enough black ones, confirmed that the gesture was strictly in imitation of the Gang of Four, it was widely misinterpreted. Even the party got its wires crossed: an English booklet printed as late as 1985 by Peruvian party sympathizers abroad, who were in direct contact with Shining Path, referred to hanged dogs being an "Inca symbol of contempt and attack."

The incident was a bizarre example of a cultural and ideological synthesis, both conscious and unconscious, deliberate and accidental, which is responsible for much of Shining Path's potency and support. The spectacle of the strapped-up dogs with their throats cut just looked out of place amid the colonial trappings of the coastal capital. Andean traditions are reflected in Abimael Guzmán's speeches and Shining Path's tactics; they have also emerged in propaganda, poems, and songs. It is the symbiotic nature of the relationship between Maoism and Andean tradition that has conspired to turn centuries of hate into action, that has transformed chaotic rebellion, sometimes supine, other times blindly vengeful, into organized revolution.

Maoism essentially comprised a development of Communist thought and its application to the realities of China as Mao perceived them, incorporating Sun Tzu, a fourth-century B.C. Chinese sage whose essays on the art of war are considered among the finest ever written. To help his analysis, Mao used China's myths like a modern opinion pollster: to see what the people wanted and to communicate complex ideas to them. Shining Path's ideology comprises Abimael Guzmán's application of Marxism-Leninism-Maoism to the situation of Peru as he sees it—Guzmán has gradually replaced José Carlos Mariátegui as the "shining path" the party follows. Guzmán was surrounded by anthropologists in Ayacucho; the most notable was the radical Marxist university rector, Efraín Morote, who was considered a brilliant academic and is believed by many to be Shining Path's spiritual father. His son, Osmán Morote, who is also an anthropologist, is a prominent member of Shining Path and is serving twenty years in jail for terrorist offenses. Such is Guzmán's emulation of Mao that it would be inevitable for the party's central committee to employ his populist methods. However, as will be seen, its task is rendered easier by the innate structural similarities of Maoism and Andean culture.

Guzmán converts what his Communist forebears regarded as historical inevitability into a millenarian utopia. Such a utopia is integral to Andean mythical tradition. The Shining Path leader, typically simplifying and historicizing world events, cites Beethoven's Ninth Symphony to suggest that, in the same way that only in this century could somebody sing the highest of the choral notes as they ascend toward a "musical explosion" and the triumph of the bourgeoisie, only now is the proletariat ready to triumph in turn. Guzmán perceives Shining Path as the vanguard of the international Communist revolution, which will be ushered in under "humanity's third millennium." In his speech "For the New Flag," to a Shining Path conference in December 1979, Guzmán splits up Peruvian history into "How Darkness Prevailed," "How Light Emerged and Steel Was Forged," and "How the Walls Were Destroyed and the Dawn Spread." The three ages confirm to the transformation in colonial times of the original five ages of the Andean world. Guzmán uses the same tripartite structure but colors it in with a Marxist vision of Peruvian history.

According to Indian chroniclers in the seventeenth century, each of the five ages lasted a thousand years and comprised two halves, which were heralded by a *pachacuti*. The *pachacuti* was both the end of one world and the start of the next, a cosmic upheaval. In some areas, under Christian influence, it had already, by the seventeenth century, become associated with the Last Judgment. By the time of Juan Santos Atahualpa in the 1700s, the ages had been reduced to three: that of the Father, the Son, and the Holy Ghost. The first two were the pre-Hispanic and the present-day post-conquest eras.

The third was an age in which the division between the Indian and European worlds would be reestablished, in which the proper balance between them would be resumed; when, according to myths, "men would have wings and fly." Felipe Guamán Poma, an influential and famous Indian chronicler writing in Ayacucho around 1610 believed that order would only be regained when the Spanish returned to their legitimate lands and all intermarriage was rejected. Today, myths and ceremonies as well as the social structures of the Peruvian Indian communities, where about six million people live, attest to the prevalence of the same view. Those who marry an outsider become outsiders themselves.

The Indians' system of communal agriculture, based of the *ayllu* division of land, is virtually idealized by Guzmán. In his "For the New Flag" speech, even the Inca Pachacútec is recognized for bringing order, albeit an exploitative one. Foreigners are condemned for pulling the "agrarian order" apart.

Guzmán declares: "People were carried off to the mines and their blood was converted into gold and silver, when [the Europeans] took to Europe." His language reflects the myth of the *pishtacos*. The myth itself conforms neatly to Marxist analysis of capitalism.

According to Marx's theory of surplus value, the true value of a worker's labor is reflected not in what he is paid by the capitalist but in the price of the final product. Where social and legal conditions permit and the labor supply is constant, workers may be paid so little and treated so badly that they are in effect sacrificed for the capitalist's profit, as happened for centuries in the Andean mines, where conditions have improved only recently. The *pishtaco* myth of the white man's extraction of the Indians' grease and blood is a metaphor for the same analysis of economic exploitation.

Guzmán contends that the age of darkness in Peru began to be lightened by the emergence of the industrial working class; that with the influence of Marxism, "light became steel." He says: "There began to appear a purer light, a shining light: That is the light we have, in our breasts and in our soul. That light fused with the earth and the mud became steel. Light, mud, steel, the Party rises up in 1928. . . ." Elsewhere, in his "We Are the Beginning" speech, Guzmán asserts that the masses are the "light of the world" who were "orphans" until they had a party to lead them. Now at last, he says, they have their "longed-for liberator."

The Shining Path leader maintains that, in the wake of Marx and Lenin, it was Mao Zedong who shone a "dazzling" light on the people, which only the party, little by little as its "retinas adjusted" and it "lowered its eyes" and encompassed Mariátegui, began to understand. In response, the party in Peru "reconstituted" itself to illuminate the path for the people: "Communists were convoked from all parts, they assembled a national system; the Communists got to their feet and the earth rumbled, and when it rumbled the comrades advanced."

The party's identity is presented as inseparable from the "armed struggle" and its leadership. Its reconstruction and its personalized role as a long-awaited liberator and guiding light of the masses, together with whom it will "spread the dawn" to put an end to the oppression that "kills the masses, consumes them by hunger, shackles them, and cuts their throats," mirrors the myth of the anticipated return of the Inkarri, who is said to be putting his body together again below the ground in preparation for settling accounts with Pizarro and the *pishtacos* —when, as the legend goes, there will be a *pachacuti* and "the day will dawn in the dusk."

Guzmán presents the revolution as if it were not just a fulfillment of historical laws but of myths and prophesies as well. Biblical quotations enhance the effect. "You will know them by their works," he says of the participants in the party's first military school. "Many are called, few are chosen," he intones at the swearing-in with the red-and-white hammer-and-sickle flag. His language and metaphors are often repetitive, as if to help along the accurate oral dissemination of his words. Together with the reiterated confidences such as "It is written" and "The future is assured," this lends his speeches an epic quality despite his surging and ungrammatical style.

He talks of historical necessity and obligation, of the fusing of "the history of the world, the history of our country, and the history of our Party . . . three realities, three conjunctions, and only one final conclusion, only one unshakable truth, only one future." The prophetic and historical assertions contain within them an implicit warning for those who ignore the rolling tide: They will be cast aside by history itself. The concept is central to one myth prevalent in the southern Andes in which a people called "the gentiles," who are said to have lived among the mountain peaks, were warned by their gods of a deluge of fire. They ignored the warning and were destroyed.

As in the Andean *pachacuti*, the revolution is presented as a reversal of the old order rather than solely a lineal progression in the Marxist sense: "The besiegers will be besieged and the annihilators will be annihilated and the would-be victors will be defeated," says Guzmán. The language conforms both to the *pachacuti* myth and to the present day, in which Lima is being encircled and overrun by shantytowns springing up because of the massive Indian migration from the Andes. José María Arguedas, regarded by Shining Path as the most politically articulate cultural voice of the indigenous cause, captured the same spirit in his "Choral Song" to Túpac Amaru: "We are coming down from the peaks. We are enveloping this race which hates us so much."

Guzmán's allegorical use of color to describe the reversal of the social order is also fundamental to Andean myths. Embracing, like Mao, who in turn had enlarged on Lenin, the concept of fire as a purifying force, he says in the "We Are the Beginning" speech: "We are a growing torrent against which are launched fire, stones, and mud; but our power is great, we will convert everything into our fire, we will convert the black fire into red fire, and the red is light. . . . The invincible flames of the revolution will grow and turn into lead, into steel, and from the roar of battles with its unquenchable fire, light will appear, from the blackness, brightness, and there will be a new world."

The relationship between red, black, and light is similar to that in the myth of the gentiles, in which fire is associated with day/sun (red) and rain with night/moon (black). An elemental imbalance produces drought or floods, the twin scourges of the Andes. Life, crops, and light are perceived to depend on the eternal, benevolent opposition between the sun and the moon. However, while according to Andean thought the prevalence of one of the opposites causes death and natural disaster— which at its extreme heralds a *pachacuti* and a reversal of order —in Maoism the two principal opposites resolve their difference and disappear in the violent birth of a new order.

Shining Path's texts, drawings, and posters constantly feature the red–black opposition. Red is identified with fire and the armed struggle, black with the "rotten state" and "forces of reaction." Modern history is reduced to a class struggle between "those from above" and "those from below"; the language is both typically Maoist and typically Andean. Everything is polarized, everyone is forced to take sides. But while the Andean world perceives the two sides to be part of an infinite order of life, under which their dominance can only be reversed and there can be no absolute, substantial change, Guzmán, like Mao, perceives the resolution of polarities producing such a change to be a universal law. Those who disagree are labeled reconciliators and lumped with the tiny minority, "those from above": "Reconciliation is the black flag of the [forces of] reaction; supporting the armed struggle is the red flag of the people," says a 1982 document of the central committee.

Propaganda leaflets aimed at the illiterate and semiliterate make abundant use of such symbolism. One leaflet features a rising sun that not only illuminates the people but is the people. It both leads and embodies them. Puka Inti, or "Red Sun," is one of Guzmán's names among Quechua communities. "Red Sun" was the name granted to Mao in China during the Cultural Revolution. But the sun is also the classic Inca symbol: It was considered the source and symbol of their power. Jean-Marie Ansion, a Belgian anthropologist who lived in Ayacucho during Shining Path's early years, claimed: "As the sun is linked to the Inca, it is probable that Abimael Guzmán is also understood as such—not that he recognizes himself as an Inca, which would without doubt be denied by militants of Shining Path, but that his authority is legitimate in the same way that of the Inca was."

Guzmán's ritualistic party purging is similar to the ritual fighting and sacrifices in Andean culture, too. For the Indians, sacrifices are essential in order to maintain the equilibrium of natural forces and thereby maintain life's harmony. It is a matter of balance and reciprocity. Offerings are made to lakes, trees, sun, and earth in turn, in thanks for what they produce and in order to ensure that they carry on producing. "You have to give the very, very best back in return for what you receive," said Salvador Palomino, an anthropologist and the secretary general in Peru of the Council of South American Indians.

Palomino's family comes from an Indian community in the Ayacucho department. Every August, which is the month of drought and wind when the powerful and potentially dangerous *huamani* spirits are said to be present, eight communities in the Ayacucho province of Víctor Fajardo meet for a ritual battle typical of those fought in many of the more culturally traditional and far-flung areas of the Andes. Four communities from the mountains take on four communities from the valleys. In the weeks preceding the fight, the two sides work themselves up by insulting and goading each other. In the actual clash, which is a ceremony in honor of the water divinity so that the drought will be "washed" away, two or three people are often killed. Palomino said: "Nobody cries. Rather, it is an occasion for happiness because their blood is being offered to the mother earth. The fight lets out all the social tensions and reaffirms the division of land."

Shining Path's ideological purges serve a similar purpose. In the *El Diario* interview, Guzmán asserts that without the "struggle between two lines" there is no basis for party unity. He adds: "Without a forceful and shrewd two-line struggle in the party, the ideology cannot be firmly grasped; nor can the program or the political line be established, defended, or applied, much less developed. The two-line struggle is fundamental to us and has to do with conceiving of the party as a contradiction in accordance with the universality of the law of contradiction." The rebels' purges involve humiliating self-criticism and, on the eve of the revolution, prompted desertions and expulsions. Such purges, which are usually aimed at "revisionists" or "opportunists," act as if to purify and redden the blood of the party. Regular public self-criticism before the party is practiced with all the faith and fervor of Catholic confession—by everyone except Guzmán, who not only embodies the leader and the party but, as its ideological guide, the Word itself.

Whether the sessions of criticism and self-criticism go as far as those in the Soviet Union under Stalin or China under Mao, in which Communists who strayed from the path would in some cases grovel as they demanded the death penalty in order to have the privilege of dying for the party of which, they cried, they were no longer worthy, miserable beings that they were, is not known. (During Stalin's purges, up to six million people were killed; during Mao's Cultural Revolution between 1966 and 1976, according to Deng Xiaoping, the figure was twenty-seven million.) But the self-criticism—and implicit self-sacrifice for the party—preserves both the party's status quo and the power of Guzmán as leader. Juan Ossio, an anthropologist who, unlike Ansion and Palomino, was never associated with the Peruvian left, said: "Shining Path's ritual battles are to avoid divisions in the heart of the party. They keep it together. Unity is re-created through artificial divisions into two parts, just as in the Andean village battles."

Maoist thought has had a strong grip on Peruvian Communist intellectuals ever since the aftermath of Mao's victory in 1949 over the Kuomintang government after twenty-two years of war. The Peruvian Communist party, which was officially formed in 1930, had its roots in the early Stalinist revolutionary model, according to which an alliance of industrial workers, soldiers, and peasants would topple the state through revolutionary insurrection and build a new state based principally on heavy industry. Since Peru was primarily an agricultural country, whose population lived mostly in the countryside, the party made little headway. Stalin's softening of his line by proposing alliances with the industrial middle class was equally unhelpful to Peru's Moscow dogmatists because Peru did not have such a middle class.

The development of Peruvian communism mirrored the tensions between the Soviet Union and China, whose relations were strained from the start because of Mao's emphasis on a peasant-based revolution and rural economic model, which the Soviet Stalinists considered petty-bourgeois "populist" deviations. Their antipathy later deepened amid Chinese requests for Soviet atomic technology. However, when Stalin was politically defrocked by Khrushchev posthumously in the late 1950s and his murderous purges were publicly denounced, the Chinese stayed faithful to the Stalinist line. They despised Khrushchev's flirtations with the imperialist West.

The radical Stalinists within the Peruvian Communist party confronted the rest as revisionists and warmed further to Mao, to whom they were attracted anyway because his emphasis on the revolutionary role of the peasantry was more relevant to Peru. When the Soviet-Chinese split finally came about in 1963, the Peruvian Communist party's breakup into Maoist and Muscovite factions was inevitable. The Maoists not only came away with more militants; they also came away with the brightest. It was their cadres who dominated the Communist presence in universities and schools at both staff and student levels.

Maoist communism has wielded greater influence in Peru than anywhere outside the Far East, with the possible exceptions of Mozambique and Angola; it did so even before and alongside the rise of Shining Path. The high profile acquired by the Peruvian left during the guerrilla movements of the

1960s and the seven years of General Juan Velasco's dictator-ship—when the state was swathed in official, socialist, anti-imperialist propaganda, the big haciendas were converted into agricultural cooperatives, and the juiciest oil and mining inter-ests were nationalized—helped to give it a platform. Maoist thought also struck a chord in Peru's neighboring country Bo-livia. However, neither there nor in Ecuador to the north have the Indians been quite so ethnically and economically margin-alized by the state.

Mao, following on from Engels, converted Marxist dialecti-cal materialism into a universal law of contradiction. In doing so, he utilized the general structure of the Chinese view of life to apply the Marxist concept of opposites, which was actually its inverse. Marx had converted the Western Socratic tradition of dialectical argument into not just a method of historical analysis but a set of historical laws. According to Marx, history was a process of confrontation through which revolution inev-itably emerged. Mao went further. In his essay "On Contradic-tion" he wrote: "The law of contradiction in things, that is, the law of the unity of opposites, is the fundamental law of nature and society and consequently also the fundamental law of thinking." For Marx and Lenin, revolution came about natu-rally in a critical moment when a society's internal contradic-tions surfaced and boiled over. For Mao, revolution was structural and permanent. Enemies were absolute; only the priority of the contradiction, a tactical matter, varied. Armed revolution was justifiable at all times.

Mao used the Chinese concept of the duality of opposites, which permeates every aspect of the traditional Chinese way of life, to support his thesis that the law of contradiction was the only fundamental law. But he had twisted the Chinese concept of dynamic harmony into dynamic confrontation and effec-tively turned it inside out.

In Peru, Salvador Palomino was closely acquainted with the students in Ayacucho who went on to make up the upper ech-elons of Shining Path. In the early 1960s, he witnessed the physical tortures inflicted on the Indians by landowners. He led a series of Indian land grabs. The landowners offered a reward for his death. As with Hugo Blanco and Abimael Guzmán, there arose the myth that he was in several places at once; in fact, he was often in a police jail. But in developing a deeper understanding of his own culture, he grew increasingly alienated from both Marxism and Maoism. He said: "Mao mixed Marxism with Chinese thought. He mistakenly thought the yang and yin were antagonistic opposites when in fact they are complementary, just as opposites are in Andean and other indigenous cultures. His dialectic is one of lineal confrontation and destruction. He saw history as lineal whereas in traditional Chinese thought it is cyclical. The Marxist classist view applies to vertical, individualistic Western societies, not ours."

Andean cultures have much in common with the Chinese, although they never reached such a level of development and sophistication. Parallels are to be found in customs, language, and religion. The name of the Inca empire, Tahuantinsuyo, is nearly identical to that of the first great empire in China from 206 B.C. to A.D. 221, Hanhuangtinsuguo. The Mandarin word's meaning is "The dominion of the great emperor Han"; the Quechua word means "The four united provinces." Similarities between the cultures include the religious importance of the sun and the snake, the recording of history and government through elaborate systems of knots, and mummification and funereal practices. Comparing Andean religious rites with Himalayan Buddhism, Peru's leading archaeologist, Federico Kauffman Doig, said the cultural similarities could only be put down to "the fact that the Asians and American Indians are first cousins and that in the substratum of the human mind they carried the same cultural seeds."

The parallel between Andean and Chinese thought is exemplified by the terms that express the essence of them both. The Chinese words "yang" and "yin" correspond closely in form and meaning to the Quechua words *"hanang"* and *"hurin."* *Hanang* is associated with the same qualities as yang; *hurin*, like yin, is associated with all their opposites. *Hanang* and *hurin* represent the principles of the opposites as well as specifically meaning "upper" and "lower" in a spatial sense. Manco Capac, the legendary founder of the Inca dynasty, is the founder of both Hanang Cuzco and Hurin Cuzco. He was seen as the divine-human force embodying the duality. As a creator, he was identified with *hanang*, the sky and the sun. But Manco Capac was the product of both the sun and Lake Titicaca, fire and water. Water is a *hurin* quality identified with the moon and the earth.

As in traditional Chinese culture, the unity of complementary opposites dominates traditional Andean life. Indian communities are divided into upper and lower areas; each half is classically divided into two *ayllu*s, although external influences tend to merge these and convert the original halves into *ayllu*s instead. Competition between them is deemed to generate collective dynamism. The characteristics of each half of a community are opposite but complementary to those of the other. In the Ayacucho village of Sarhua, the Sawqa are the "upper" *ayllu*; they are the Indians most native to the community and are associated with agriculture, the village center, the traditional authorities, and native religion. The Qullana form the "lower" *ayllu* and are those with weaker loyal links; they are associated with pasturing, the rural area, the official national authorities, and Catholicism. The oppositions, which are symbolic and cultural rather than real, transcend space and time. Although the Sawqa are the "upper" *ayllu*, they are linked to agriculture in the valley rather than animal grazing on the mountainsides. And although the Sawqa are the richer *ayllu*, it is the herdsmen of the Qullana who are associated with the vestiges of the supposedly wealthier outside world.

Old and new forms of government and religion are correlated into the present. Catholicism's god and saints have acquired the symbolism of the indigenous religion; likewise, indigenous gods have taken on aspects of Catholicism. The Christian god is identified with Viracocha, an asexual universal divinity that envelops all matter. In Sarhua, St. John the Baptist is the (Qullana) masculine saint and the Virgin of the Assumption the (Sawqa) feminine one. St. John is identified with the sun and the Virgin with water. The symbols and functions of each saint accord with the annual seasons and farming cycle. Mutual criticism is practiced in community assemblies, which take place in front of the church—the Sawqa on the right side and the Qullana on the left. Inside the church, whose tower is on the left in the Qullana section—since they brought its bell —the women and the female saints sit on one side and the men and the male saints on the other.

Any imbalance, any failure to reciprocate nature's favors through offerings, sacrifices, and ceremonies is believed to bring disaster and cause the death of people and animals. Indian concepts of sacrifice and rebirth are inherent in a revolutionary song by Carlos Huamán López called "Elegy (to Ayacucho)." "Bloody wheat" grows from tombs and it is said that Ayacucho's sons are born again in its flowers. In traditional Indian rituals, including Indian bullfighting that despite being banned still takes place in remote areas, it is believed that the more blood is spilled and the more people are killed, the better the harvest. Huamán López writes that "history will germinate our glory." Moving back and forth between the masculine and feminine, the huamani spirits of the peaks and the pachamama goddess of the earth, is the amaru, which is both snake and water. According to Palomino, the amaru "lives in the depths of the mountain peaks . . . from where, at god's order, it comes out at the head of a great avalanche of water and mud which, destroying all in its path, heads toward the village destined for destruction in punishment for its sins; once completed, it heads for the peaks above another sinful village, where it begins to mature for its next destructive sortie." The myth of the amaru, which means snake, could hardly be a more suitable metaphor for the activities of Shining Path guerrilla columns.

Indeed, in his "Choral Prayer of La Kantuta Negra," Feliciano Mejía identifies the narrator and the guerrillas with the snake, the amaru, and the mythical Inkarri:

> *I know today in your center, My Ande,*
> > *seethes*
> > *and roares The Snake,*
> *. . . The Great Wise Snake, our arm and soul,*
> > *fighting a guerrilla war.*
> *Each one of us*
> > *Is you, Ande, and we are a piece*
> > *tiny and complete*
> *of The Snake (you know your code name: Inkarri)*
> > *and blood boils*
> > *in your chest.*

The poem, which closes with the Inkarri's reconstitution, castigates the Pope for what it calls his "obscene" visit to Peru "ignoring our deaths and disappearances"—this moves the narrator to weep before "the Sun."

According to Palomino, no afterlife is promised the Indian because "the gods are also 'living beings like us,' with the same necessities and the same organization, who inhabit villages and marvelous palaces within the earth and the mountain peaks." He adds, "They are absolute owners of the natural things and can therefore give them to us here and now, during life and not after death." Hence, in another poem called "Wanchu," an Aymara Indian from the shores of Lake Titicaca in the department of Puno implores the creator of the Aymara universe to restore "Agrarian and Solar Socialism" and to protect them from, of all things, "metaphysics." The poet, José Luis Ayala, encounters no contradiction in the fact that while he is piously rejecting metaphysics he is invoking the same: For him, the creator of the Aymara world is an actual, living being like himself. His concept of paradise is an earthly state, a socialistic utopia obtainable here and now in this world. Shining Path spurns what Mao called the "metaphysical conception" of life. Like Marx, Mao maintained that religion was used by dominating classes to justify and keep the status quo. Myths, despite their political usefulness, were dismissed for not being "scientific" reflections of reality. However, Guzmán allows that "the freedom of religious conscience" must be respected until people know better.

One of the more bizarre political-cultural links revolves around revisionism. In "Foxes," the poet links the Peruvian soldiers and "the Reaction" with the legend of the gentiles, who are also known as "the damned." Fear of the return of the damned is a potent, mythical force in the Andes. In his "We Are the Beginning" speech, Guzmán's reference to how the past must be guarded against because "the past always tries to reestablish itself in a thousand forms" is cast in the same language as frequently recorded by anthropologists in the legend itself. The poet uses that fear to drive home the importance of stamping out every last scrap of "the Reaction":

*Hurry to cut off the fat arms of the Damned.*
*Make it rain fire and excrement on their homes. Punish:*
  *That is your destiny and being;*
  *not an order: for that Pachakuti prepares you.*
  *For that the world turns*
  *inside and outside of itself. Break all the teeth of the*
    *beasts,*
  *drink the marrow of their bones,*
  *don't leave either a drop, or the memory*
                    *of the Damned*
*. . . The Cursed Empire of the Damned*
            *sends against you*
  *warships                    warplanes*
        *war machine guns        war helicopters*
  *soldiers of war and money*
      *of war*
      *Yakarreee, Fox!*
      *Run along the top of the Andes to your point*
        *and arrival: The Guerrilla War.*
      *That is the Pachakuti Chain*

The poem carries the implied warning that unless every vestige of the damned is destroyed, they will come back. This reflects Shining Path's constant and frenzied war on "revisionists," whom Guzmán in the *El Diario* interview condemns as an "advance guard of the bourgeoisie among the ranks of the proletariat." With all the antirevisionist fervor of Stalin and Mao, he adds: "Revisionism is obviously a cancer, a cancer that must be implacably destroyed; otherwise we will not be able to move forward with the revolution." The Peruvian left is therefore as much a target as the right, if not more of one. The left is fighting for the same social bases. The left, particularly the pro-Moscow Peruvian Communist party with strong influence in the mines, and the more radical, revolutionary factions prevalent in the Lima shantytowns and some parts of the Sierra, has, along with the progressive Catholic and Evangelical churches, been the most effective block to Shining Path's expansion.

For Salvador Palomino, the illegitimate son of an Indian peasant by an urbanized Indian tailor, the structure of Andean duality expresses a universal dialectic that is alien to European culture and an inverse of Maoism. Writing in 1964, amid the increasing hostility of the future founders of Shining Path as well as of most of the rest of the left, which accused him of "aborting the revolution" by conducting peasant land grabs, Palomino said: "The complementary duality of the two different parts of a unit serves for development and balanced and harmonious change, from the unit itself to a new state; and not for mutual conflagration of the parts or categories in which one of them destroys or dominates the other, producing a new reality in which one part alone is triumphant, a characteristic of the European societies which came to us with the invasion." A quarter of a century later, Palomino is not only occasionally hauled off to jail by the police because as an Indian leader he is suspected of being a Shining Path militant, but he is also, with steadily greater frequency, receiving telephone threats from the guerrillas. The rebels have told him he is sentenced to death for the being a "treacherous dog." The Indian leader, who was brought up by his grandfather in the Ayacucho countryside, was adopted by relatives as a servant in a run-down district in Lima before being returned again to Ayacucho. There he grazed his grandfather's bulls, learned which seeds suited which soil, which plants grew best with which plants, which foods most complemented which foods, and what sacrifices were demanded by which gods. Time was told by the buzzing of insects, the changing colors of leaves, the direction of the wind, and the singing of birds. He said, "Shining Path attempts to penetrate Andean thinking using a certain type of contradiction, but it is not ours and the guerrillas are doomed to fail. Our time will come, and we will be unstoppable. Lima is being Andeanized even now." A historian, Manuel Burga, said: "The culture of the poor is an Andean one; Shining Path's success is based on the erroneous belief that it is 'pro-Indian.' If it really assimilated Andean discourse it would sweep the board."

Shining Path's constant and assiduous development of the ideological and cultural identities of its militants and sympathizers is conducted by its newspaper, *El Diario*. Not only does the party diffuse poems and *huaynos* up and down the country informally, in village meetings and during party training, but *El Diario* is replete with revolutionary poems, essays, and prose. Articles in the paper are always careful to refer to Shining Path—preferring its official title, the Communist Party of Peru—in the third person; but in private conversations before the paper was forced to go underground its staff would slip into the first. The newspaper was born out of an aggressive but respected forum of the left that was slowly transformed from within into the rebels' mouthpiece despite remaining independent of the party structure.

From the mid-1980s, *El Diario* was on sale daily, in its pro–Shining Path format, at any street kiosk; its most strident calls to arms were to be found in the cultural pages. A poem by Luis Placencia called "Terrorism," which appeared in June 1988, included the lines:

> *Onward guerrilla, ignore them*
> *if they call you "terrorist" or "criminal." . . .*
> *Terrorism . . . this is terrorism?*
> *What peace and calm existed? . . .*
> *You are terrorists*
> *who make a man a slave. . . .*
> *Terrorism is terror,*
> *and I feel that daily*
> *when hunger and pain*
> *take children to the grave. . . .*
> *Terrorism! you will shout*
> *you will kill . . . you will accuse*
> *but history will sing*
> *of glory, of freedom*
> *of another land*
> *of another sea.*

In the same month, the Lima and provincial editions of *El Diario* were selling more than 25,000 copies a day, according to the director, Luis Arce, who fled to Belgium to escape police pressure. After a few years of total freedom, marred only by threats, the occasional detention, and inept bomb attacks on its offices by government-backed hit squads, the paper went clandestine in late 1989 after its staff were arrested following the passing of a law against the "defense of terrorism." Thereafter, progressively hounded by the police, *El Diario* first became a weekly, then a monthly, and increasingly hard to procure.

The newspaper, which police at times have claimed conveys coded messages to militants, enthusiastically vindicates assassinations, bombings, sabotage, and other guerrilla actions on behalf of Shining Path. It has helped to institutionalize the party, forge a public identity, and communicate information quickly and more safely than the party's clandestine, cellular structure allows. In July 1988, it caught the world's headlines when Arce and the assistant director, Janet Talavera, conducted what they called the interview of the century with Abimael Guzmán. It is the only media interview "Chairman Gonzalo" has given and, like *El Diario* itself, was eagerly devoured as much by Shining Path activists as by intelligence and counterinsurgency specialists, diplomats, and journalists alike. The forty-thousand-word interview was reprinted many times by *El Diario* and translated into several languages abroad.

*El Diario* announces general "armed" strikes decreed by the party, whips up labor unrest, denounces massacres and human-rights abuses, and condemns with vitriolic fury all the other political parties, the president, judiciary, army, and police, and, in its international section, "revisionists" and "imperialists" such as the governments in Cuba and the United States. In response to the awarding of the 1990 Nobel Peace Prize to the then leader of the Soviet Union, Mikhail Gorbachev, *El Diario* damned him as "a reactionary element of the worst species (genocidal, professional twister and opponent of Marxism, a corrupt bourgeois of rotten morals disguised as a socialist)."

"Without doubt," *El Diario* continued with characteristic sarcasm, "the peace to which [the Nobel Peace Prize resolution] refers is the existence of the tombs of the thousands who fell resisting the invasion of Afghanistan; or the peace of its military forts and engagements in Angola and Mozambique, adorned with massacres and outrages against the minority nationalities; and the fight for emancipation waged by the republics that form the now dilapidated Soviet Union." It concluded threateningly: "The announcement of Gorbachev's visit to Peru in 1991 represents a true affront to the Peruvian people, although it will have a brighter aspect in that this sinister character will personally witness the land in which revisionism is being crushed, swept away, and buried by the victorious People's War. In return for his award . . . his planned visit to Peru will perhaps be his last nightmare."

As in the speeches of Abimael Guzmán, the opposition is commonly labeled "black," and the idea is stressed that it can only be overcome by the spilling of blood. "There is one sole reason for this," writes the author of an article asserting that the actual Peruvian president, Alberto Fujimori, is the servant of imperialism. "The people's war is the concentrated expression of both the crisis and the solution of the great evils in contemporary Peruvian society." With its black and red typefaces laden with Maoist rhetoric and analysis, *El Diario* is an articulate purveyor of Shining Path's ideas whose eloquence is broken only by bursts of stuttering rage. But insults surge as from an artesian well. Shining Path's enemies are branded everything from "worm" and "cockroach" to "executioner," "man-eating imperialist lackey," "murderous vulture," and "*pishtaco.*" A year after it went into clandestine production, its publication increasingly sporadic amid effective police persecution, *El Diario*'s self-righteous sense of destiny and historical legitimacy was still evident: "We will continue advancing along the path that the revolution has shown us; and, whatever the cost, we will continue informing of this magnificent epic that our country is living, because, unlike that of the reactionary press, the future of the revolutionary press—and within that this newspaper—is assured."

Party militants are brainwashed by the stock of rituals and commandments enforced to ensure ideological purity and to secure total dedication to the cause. In a Shining Path funeral tribute, according to a sympathetic witness, four burning torches are placed in a square around which the rebels stand in a circle. The torches are enveloped in red paper to protect them from the wind and let them burn for longer. In their center, there is another torch, beside which stands a guerrilla leader who reads out the list of those comrades who have fallen in battle. The other rebels shout in response: "Present in the armed struggle." A tribute is read out asserting that the guerrillas had emerged from the fire of class struggle "whose highest expression is the armed struggle." Hereupon, the master of ceremonies makes the central torch flare up by pushing the paper into the flame. He declares that the dead guerrillas should return to the armed struggle "to give it new life, to stroke it up, to feed it and thereby generate new combatants, new red soldiers to apply the thinking of Chairman Gonzalo so that the revolution will be irreversible, invincible, and finally triumphant." There is a marriage ritual, too. Dewy-eyed couples marry "in the name of Chairman Gonzalo and the Communist Party of Peru." According to *El Diario* the party commissar continues: "I declare them husband and wife, so that they will support, help, and assist each other and thereby better serve the revolution." An oath of fidelity is taken not only to each other but also, implicitly, to the party and its leaders. The ceremony is sealed with a quotation from Marx comparing a couple's relationship with that between people and nature.

Shining Path maintains discipline and morale through the imposition of internal laws and ceremonial party greetings. The laws are known as the "eight warnings." They derive from revolutionary China but there is a more fanatical, biblical edge. According to a teenage guerrilla in the department of Huánuco, the "warnings" are: (1) Do not take liberties with women or men; (2) Do not steal either a needle or a yarn of thread; (3) Do not take the name of the party in vain without being a member of the party; (4) Be just, correct, and honest; (5) Return alike all which is lent; (6) Do not cause street rows among the masses; (7) Serve the revolution according to the law of the party; (8) Do not be relaxed or opportunistic.

The guerrilla, whose alias was Homero, said there were twenty-seven "Chairman Gonzalo greetings." These included: "Greetings to Chairman Gonzalo, the greatest Marxist-Leninist-Maoist-Thoughts-of-Gonzalo living today, grand strategist, politician, military, philosopher, master Communist" and "To the all-powerful and invisible, to the Marxist-Leninist-Maoist-

Thoughts-of-Gonzalo ideology." Most of the rest of the greetings are related to Shining Path's celebratory calendar of historic dates: March 4, the freeing of two hundred "prisoners of war" from the Ayacucho jail; May 17, the start of the armed struggle; June 7, the hoisting of the flag; June 14, the birth of Mariátegui in 1895; June 19, Heroism Day, the "genocide" of up to 250 "prisoners of war"; October 4, the massacre of another thirty "prisoners of war"; October 7, the founding of the party; December 3, the birthday of Abimael Guzmán, which also marks the closing of the first military school. Each occasion is celebrated with the blowing up of electricity pylons, general strike decrees, and other shows of force. However, the occasions are mainly considered by Shining Path as opportunities to reaffirm its revolutionary identity and commitment.

Guzmán defines Peru as a semi-feudal and semi-colonial country in the death throes of "bureaucratic capitalism." In claiming Peru to be semi-feudal, he asserts that sixty percent of the population are peasants who through having too little land of their own are forced into servitude. Either they live precariously by self-subsistence or they form part of the big cooperatives and other agricultural associations still left over by the Velasco military government in place of the haciendas. For Guzmán, only the intermediate bosses have changed: The *patrón* has been replaced by a state functionary of one kind or another. The bankers and imperialists are still in ultimate command. According to Guzmán, Peru is semi-colonial in that although it has political independence, the country has failed to throw off the economic yoke of (mainly "Yankee") imperialism. The blood is sucked from the people by imperialist and "social-imperialist" countries' (that is, the former Soviet Union's) control of Peru's industry, exports, banks, finance, and natural resources.

By "bureaucratic capitalism," Guzmán means capitalism as he perceives it inflicted on underdeveloped countries by imperialist ones. In alliance with landowners, bankers, and the upper echelons of the bourgeoisie, the imperialists have, he maintains, imposed on Peru a bureaucratic capitalism that exploits the proletariat, the peasants, and the petty bourgeoisie while cramping the movement of the middle bourgeoisie. Guzmán sees bureaucratic capitalism as a seesawing combination of private and state monopolies, which is doomed to destruction at the hands of the people's war now that, for Guzmán, the stage of bureaucratic capitalism has passed its point of maturity and, like an overripe apple, has rotted to the core.

Shining Path envisages three revolutionary phases: democratic, socialist, and communist. The three objectives of the democratic stage are to wipe out "imperialist domination," to destroy bureaucratic capitalism by confiscating monopolistic private and state capital, and to overthrow the big landowners and agricultural cooperatives in order to redistribute land to those "who work it," the poor peasants. Those with "middle capital" would be supported but controlled. In order to achieve the democratic revolution, Guzmán holds that a people's war led by the Communist party is needed to destroy the old state while the party simultaneously builds a new one within it.

Guzmán aims to unite industrial workers, the peasantry, and the petty and middle bourgeoisie against landowners and the "bureaucratic and consumer" upper bourgeoisie (by which he means both its public and private sectors). The driving force of the revolution is the peasantry and the poorest of the urban poor who together form the bulk of the party, the People's Guerrilla Army, and the People's Committees, which are to be the backbone of the People's Republic of New Democracy. However, the workers or proletariat are the "leading class," which "through the party" is given the role of directing all stages of the revolution. The first stage of the revolution is said to be "democratic" in that the interests and property of the cooperating members of the middle bourgeoisie are to be respected. Once power is taken, it will become a "socialist revolution" in which the state is ruled by the "dictatorship of the proletariat" and all forms of capitalism and private ownership are terminated. This entails the middle bourgeoisie's liquidation. The revolution will be continued through successive "cultural revolutions" until Peru joins up with other socialist states in the third stage to make up international communism.

The main "contradiction" that Guzmán seeks to resolve

through Peru's "people's war" is that of the "masses and feudalism"; this in turn is a "contradiction" between the masses and government, the new state and the old state, and the party and the "reactionary armed forces." War is believed to be the only means of solution. "Except for power, all is illusion," says Guzmán. There will never be any dialogue. Power acquired and exercised by the people's committees at people's assemblies is to be defended by violent, surgical dictatorship.

Guzmán's greatest political innovation is regarded by his followers to be the concentric relationship between the party, the guerrilla army, and the new state. "With Mao, the three were interrelated," said one Shining Path activist, "but that is not enough. The party has to be the hub around which the army and then the state are built. Each militant therefore has three functions: Communist, fighter, and administrator." The state is based on "people's organizations" envisaged as a united front that the party generates; few of their members actually belong to the party. They are the source of party recruitment: Prospective cell members undergo lengthy and extensive evaluation and training and perform many tasks, which culminate in an action that puts him irretrievably outside the law, such as the killing of a policeman and the seizure of his weapon. At the same time as building a new state during the people's war, a "new economy" and "new culture" are introduced. Collective land use, planting, and harvesting are supposedly conducted in such a way as to help the poorest of the peasants, among whom the excess fruits of rich harvests are redistributed. The system comfortably embraces traditional Indian concepts of communal work and land use, although it seeks to reduce to a minimum the production aimed at markets in the towns and cities. This is both to blockade the markets and to try to stifle the profit initiative.

As the young state expands and land is confiscated from the old cooperatives—the land of the richer peasants is to be respected as long as they abide by the new conditions—its economy is supposed to become more sophisticated. A party document enthuses: "We have escalated land invasions all over the country. Furthermore, we have managed to organize the production of whole villages, the exchange of products or seeds, the collection of firewood or cochineal, for example, communal shops, trade, animal tending." It runs on: "The process is served by actions in the towns, sabotages against democratic-bourgeois state organizations or fascist cooperatives, state or private and imperialist banks, imperialist centers of superpowers or powers, whether factories of 'research,' businesses of bureaucratic capitalism; also, by selective annihilations and campaigns of agitation and armed propaganda."

For Shining Path, "new culture" means education, mainly of the peasants. That education consists of attacking incipient capitalistic tendencies and preaching what it regards as the universal, scientific truths enshrined in its ideology. The central "truth" is the "law of contradiction." Convinced that its ideology is scientific, Shining Path legitimizes itself and finds no difficulty in committing the worst atrocities. In the *El Diario* interview, Guzmán says: "The ideology of the proletariat, Marxism-Leninism-Maoism and today mainly Maoism, is the only all-powerful ideology because it is true, and historic events are proving it." Game, set, and match. Guzmán's is the immutable argument of a religious bigot rather than a philosopher. To assume Shining Path's ideology is to follow a faith and calling rather than just a set of intellectual ideas. Almost immediately afterward, Guzmán continues: "Without the ideology of the proletariat there is no revolution; without the ideology of the proletariat there is no prospect for the class and the people; without the ideology of the proletariat there is no communism." The ideological struggle has all the fervor of a religious crusade.

Fanatical self-righteousness born of a religious-style ideological conviction has helped to give Abimael Guzmán and Shining Path the tenacity and determination to corrode the power of a state which for all its superiority in military hardware is totally lacking in heartfelt national purpose and identity. Allied with the centuries of racial and cultural resentment, the grinding poverty, and the fact that the Maoist universal view accords pervertedly with the traditional Andean one, Shining Path has everything to fight for. A Peruvian naval officer said after the 1986 Lima prison massacre in which the rebels were slaughtered after a vigorous struggle: "With five thousand like these, we would have won the war against Chile."

Shining Path's aim is for the new "state" to grow within the official one alongside the expansion of the People's Guerrilla Army and its territorial influence. The rebels' organization and military strategy are founded mainly on Maoist models. "People's committees" are set up secretly in villages, communities, and urban districts; dozens of these in turn form a "support base," of which in February 1990 there were twenty-four, according to reports from what the party called its First Session of the Central Committee of the First Congress. In the same meeting, the party resolved to set up a national governmental tier for the "support bases," the Organizing Committee of the People's Republic of New Democracy.

Each "people's committee" comprises five "commissars." The most important are the committee secretary and the security commissar, both of whom are members of the Communist party itself. The former is responsible for political orientation and the latter for internal security and the coordination of the People's Guerrilla Army. The production commissar organizes agriculture and trade as well as the exchange of goods with other committees; he looks after widows' lands and the "orphans of war." The commissar of communal affairs resolves judicial problems, officiates at marriages, issues divorces— which are granted when one of the parties so requests—and runs the health service. Medicines are obtained by "confiscation" from hospitals and health posts; traditional, herbal medicine is encouraged.

A senior Shining Path militant related to the family of Abimael Guzmán and using the name of Enrique said, "The commissar of communal affairs sets up the Damages Commission, whose members are rotated. If a peasant's cow eats somebody else's crops, the commission makes him pay for the damage. If it happens again, the peasant is again made to pay compensation and warned that the cow will be killed if it happens once more. The third time, the cow is killed, the proceeds are given to the people's committee, and more compensation is enforced." Wife-beaters, he added, were liable to have their heads shaved or, in the worst instance, to be executed. The same commissar organizes sports and recreation, traditional fiestas and education. "Spanish is taught because it is a universal language, although Quechua is protected at the same time," said

Enrique. "Basic mathematics skills are taught, as are natural sciences from the viewpoint of dialectical materialism and social sciences from the viewpoint of historical materialism. All education links theory with practice in order to mold the people into Marxism–Leninism–Maoism–Thoughts of Chairman Gonzalo."

The fifth commissar is responsible for coordinating the activities of the "people's organizations." In rural areas, there are six of these fronts: the Movement of Classist Workers and Laborers, the Movement of Poor Peasants, the People's Women's Movement, the People's Intellectual Movement, the People's Youth Movement, and the Pioneers Movement (for children —a term from the Soviet and Chinese revolutions). In the towns, there is also the District Classist Movement (for the shantytowns) and the People's Revolutionary Defense Movement, which coordinates the "people's organizations" nationally. Overseas semi-clandestine support groups are known as the People's Movement of Peru of Sweden, France, Spain, and so on. In the countryside, the delegates of the "people's organizations" in a village form a "people's assembly," which in turn elects the commissar on the "people's committee."

The support bases are ringed by guerrilla zones in which, theoretically, the guerrillas have reached an equilibrium with the national forces. They conduct actions outside that band, successively attacking and retreating, until they slowly push back the national forces and enable the support base to expand and incorporate more people's committees. Towns are gradually encircled.

Shining Path has divided up Peru into several military regions that contain the scattered support bases. The People's Guerrilla Army comprises three kinds of militia: "principal forces," "local forces," and "base forces." Each military region has a principal force, which moves throughout it; the regions are split into zones, which each have a local force; and each village inside a zone has a base force. The guerrillas follow military plans strictly laid down by the party, in line with Mao's dictum "Our principle is that the party commands the gun, and the gun must never be allowed to command the party." Plans are formulated by the central committee; they comprise overall strategic political-military objectives and are subdivided into more specific ones. Except for important actions, the plan's application is left to the party's regional committees, whose areas correspond to the military regions. The regional committees comprise local committees, which correspond to the areas of the local forces; these in turn comprise local cells, which conform to the base forces.

As far as possible, it is the base forces that carry out actions. Enrique said, "The assassination of a torturer would be organized by the local committee following orders from above. The aim of incorporating the base forces or militia into the army is to make them 'an armed sea of masses.' The party wants all the masses armed so that in the future there will be no necessity for an army as an élite. Once the revolution triumphs, the army could be subverted by infiltrators and controlled by reactionaries, as happened in China and the Soviet Union. Mao had eighty million highly equipped militia but it was not enough to consume the army of four million. Because the immense part of the masses were still unarmed, the bourgeoisie was able to use the army to knock out the militia and take power. Eventually we will do away with the principal and local forces. Peru has a population of twenty-two million people. Once they are armed, who will take power from them?"

Shining Path conceives of its "democratic revolution" happening in three stages in accordance with Sun Tzu's concept of war as absorbed by Maoism. The first and longest stage is that of the strategic defensive, in which the destruction of the official state and the creation of the new one are to bring about a position of strategic balance in which the political and military power of each state is at an equilibrium. At such a point, the guerrilla war is to convert into a "war of movements," in which large columns of the People's Guerrilla Army take on the dwindling national-security forces directly and endeavor to hold their ground; "people's committees" start to govern openly and, in a departure from Mao and a return to Lenin, insurrections begin in the towns and cities. The final stage, the strategic offensive, would involve the rebels taking the full military initiative and would lead to mass national-army desertions, the collapse of government, and the destruction of the actual state and its replacement with the People's Republic of New Democracy or the "New Government."

Guzmán has so far employed four political-military plans and wrong-footed the state for more than a decade. His overall strategy is to encircle the towns from the countryside. However, his plans depart from Maoism in that, although the countryside is Shining Path's main chosen battlefield, actions are also carried out simultaneously in the towns because their poor are deemed too numerous to be ignored. Shining Path's first plan was the Starting Plan, which opened with the burning of the ballot boxes in Chuschi in May 1980. Its aim was to militarize the party, to take it past the point of no return into the "armed struggle" and to make that the principal form of revolution. Guerrilla warfare was initiated and weapons were acquired in the course of political and military "actions," which, according to Enrique, totaled 1,342 from May to December 1980 (according to official government sources, violent attacks numbered about 220). Sabotage, the redistribution of land and harvests, and intense political propaganda and mobilization took place in almost every department but mainly in those of Ayacucho, Lima, and Junín. Mining dynamite was stolen as the rebels, who were equipped mostly with traditional Indian weapons such as *huaracas*—hunting slings—pointed sticks, and machetes, made their guerrilla debuts. As their dynamite supplies increased, mines, government offices, banks, electricity pylons, General Velasco's tomb, and police posts were blown up. By the end of the year, with its Boxing Day celebration of the dead dogs decorating Lima lampposts, the revolution had surreptitiously killed just three people: a policeman, a mining employee, and a landowner. Only a handful of rebels had been caught and jailed.

Guzmán initiated the "Plan to Develop the Guerrilla War" in January 1981. Guerrilla zones for eventual support bases were established where "operation zones"—those where the guerrillas fought and withdrew—had already been set up. The party's accumulation of political power, and its erosion of the state's, is meant to coincide and depend on the increase in people's committees, which merge together in zones earmarked for support bases. Campaigns have a cyclical pattern comprising preparation, intensification of actions, guerrilla warfare, a climax, and complementary actions. Party documents captured by the police reveal Shining Path's military flexibility, precision, and foresight. The central committee stipulates that the "key question is when and for how long to apply momentum, defining how to face the response of the [forces of] reaction" and "to withdraw in order to consolidate, to readjust in order to rearm, and to prepare in order to advance; all in gradual and periodicized actions, with initiative, flexibility, and planning, applying the principle of concentrating and dispersing." Eventual participation and repression by the armed forces was taken for granted; it was eagerly anticipated to fuel the "polarization" between the two sides. Apart from increasing guerrilla actions and preparing for the support bases by organizing more and more people's committees, a particular objective of the second plan was to build up supplies of weapons and dynamite.

Over the next two years, Shining Path embarked on 5,350 "actions," according to Enrique. Of these, 1,100 acts of violence were recorded by the Ministry of Interior. They were aimed at all vestiges of government, "bureaucratic capitalism," landowners, and "imperialist domination." Courthouses, state companies, local government buildings, political party offices, banks, union headquarters, hotels, factories, shops, embassies, and churches were dynamited or firebombed. Telephone, television, and electricity installations were blown up, as were water tanks, dams, railway tracks, and bridges. Molotov cocktails were flung around in the streets of the predominantly upper-class Lima district of Miraflores; newspaper offices were bombed and radio stations occupied. The horse track in the southern city of Arequipa was dynamited, a synagogue attacked, Congress bombed, and Ayacucho's airport control tower dynamited. Haciendas were raided and their livestock and harvests shared out among the poorer peasants. Richer and uncooperative landowners were killed; so were peasant leaders deemed to be on their side or the government's, as well as political and state authorities. Mining dynamite continued to be plundered. Police patrols were ambushed and police stations raided. In March 1982 Shining Path took control of the city of Ayacucho and held it for over an hour, during which time it freed 247 prisoners from the police jail, at least 78 of whom were allegedly Shining Path militants. Although the violence was mostly in Ayacucho, Lima, Junín, and Apurímac, only two of the country's twenty-four departments remained unaffected.

By Christmas 1982 the guerrillas had routed most of the police and civil authorities from the villages around Ayacucho after a wave of attacks that left the poorly equipped police holed up in the city and concerned primarily for their own safety. A predeliction for drunkenness and prostitution as they grew ever more desperate and demoralized had won the police the scorn of the local population. According to the Ministry of Interior, Shining Path now had two light machine guns, fifty-four submachine guns, an assault rifle, fifty-two revolvers, and an unknown quantity of rifles and shotguns. The guerrillas had also amassed a huge amount of dynamite. Clandestine people's committees multiplied all over Ayacucho's countryside. The death toll had reached about 180. According to official figures, half of the victims were civilians, a quarter were police, and a quarter were guerrillas. The New Government had emerged.

As Chairman Gonzalo had anticipated, the armed forces took to the fray. At the behest of President Belaúnde, five provinces in Ayacucho and one in Apurímac were placed under a state of emergency in which the military was given overall political control. Genocide ensued. Pursuing a doctrine inspired by Argentina, under which human rights were ignored in a wholesale, random slaughter of mainly middle-class intellectuals in the 1970s in order to crush left-wing revolutionaries, the armed forces embarked on a series of ferocious massacres of Indian peasants. Over the next two years, at least 7,126 people were killed, according to official figures. About 200 of the victims were members of the security forces; 2,507 were listed as civilians, while 4,428 were claimed to be guerrillas.

Meanwhile, Guzmán had put Plan Three into effect: the Plan to Conquer Support Bases, which lasted from early 1983 until late 1986. Its overall objectives included the reorganization of the party, the formal creation of the People's Guerrilla Army, and the establishment of the first fully fledged support bases. The more blood was spilled, the more Shining Path prospered. "Bloody wheat" flowered from tombs. "There is no construction without destruction, they are two aspects of one and the same contradiction," said a Shining Path document in 1985. It accused the government of behaving "worse than the Spaniards who quartered Túpac Amaru" and added: "That cruel form which the war is taking is just the bloodbath which we had posed, and the resolution is to cross it . . . and conquer the other side." In another document, a rebel wrote that the bloodbath in which they were plunged by the armed forces was "not doing us damage, but fortifying us."

In the *El Diario* interview, Guzmán commented: "When the armed forces joined in, we had to wage a tough struggle. An extremely bloody and ruthless genocide took place. We fought hard. The reactionaries and the armed forces in particular thought that they had defeated us in 1984. But what has been the result? The people's committees and the support bases multiplied, and this prompted us subsequently to develop the bases, which is what we are doing today." Despite all the armed forces' torture and massacres and burning down of villages, the number of Shining Path attacks in the Ayacucho department in 1984 was, according to official state figures, stepped up. They were double those in 1982. Nevertheless, in May 1984 Shining Path decided to withdraw, readjust . . . and advance. In Ayacucho, where "consolidation" was the order of the day, attacks declined by nearly half in 1985 compared to the previous year; in Huancavelica and Apurímac, which were under similar instructions, the number of attacks also fell. Meanwhile, guerrilla operating zones were opened in the upper Huallaga valley (which embraces parts of the Huánuco and San Martín departments), the departments of Pasco, Cajamarca, La Libertad, Junín, Puno, and Cuzco. By the close of 1985, officially registered attacks by Shining Path had increased by nearly fifty percent in those areas compared to 1984. And in Lima, over the same period, the attacks had almost doubled.

The election campaigns that resulted in presidential victory in 1985 for the center-left populist Alan García, of the American Popular Revolutionary Alliance party (APRA), and his initial period of office, were specifically targeted by Guzmán within his third plan. Shining Path's attempt to boycott and sabotage the elections, in which voting is compulsory, wherever they had the power to do so, rendered the elections almost meaningless in Ayacucho, Apurímac, and Huancavelica. In those departments, aside from the third of the eligible voters who were not registered, a fifth of those actually registered failed to turn out to vote and an additional thirty-five percent either spoiled their ballot papers or left them blank. This was despite a huge mobilization by the armed forces, and followed a wave of guerrilla attacks and killings. "Conquering support bases" meant just that: Power was secured by terror where mere persuasion was not enough. But with the population neutralized, it was power all the same. In a corner of Peru, Guzmán had undermined the democratic legitimacy of the elected government.

Futile attempts at dialogue, in which the later prime minister Armando Villanueva vainly tried to contact Peruvian exiles connected with Shining Path in Sweden, chimed with car bombs, assassinations, and jail riots by Shining Path prisoners. Amid the soaring number of attacks in Lima, with the dynamiting and firebombing of police stations, clubs, department stores, gas stations, embassies, restaurants, banks, hotels, offices, and factories; and amid the killing in the capital of dozens of police officers and political leaders, a night curfew was declared in February 1986. The violence was stepped up, Guzmán launched what he called the Gold-Sealed Finishing Stroke of the Great Leap and, in fulfillment of predictions by the prisoners themselves in the face of harsher treatment, at least 210 were massacred after riots broke out simultaneously in three separate jails.

Guzmán hailed the slaughter as a moral, political, and military victory. He said, "The supposedly devastating and decisive blow ended up falling on the heads of those who engendered it, submerging the fascist and corporate APRA government and engulfing the president—violating the rules of his state—in a grave political crisis and in great disrepute; thus the rebellion of the prisoners of war, at the cost of their own lives, won a great triumph for the party and the revolution." It contributed, he continued, to the success of the Gold-Sealed Finishing Stroke of the Great Leap and laid the foundations for the next overall plan, "To Develop the Support Bases." Guzmán concluded: "The prisoners of war . . . carry on winning battles beyond the grave, they live and fight in us gaining new victories; we feel their robust and indelible presence, throbbing and luminous, teaching us today, tomorrow, and for ever to give our lives to the party and the revolution. Glory to the Day of Heroism!"

Shining Path had notched up 28,621 actions by the close of the third military plan in late 1986, according to its official scoreboard. Another 1,268 people had died during the year, according to the national government. Four departments were under a state of emergency. Under Guzmán's fourth military plan, To Develop the Support Bases, Shining Path made deeper inroads still. By its close in May 1989, the campaign had, according to the party, nurtured 98,365 actions. The unions, judiciary, state companies, schools, colleges, and universities were heavily infiltrated, the economic infrastructure was severely eroded, official government was absent from vast tracts of the Andes, and the morale of the security forces was sinking ever lower. Nine departments were under a state of emergency. Meanwhile, Shining Path had discovered new sustenance in the upper Huallaga valley: cocaine. The sacred plant of the Incas provided the guerrillas of the *pachacuti* with just the extra social nourishment—and maybe, although they strenuously deny it, the economic nourishment—they needed.

# 4

# Gunning for the White Goddess

The decade that marked the decline of tobacco smoking in Europe and the United States coincided with the boom in the popularity of the innocuous little coca leaf. Even as the drug that Sir Walter Raleigh triumphantly presented to England's Queen Elizabeth I after his first visit to the Americas in the late sixteenth century was slowly but surely being cast aside by the developed world in the 1980s, millions of the "First World's" rich and poor were turning for a panacea to coca-leaf derivatives such as cocaine and crack.

The coca leaf, which nurtures an industry estimated to gross, at street level, between $50 billion and $80 billion annually worldwide, attracts direly needed foreign exchange to the Andean countries where it is cheaply grown and processed. In 1988 the coca trade accounted for seventy percent of Peru's total export earnings, although this dropped to forty percent and twenty-five percent in the subsequent years. Because of the apparently unquenchable demand from overseas consumers, cocaine paste has become the principal export of Peru, which is where most of the world's coca leaf is grown.

Yet the coca trade, which contributes to the deforestation of the Amazon rainforest and pollutes it with processing chemicals and which, because of its illicit nature, generates violence and corruption, is founded on a plant whose chemical properties have made it a central part of Andean culture for thousands of years. Coca is a symbol of Indian identity and prestige. It has social, financial, and religious value. Considered a luxury item, coca is used not only in direct barter for other goods, principally food, but also as a form of money in communities that are still only partially absorbed into the official economy. The chewing of coca, which dulls physical pain and produces energy, is integral to everything from community building projects to social occasions such as marriages and community meetings. It creates a sacred, ritualistic bond. "Mother Coca" is also chewed during religious ceremonies and is offered up to the deities, be they the *huamani* spirits, Jesus Christ, or the Virgin Mary.

Coca bushes thrive on the eastern slopes of the Andes, which in Peru are called the Eyebrow of the Jungle. Formerly, coca was only grown in any quantity, for traditional and medical purposes, in the valley of La Convención in the department of Cuzco; but coca plantations sprang up in the jungle in the departments of Huánuco and San Martín alongside colonization in the 1940s. The migrants were mainly from the Andes, but some came from the coast. As they settled, demand began to grow for the coca leaf, not just because of its natural properties. With the help of kerosene and chemicals such as sulphuric acid and ammonia, coca leaf could be turned into a fine white powder that fetched a high price overseas. Its profitability and narcotic effect won cocaine the sobriquet "White Goddess."

By 1975, the basin of the Huallaga River in Huánuco was planted with about 2,500 acres of coca. Five years later, as the plantations spread down the valley, the figure had sextupled. In the same period, coca cultivation was intensified in river basins to the north and south, mainly those of the Maranon, Ene, and Apurímac. By 1990, according to United Nations agricultural experts, coca plantations occupied almost 200,000 acres in the Huallaga valley and up to 500,000 acres nationally. The Huallaga valley is the world's single largest coca-growing zone and is home to the bulk of the 580,000 Peruvians who, according to the United States Department of State, depend on coca directly for a living. The leaf is turned into paste in jungle laboratories and then flown out by Colombian traffickers, who later process it into cocaine. Some is shipped down-river. Little cocaine is produced in Peru itself, although the quantity is growing.

Neither Shining Path nor the United States has stood idly by. The guerrillas have encountered a golden opportunity to capture popular support and, according to the government and local reports, finance. Meanwhile, the United States' drive to stamp out drug production has gradually displaced the defense of democracy as its primary, stated political priority in Peru. The U.S. government has put itself in the front line.

When the guerrillas moved into the upper Huallaga valley in the second half of 1983, the Peruvian police, backed by the U.S. Drug Enforcement Administration, had already formed a specialized antidrug unit, UMOPAR, and stepped up the erad-ication of coca plantations by deploying large squads of workers armed with picks and shovels around the coca boom town of Tingo María. The town, whose drug wealth was such that in 1975 its Datsun dealer's sales reportedly won him an interna-tional dealer-of-the-year award, fell into relative decline and the coca plantations moved north down the valley, deeper into the jungle, around the towns of Uchiza and Tocache. As the police repression grew, the first evidence of Shining Path "peo-ple's schools"—political-indoctrination and guerrilla training camps—emerged. And following the rebels' assassination of the mayor of Tingo María, Tito Jaime, who had tried to orga-nize a coca growers' defense front, thereby usurping the politi-cal role of Shining Path, the department was declared in a state of emergency and placed under political-military control in late 1984. The rebels had dynamited a string of police stations, killed about twenty policemen, and forced many public officials to resign.

The peasants turned to coca leaf not only because its high harvest rate and average price of two to three dollars a kilo made it the most profitable crop. The popularity of coca, whose price plunged after demand was severely reduced following the Colombian government's crackdown on its drug barons in 1989, also stems from the failure of the Peruvian state to fulfill its promises to buy the peasants' perishable crops, such as rice and corn, locally. The fall in international prices of other crops such as coffee and cacao, coupled with the peasants' difficulties in marketing them, have helped to compound their dedication to a crop that grows like a weed, can be harvested from three to six times a year, and needs minimal tending. While coffee and cacao take several days to be transported over the Andes to the coast along dangerous roads that are frequently rendered impassable by landslides, and finally at the ports encounter bureaucratic barriers erected by monopolistic business cartels, coca leaf is bought by middlemen directly from the peasants' smallholdings.

When the armed forces moved in against the guerrillas, they turned a blind eye to the coca trade in order to secure the population's support. Police repression was curtailed. While Shining Path adopted a low profile and the Americans fumed with fury, dollars continued to pour relentlessly into Peru's grateful, debt-ridden economy.

The illicit trade was already demonstrating its corruptive power. Carlos Langberg, a businessman who had close links to the last military government, the army, and the police, and who is in jail for cocaine trafficking, largely financed APRA's 1980 electoral campaign. If his drug network had not been uncovered in 1982, he would have enjoyed a strong base within the party that later took over government under Alan García. Shortly after García came into office, a cocaine laboratory blew up in Lima, leading to the imprisonment of Reynaldo Rodríguez, the "Godfather," who was an adviser to a top police chief. Gustavo Gorriti, a Peruvian journalist who investigated Langberg and Rodríguez, said, "In those decisive months of 1980–81, when an intelligent effort could have substantially curbed the Shining Path insurrection, the leadership of both police forces . . . dedicated a good deal of their energies and efforts to collaborating with the drug-trafficking business headed by Rodríguez."

Drug-related official corruption intensified in the latter half of the decade. In September 1988 an APRA congressman, Manuel del Pomar, was arrested in West Germany while cashing checks signed by a Peruvian businessman who was awaiting trial in Lima on drug charges. Del Pomar was the former president of the deputies' Commission of Justice and Human

Rights and president of the National Federation of Lawyers' Colleges of Peru. He was released under diplomatic immunity, protected by his party, and disappeared. A Peruvian diplomat, Gastón Pacheco, was less fortunate. He was sentenced in London to twenty years after being detained in March 1989 while in possession of twenty kilos of cocaine. Meanwhile, four judges of the Supreme Court faced charges in connection with the freeing of Perciles Sánchez, who was absolved of drug trafficking six times running before being gunned down in a drug vendetta in February 1991. According to Western diplomatic sources, drug-related corruption under Alan García's government went "right to the top." A Peruvian intelligence source said that General Julio Velásquez, a former minister of defense under García, was the "visible head" of a group of army officers who offered protection to drug trafficking. "He is a criminal," said the source. "When he was nominated for the Ministry of Defense, some intelligence officers raised the possibility of trying to kill him for fear he would cripple the armed forces." Under the government of President Alberto Fujimori, suspicion fell on one of the president's closest advisers, Vladimiro Montesinos. A shady former army captain who was said to have passed military secrets to the Americans, Montesinos was expelled from the army before becoming a lawyer and entering into compromising links with a Colombian cocaine trafficker.

Bitter institutional rivalry between the armed forces and police is reflected in the mutual accusations of corruption at all levels. Following the demise of the García government, twenty-six generals were among more than 150 police officers fired by the incoming regime of President Fujimori at the behest of the army. The move was interpreted as an attempt to break up the power structure implanted by the former minister of interior, Agustín Mantilla, whom intelligence sources pinpointed as the head of a government-linked death squad under García, the Rodrigo Franco Command (Comando Rodrigo Franco). Mantilla was believed to have acted as a Mafioso-style beneficiary of drug protection money which was probably siphoned off to APRA and the death squad.

The police were also close to the Americans—"We have to make friends somewhere," muttered a U.S. antidrug official—

whose plans to step up eradication and interdiction through a military agreement in 1990 were stymied by Fujimori with the backing of the dominant sectors of the armed forces. Military pressure was also widely suspected to lie behind the indictment of the former general of the antidrug police, Juan Zárte, on charges linked to the alleged disappearance of seventy-two tons of confiscated cocaine.

Fujimori's spurning of the $37 million military-aid package in 1990 was followed by his promises of profound legal reforms in order, said the president, for Peru not to repeat "the errors of President Ngo Dinh Diem in Vietnam, who in the 1950s launched himself against the habitual, informal order of the peasants in central Vietnam . . . and invalidated the property order that they had established. . . . We do not want to throw the peasants and their families into the arms of the terrorist subversion and the drug traffickers." The military agreement would have been the first of its kind since General Velasco switched such links from the United States to the Soviet Union. Its rejection added to the State Department's deep frustration with the Peruvian military. It followed insinuations in the Congress by Melvyn Levitsky, the assistant secretary for international narcotics matters, that Brigadier General Alberto Arciniega, the political-military commander in the Huallaga valley in 1989, was implicated in drug trafficking. By late 1990 the Americans were increasingly leaking stories of military involvement in the trafficking. In December State Department sources were quoted by *The Washington Post* as saying that Peru might lose its annual certification as a collaborator in the war against drugs. This would have cut its access to fresh credit from international financial institutions just as the country was augmenting its external debt payments and repairing relations with the foreign financial community. Peru was declared ineligible for further credits by the International Monetary Fund after García froze debt payments and passed legislation to nationalize the banks. The threat of U.S. economic sanctions against Peru if the latter fails to take determined action against cocaine trafficking has grown ever more real, although it was alleviated by an antidrug accord signed by the two countries in May 1991.

Meanwhile, once the armed forces gave the coca trade its head in mid 1984 in order to concentrate on weeding out Shining Path—a policy that was revived by Arciniega—the Colombian drug traffickers unleashed a reign of terror in the valley. Peasants were forced to accept low coca prices on pain of death. The local drug barons, among the most notorious being those nicknamed the Vampire and the Minister, carved out their coca fiefdoms in blood and bullets. Bodies appeared on the roads daily as the villages in the upper Huallaga valley were racked by murder, rape, and theft in an endless cycle of violence in which the poorest peasants came off worst. These circumstances, when combined with the corruption of the police, who extorted money from the coca growers and extracted payoffs from the traffickers, made the environment ripe for the intervention of Shining Path and its imposition of order.

The rebels' moment came with the government of President García. Under pressure from the United States, the police operations were stepped up. At the same time, thirty-two army officers, including the political-military commander of the region, Brigadier General Julio Carbajal, were subjected to internal investigations for alleged links with drug trafficking. The army crackdown on the guerrillas was lifted. By late 1985, Shining Path's political presence had resurfaced: The UMOPAR antidrug police were ejected from the small towns of Tocache and Uchiza. But over the next two years, the Peruvian police in coordination with American antidrug agents blew up dozens of jungle airstrips; confiscated weapons, processing chemicals, motor boats, and hundreds of kilos of coca paste; destroyed light aircraft, cocaine laboratories, and coca processing pits; and eradicated, by hand, several thousand hectares of coca bushes.

Shining Path prospered out of the hatred and fear generated by the brutal lawlessness of the coca barons, the corruption of the police, and the government's U.S.-sponsored drug busts. The guerrillas sought to convert the peasants into Shining Path militants. They offered them protection against exploitation by the Colombians and their Peruvian minions and against repression by the Americans and the Peruvian government. The rebels, whose people's committees were established over a wide area north of Tingo María, broke the back of the drug barons by uniting the coca growers. They demanded a higher price for the coca crop and, with the help and cooperation of the peasants, massacred the drug trafficking gangs that resisted them.

As for the attacks on the beleaguered coca-eradication unit, CORAH, it was often unclear whether they were conducted by Shining Path militants, the peasant growers, or the middlemen; the distinction itself started to fade. All were on the same side, a side that was bonded together by economic interest but granted political cohesion by the rebels. An auto-repair shop owner in Tingo María, whose family originally made its money out of the town's coca boom in the 1970s, said, "What used to be a business is now 'trafficking.' CORAH is hated. Shining Path says we are going to support you if you support us, so it is simple. Nobody could give a damn if coca badly affects the United States. The imperialists are the drug addicts, not us. They repress us economically so its serves them right, they are paying the consequences. They just do not like it because they are not the ones in control of the business."

The rebels view coca itself rather as they do religion: It is an opium of the people whose cultivation must be eradicated systematically where circumstances permit and whose excessive consumption must be punished with exemplary penalties. They adhere to an opinion commonly held by the Peruvian left that although coca was originally a mystical plant—and hence part of an "unscientific" and folkloric view of life—it came to be used by the Europeans and their descendants as an instrument of Indian oppression. The left's founding father, José Carlos Mariátegui, in subscribing to the view that coca chewing was encouraged because it stifled hunger and fatigue while numbing pain and boosting energy, in some cases thereby enhancing the Indians' productive capacity, wrote: "Coca-mania and alcoholism in the indigenous race . . . are purely consequences, results of white oppression. Local despotism foments and exploits these vices, which in a certain way are fueled by the urges of the fight against pain." As for coca's intrinsic cultural importance, Shining Path regards it as part of the Indian popular culture, which, like religion, time and a "scientific" understanding of life will erode.

Parallels with the history of opium in China are relished. In the aftermath of the Cartagena drug summit in Colombia between President George Bush and the presidents of Bolivia, Peru, and Colombia in February 1990, when the United States guaranteed economic aid to the cocaine-producing countries in acknowledgment of the "coresponsibility" of itself and other consumer nations in resolving the problem, *El Diario* ran an article on the Chinese opium wars in an endeavor to demonstrate the hypocrisy of all parties. In highlighting how the British addicted China to opium, which Britain traded in exchange for tea and porcelain mostly during the nineteenth century, and how the British waged wars on China when opium was banned, the article purported to show that then, as now, the interests of the "imperialist" countries are dominated exclusively by profit and power. "These are the [historical] roots of those who make a great show of being shocked and want to appear—along with the governments of their colonies and semi-colonies—as the standard-bearers in the fight against drugs," said the article. "Those who once enriched themselves by opium are the same as those who today feather their nests with cocaine."

Shining Path views cocaine consumption and alcohol addiction as symptoms of politically bankrupt societies. In another *El Diario* article, the rebels cite the Chinese revolution to suggest a cure: the adoption of full state power by the Communist party. Prior to Mao's foundation of the People's Republic in 1949, Chinese society had been saturated by opium. It was as common as tobacco, for sale almost everywhere, and used by up to seventy million addicts. Three years later, after Mao had prohibited opium's cultivation and sale, punished both with the death penalty, and embarked on a huge treatment program for addicts, the problem was all but resolved. The opium barons and their "imperialist" masters were systematically killed while the populace was subjected to the party's vigorous mass methods of education and persuasion: Everybody ordered everybody not to do it.

The guerrillas' cynical scorn for the hawkish public attitudes of the U.S. government toward the repression of the coca trade is encouraged by U.S. duplicity. In Iran-gate, Colonel Oliver

North, a staff member of the National Security Council, was alleged to have knowingly allowed cocaine-trafficking funds to be used by the Nicaraguan contras. The Panamanian dictator, General Manuel Noriega, who for a long time was widely believed to be involved with drug traffickers, was left to his own devices in return for his cooperation with the U.S. Further, Shining Path likes to believe that the United States is simply jealous that it is not in the driver's seat of a major international industry despite providing its biggest market. Shining Path is also convinced that neither Peru nor the United States wishes to lose the money that the coca trade produces. President George Bush's "War on Drugs" has concentrated on attacking the drug's consumption and supply. Meanwhile, cocaine's U.S. distributers and the money-laundering banks, who between them swallow the lion's share of the profits, have been left almost unscathed. It was Great Britain that brought down the fraudulent Bank of Credit and Commerce International, a bank that was not only laundering drug money on a massive scale but was also used by the CIA.

In the *El Diario* article on the opium wars, the author enthusiastically quotes García from an article in which the former president cited estimates of the value of the coca trade. García wrote in the aftermath of the Cartagena summit, "It is calculated that the value of street cocaine in the United States is $100 billion annually. It is the most profitable business in the United States. . . . Of the $100 billion, perhaps $10 billion reaches Latin America. The other $90 billion constitutes an informal market in Miami, New York, California or is deposited and laundered in North American banks. . . . If one accepts that Peru only receives $700 million for the basic cocaine paste, that sum is greater than that produced by the legal exploitation of copper, fish meal, or silver. Furthermore, millions of Peruvians directly or indirectly are linked to the 'coca-ized' economy." Shining Path interpreted the summit as the basis for an agreement between the cocaine producer and consumer countries on how to share out the proceeds.

The rebels' argument was bolstered by García's claim, in the same article, that Peru had become addicted to buying dollars in order to service its external debt. The national-debt burden, said García, had fallen on the shoulders of the peasants, who in growing coca had encountered a solution to their poverty. Making the link between coca earnings and debt payments to the international financial institutions became increasingly orthodox in Peru in the late 1980s. When García resumed current payments to the International Monetary Fund in October 1989, it not only coincided with the period preceding the Cartagena summit but followed several months of his government's soft-pedaling on coca eradication and interdiction in the Huallaga valley.

President Fujimori's full restoration of current debt payments in late 1990 helped to endear him to the IMF. But his rejection of the U.S. military-aid package and ambiguous, lackadaisical attitude to the repression of the coca trade won him the hostility of the DEA and the State Department. Peru's monthly debt obligations of about $37 million were easily covered by the millions of "coca dollars" purchased daily by the Central Bank. Using local banknotes straight off the printing press, the government is accustomed to buying dollars from the clearing banks and foreign-exchange houses. The dollars come almost directly from the drug trade. Both the foreign-currency exchange houses and the banks buy the dollars cheaply in the Huallaga valley, where the flood of dollars depresses their value, and bring them to Lima. The valley population needs to sell the dollars—which are brought in by the Colombians as payment for the coca paste—in order to buy local currency for everyday living. Often it is the networks of the big Peruvian intermediary traffickers themselves who distribute the dollars in the capital. When President Fujimori was finally persuaded to sign an umbrella agreement against drugs in May 1991, a document that was little more than a bilateral version of Cartagena, it was rigidly understood—although never publicly acknowledged—that otherwise the United States would not assume the initiative in the formation of a support group of countries willing to plug the budget deficit caused by the debt payments. That would have torpedoed the support group and hence Fujimori's entire economic-adjustment program.

Shining Path believes that the United States is using cocaine trafficking as a pretext to intervene against it. The guerrillas argue that the United States' true intentions are proven by the fact that its emphasis on military aid is out of all proportion to economic assistance. An *El Diario* article in June 1990, head-lined "People's War Will Crush Imperialist Aggression," com-pared the Peruvian situation to the 1989 U.S. invasion of Panama which led to the arrest and deportation of General Noriega for drug trafficking. The United States had initially backed Noriega and ignored his supposed illicit activities, not only in exchange for Noriega's political support but also appar-ently for his connivance in CIA operations. The Americans changed tack once Noriega became too powerful and turned from a puppet dictator into a Frankenstein beyond their con-trol. The drug-trafficking charges were widely seen in Latin America to have been applied purely as a means to secure his removal.

"The pretext [for armed intervention in Peru] remains the same 'antidrug' ruse," said the *El Diario* article, "the same trick of blaming the oppressed countries for the moral misery and social breakdown in North American society, the den itself of Yankee imperialism. The real intention is to confront the Peo-ple's War, to obliterate its social base, the poor coca-growing peasantry." Guzmán, at a meeting of Shining Path leaders in September 1989 to celebrate the fortieth anniversary of the Chinese revolution, welcomed the prospect of U.S. interven-tion: "Yankee aggression, direct or using puppets, takes us to a war of national liberation," he said. "And in spite of the sacri-fice and effort which it will demand, it will be a magnificent development to unite ninety percent of the Peruvian people." The scale of the rebels' confidence and ambition is demon-strated by the banner headline over the *El Diario* article: THERE WILL NOT BE ANOTHER VIETNAM IN PERU. Shining Path regards the Moscow-inclined revisionism of Vietnam's post-reunifica-tion regime as a partial failure on the part of the Vietcong and a partial triumph for the Americans, rather than the resound-ing thrashing that has usually been attributed to the United States.

Official U.S. policy in Peru toward Shining Path is shrouded in ambiguity and summed up by the pan-American invention of the term "narcoterrorism." Directly associating the guerrillas with narcotics enables the Americans to claim that in combating the rebels they are simultaneously fighting the drug trade. Similarly, it helps the Peruvian security forces, who thereby can enlist U.S. support to fight the guerrillas, a marginally less controversial excuse for foreign intervention. Uniting the phenomena resolves the apparent difference in priorities between the countries' governments: While the Peruvians see Shining Path as the major target, the main priority for the United States is, officially, the drug trade.

The thrust of U.S. policy became evident in the unsuccessful campaigns in 1990 to persuade first the García and then the Fujimori government to accept the $37 million military-aid package. According to a U.S. embassy source in Lima, the aid was to include the setting up and running of a counterinsurgency training site in the upper Huallaga valley, the handing over of river patrol boats and light artillery, and the refurbishing of U.S.-built Peruvian ground-attack aircraft, which were to be transferred to the Huallaga valley. Uniforms, machine guns, trucks, ammunition, and communications equipment were also to be part of the package, which, said the embassy source, was designed "to provide security for the antidrug activities." The policy thesis was encapsulated by the U.S. assistant secretary of inter-American affairs, Michael Skol, who told a meeting in Washington in February that year, "One cannot fight drug trafficking without fighting Shining Path."

Suspicions of the real U.S. motives in the Latin American drug war were voiced at the time by the Colombian writer Gabriel García Márquez. Shortly before the Cartagena summit, he asserted that the attempt to demonstrate that drug traffickers and guerrillas were one and the same thing was meant to enable American troops to be sent to Colombia "with the pretext of capturing the one and in reality fighting the other." But when the U.S. ambassador to Peru, Anthony Quainton, an ambassador in Nicaragua after the Sandinista revolution and a former director of the State Department's Office for Combating Terrorism, inaugurated the Santa Lucía police antidrug base in the Huallaga valley that same month, he stated unequivocally in front of television cameras: "We have come to fight against drug trafficking and terrorist subversion." However, the military-aid package itself ran foul of the Congress and public opinion on the grounds of the Peruvian military's human rights abuses, and fears that the United States might become bogged down in another guerrilla war. It was rejected by Peru mainly, it was claimed, because it failed to come hand in hand with economic aid and because it was believed that physical repression of the coca trade alone would engender still greater support for Shining Path.

After the guerrillas had proved their status as the protectors of the coca-growing peasants and had ended the Colombian drug barons' bloody dominance in the mid-1980s, they installed their own form of law and order in the valley. Basic justice, administered under the threat of the death penalty for severe offenses or regular offenders, won Shining Path considerable popular goodwill. Drug addicts, prostitutes, thieves, and swindlers were treated with summary harshness. The auto-repair shop owner in Tingo María whose family made its cash out of the coca boom said: "Shining Path says such people are like fertilizer. Their eradication feeds the growth of the plant [the revolutionary state]. There is much less common delinquency around here. The party is liked everywhere; people feel protected by it and believe in its justice rather than the police, who let delinquents go free and use them as informers. People complain of thieves to the people's committees instead."

Punishments are meted out with exemplary brutality when Shining Path's "eight warnings" are ignored. Tales abound of the party's "people's trials" in which the accused is denounced by the community and investigated by the "people's committee." The accused is condemned by delegates from the support bases. If the community wishes or dares, it may be given the chance to pardon the condemned person. Sometimes a pardon may be offered in exchange for joining a guerrilla column for a few months.

Witnesses in Tingo María gave examples of the rebels' justice: of how a man was beheaded for beating up his mother and wife while he was drunk; how a man who had been less than diligent with maintenance payments for his children became a good deal more so after the party warned him; and how two women and a man who were taken from their homes to a hamlet where a pair of columns comprising a few hundred guerrillas had converged, were accused of prostitution and armed robbery and were hanged, beheaded, and buried in the jungle. "The party does not like prostitutes and it does not waste bullets," said Homero, a sixteen-year-old guerrilla present at the latter event.

A lawyer in Tingo María said that Shining Path had lost him all his clients from the countryside. "They used to come because of theft, land, and family problems, but none do anymore. They have their own form of justice, which is logical because official justice is expensive, time-consuming, slow, corrupt, and inefficient. The police are underpaid and request money from both the aggressor and the victim and in the end nothing much happens. Shining Path educates the peasant, disciplines him, teaches him respect for work, and provides him with effective justice in the absence of official justice." According to local reports, police are killed by the rebels mainly in cases where it is believed they are corrupt and abusive: for demanding money when people are found without identity papers and for systematically robbing bus travelers or raping women.

Shining Path's habit of policing the police was highlighted by a guerrilla attack on Uchiza's police station in March 1989. It was a late Monday afternoon. Several policemen were kicking a soccer ball around near the Plaza de Armas as others lounged at their lookout posts or dozed, off duty, behind the station's low, sky-blue concrete walls. A guard's eye was caught by the sudden withdrawal of the moneychangers, who were rushing from the square. The guard died of a grenade blast as he raised the alarm. A barrage of machine-gun fire and grenades was unleashed as at least two hundred guerrillas emerged on all sides. The rebels picked off the policemen on upper floors and rooftops, assumed the police positions, mounted the church roof and other buildings, and bombarded the station as the police fled inside.

A few hours later, the police surrendered after a final burst of grenades left the survivors too stunned to respond, sprawled bloodily on the floor. Their calls for help had failed to elicit reinforcements, apparently because the army helicopters were not equipped with night sights and those at the Santa Lucía antidrug base were grounded by torrential rain. Once the police had been dragged outside, they were forced to shout "Long live Chairman Gonzalo!" and three officers were machine-gunned in the head. Some "informers" were also killed, bringing the number of the rebels' victims up to sixteen. The remaining police, fourteen of whom were badly injured, were freed as the guerrillas proceeded to dynamite their vehicles and to rob and blow up the banks. After collecting the rebels who had stayed on watch at the airport and approach road, they retreated in trucks sometime after midnight.

Shining Path's motives for the attack, which was greeted with pleasure by many of Uchiza's inhabitants, revolved around the police's alleged extortion of the population. According to an army report, it also resulted from the Colombian traffickers' anger at the police's doubling of the protection money they paid the police for the drug flights out of Uchiza. The police themselves, who were mainly members of a highly trained special operations unit, claimed it followed their recent arrest of some Colombian traffickers. In both versions, it appeared that the security forces were trying to link Shining Path to drug trafficking in a bid to deflect blame from themselves. The substance of none of the claims was ever proved.

Shining Path views itself as a defender of the peasants' right to grow and trade coca at fair prices until such time as political and economic circumstances permit the peasants to abandon it. The party does not market coca: As an aspirant state, it taxes the trade by way of requesting collaboration money from it as well as other businesses. In defiance of the evidence from many areas of the country, the rebels deny coercion. In any case, it may be argued that one man's protection money is another man's tax. In protecting the peasants from the low prices forced on them by the traffickers on the one hand, and from police repression on the other, Shining Path perceives itself to be doing its job as a nascent national government. Although in doing so the guerrillas are intrinsically regulating the trade, they insist that they are slowly pushing the drug traffickers out of the areas under their control and reducing the proportion of hectares devoted to coca cultivation by the peasants. Meanwhile, in exacting dues from the traffickers, the army and police break their own government's laws, which the official state is little inclined to enforce because of the economic dependence on coca by all concerned.

While citing the corruption and hypocrisy of its enemies, Shining Path makes no bones about its own present—and future—policies. A party member, "Elva," said: "Where the party has control we are teaching peasants how to cultivate other crops and reeducating people who have a problem of drug addiction. In our areas there used to be delinquency and bodies floating in rivers because of fights between drug traffickers, but they no longer enter and it is now safe. There is no alliance with the drug traffickers; on the contrary, there are clashes in defense of the peasant. The party does not take money from the traffickers; what happens is that groups of the lumpen use the name of the party to extract money. They cause confusion. The party liquidates those who take its name in vain. It defends the poor peasant who grows coca for survival, but it has nothing to do with the big plantations or laboratories, which are controlled by the authorities and in the areas of the Reaction. We kick out the drug traffickers when and where we can. Drug planes do not enter zones where the party is in control. There is no collaboration. That is a pretext to attack the party. Even to think of it . . . where would the party's principles be? In no way can we permit it, but there are people who try to justify the unjustifiable. It is they who become subject to the drug traffickers; that is why they put the blame on us. The territory of the big traffickers is never touched—the Reaction only enters when there are clashes of interests and informers pass information.

Shining Path's espoused ambition to ban all drug trafficking once in power coincides with that of the coca growers themselves, although evidently not with that of the intermediaries or the richer traffickers, who depend exclusively on the growers for their livelihood. The coca growers wish to substitute coca for other crops. They dislike the violence generated by the trafficking, and the unpredictable nature of the price, but in the absence of technical development and efficient means of transport and marketing find coca cultivation the easiest way to survive. Nevertheless, they grow other crops as well and, according to United Nations agricultural experts, the volume of legal crops has outpaced the expansion of coca plantations in the upper Huallaga since the drop in the coca price in late 1989. This tends to fortify Shining Path's claims that, rather than bolstering the cocaine trade, the guerrillas are undermining it.

Justo Silva, the president of the coca growers' cooperative in the upper Huallaga, said, "We want to replace the coca, but only when we are guaranteed credit and technical support and are assured a market for the space of ten years." Coca prohibition, economic development, and rock-solid security are what Shining Path promise their Communist government would bring about once in power. The level of support for the rebels by the peasants is almost impossible to ascertain either in or out of the area because of the conflicting dangers posed by the security forces, the rebels' strength, and the drug-trafficking network. The situation is neither static nor uniform, and the communities survive by adhering to the strongest master while paying lip service to the rest. But they are reticent in discussing Shining Path. Instead, the population is much more eager to condemn abuses by the security forces and is especially critical of the police and the American antidrug agents.

U.N. experts claims that the guerrillas' popularity has slipped since the advent of lower coca prices stripped coca of much of its profitability, lessened its cultivation, and hence cut the need for protection. They report corruption within Shining Path's own ranks, growing resentment of the rebels' violent domination, and hail the policy of Brigadier General Arciniega, who channeled drug-trafficking money into local development in Uchiza, at the same time trying to wean the peasants voluntarily off coca and encourage crop-substitution projects. In effect, Arciniega applied a development of the old 1984 policy: He permitted drug trafficking in order to win local support and undermine that for his main target, the rebels. At the same time, his policy ensured his troops were properly fed by the town. Under Arciniega's command in 1989, the army killed about eleven hundred alleged guerrillas. No prisoners were taken. The young, charismatic general was widely believed to be guilty of extensive human-rights abuses. Villages were bombarded with heavy machine-gun fire from helicopters before being burned to the ground. U.S. embassy sources reported evidence that Arciniega was responsible for scores of headless corpses that floated down the river past the antidrug base.

All sides agree that, mainly because of the police antidrug operations, the coca trade continues to move north down the valley, which eventually joins the Amazon basin. But while the U.N. experts claim that both the trafficking and Shining Path's influence have fallen away around Uchiza, the rebels maintain they have simply adopted a lower profile in the face of army repression that, although damaging, failed to uproot them. Similarly, the rebels claim that their own advance northward corresponds to their natural expansion rather than just the movement of the coca trade or their repression by the army; that it is indeed they who have displaced the coca trade, but deliberately, and that popular discontent provoked by the drop in the coca price has simultaneously swelled the guerrillas' ranks.

Apart from encountering a social base ripe for taking up arms in order to protect its principal livelihood, Shining Path is claimed by the government, the security forces, and the United States to have captured a huge source of income not only in the valley but in the other coca zones as well. Although the guerrillas deny it, local evidence suggests that, even if the party itself does not officially elicit protection money from the traffickers, it too suffers from local or individual corruption. Small airplanes fly in and out on average several times a day, mostly from Colombia but also from Brazil, to collect cargoes of the semiprocessed cocaine awaiting them at both legal and illegal airstrips. According to reports from residents and visitors to the region, the airstrips' controllers charge anything between $6,000 and $20,000 a flight; in return, they offer the aircraft ground protection. The rich pickings are at the heart of much of the conflict between Shining Path, the army, the police, and the other Peruvian guerrilla group, the Túpac Amaru Revolutionary Movement (Movimiento Revolucionario Túpac Amaru or MRTA). MRTA, a Cuban-inspired group with close historic and family links with the APRA party, was originally dislodged from the head of the valley by Shining Path. It has built up a stronghold in the valley's north around the towns of Juanjui and Tarapoto; beyond the valley northward on the edge of the Andes, they also control a substantial area around the town of Moyobamba. Whenever MRTA has clashed with Shining Path, the Maoists have almost invariably come out on top.

Neither the amount nor the whereabouts of the money that Shining Path has supposedly gathered from the coca trade can be ascertained at all. But if the guerrillas were to have controlled just one third of the flights coming in and out of Peru since 1987, they would have earned themselves approximately $40 million. Yet they have apparently failed to purchase any sophisticated weaponry in Peru or abroad, and despite all attempts, it has never been proved that any such relation exists between them and the traffickers.

The rebels continue to rely on stolen dynamite—by 1991 they were estimated to have stolen about one million cartridges and to have used just one fifth—and the arms and munitions "confiscated" from police and soldiers. In the Huallaga valley, there are also regular reports by residents of soldiers selling their weapons to both the guerrillas and the drug-trafficking middlemen. Arms and ammunition are said to be bought by Shining Path from the international cocaine dealers, who allegedly provide them in exchange for both money and protection. Any money from the drug flights is supplemented by the guerrillas' extraction of collaboration cash from the peasants, intermediary traffickers, travelers, and businessmen, who, as in other areas of the country where the guerrillas have sufficient power, are expected to offer what they can afford. Failure to comply with the payments requested by the people's committees is said by local inhabitants to be punished with execution, although this is denied by Shining Path.

In the *El Diario* interview, Abimael Guzmán said that Shining Path was fighting "the most economic war on earth." Embracing what he called "the humble dynamite" as the party's major weapon, he stated that its three forms of arms procurement were to wrest them from the enemy, to fabricate them, and to buy them. "There is a problem here because they are expensive," he added. Communications equipment is also believed to be obtained mainly from the drug traffickers. Outward signs of wealth by Shining Path are few and far between: the rented upper-middle-class house in Lima where Guzmán was alleged by police to have his headquarters; the golden trophies confiscated there; the other rented houses raided by police in January 1991, as well as a computer and cellular telephones, are relatively modest examples. No weapons other than those used by the Peruvian security forces have ever been found on Shining Path. According to the guerrilla Homero in Tingo María, the rebels live mostly off water, sugar, and biscuits when traveling in an "unorganized" zone. It is widely presumed that Shining Path, whose logistical organization is rigidly and adroitly controlled from the top, must be hoarding its money in national and overseas banks, if indeed it has any to spare.

The U.S. presence in the Huallaga valley is embodied by the anti-drug base, Santa Lucía, a hundred-acre fort whose wooden watchtowers on the banks of the Huallaga River gaze across toward the unseen dangers lurking in the rainforest on the far side. American UH-1H helicopter gunships lurk behind black plastic sandbags as others land in clouds of dust on the ample, 1,750-yard runway. The runway hosts C-123 transport planes and is patrolled by a British government–donated Hotspur Hussar, a tanklike radio command module. Barrack buildings line up behind the rows of concrete bunkers; barbed wire and mine fields ring the base's ground perimeter. Santa Lucía, an ambitious stronghold from which to launch antidrug operations throughout the valley in coordination with the Peruvian police, is in the heart of the guerrilla zone. It is manned by up to five hundred Peruvians and forty Americans. A sign in Spanish reads, "Here you work for Peru and the world."

Built in 1989 after logistical weaknesses and successive attacks on coca-eradication workers had forced antidrug operations to be suspended for several months, the base is fifteen miles north of Uchiza and safely accessible only by air. Its

Peruvian personnel comprises the CORAH coca-eradication workers, UMOPAR antidrug police, and general workmen. Peruvian troops are also present from time to time, as is the air force. The fort's U.S. contingent comprises agents of the DEA and Narcotics Assistance Unit (NAU) as well as helicopter pilots and mechanics working for a private U.S. company, National Air Transport, which is contracted by the State Department. Several of the U.S. air and maintenance crew are veterans of the Vietnam War. The full American complement involved in Peruvian antidrug operations is about eighty; they take turns at the base while the others are in Lima. U.S. antidrug efforts in Peru were launched by the DEA in 1978. Intelligence and advisory work in coordination with the police and customs expanded in 1981–1982 into the setting up of CORAH, UMOPAR, and the Upper Huallaga Area Development Project (PEAH), which concentrated on economic aid. This included road and bridge maintenance, communications development, seed distribution, and the establishing of agrarian cooperatives and agricultural research programs. Dogged by Peru's inadequate market conditions and the government's failure to match the American money, and amid the regular destruction of its equipment and the killing of its workers by Shining Path, PEAH had virtually collapsed by 1988. It has seen been reduced to repairing the surface and bridges of the Marginal Highway under military escort. The road was wrecked by dynamite during the rebels' initial seizure of power in the valley. Occasionally, said a disconsolate American source pointing an accusing finger at the military, PEAH workers are forced to widen the road to allow it to be used as a landing strip for drug flights.

CORAH was designed to be the eradication arm of the U.S.-trained and U.S.-equipped UMOPAR antidrug police. Hundreds of men hacked at coca bushes with everything from picks and shovels to machine saws, which were useless because they failed to kill off the roots: The plant grew back all the stronger for its pruning. By late 1988, when eradication was suspended until the opening of Santa Lucía, a mere 45,000 acres of coca bushes and seedlings had been cut down or pulled up. It was enough to make CORAH hated by the peasants but too little to keep pace even with the rate of coca's displacement and expansion. Thirty-five CORAH workers had been killed by the peasants, traffickers, and guerrillas; wage increases were frozen because the Peruvian government refused to pay its share of the budget; and the workers quit in droves. Since CORAH resumed operations from Santa Lucía in September 1989 it has solely eradicated seedlings. Small teams swoop from the U.S.-piloted helicopters as machine-gunners spit fire if attacked during the frantic razing of the patches of fragile shoots. Eradication in 1991 was running smoothly, and blissfully ineffectively, at 125 to 200 acres per month.

Faced with the futility of manual eradication efforts, the Americans have lobbied heavily for the use of herbicides. The favored choice is Tebuthiuron, marketed as Spike, which according to its worried U.S. manufacturers, Eli Lilly and Co., "could cause irreversible damage to the flora and fauna and even affect human beings if it is not applied with painstaking precaution." Although test results from both manual and aerial spraying of low doses in the Huallaga have not done "any measurable environmental damage" except to the coca plants, says the U.S. embassy, its application triggered off a national furor and was a propaganda gift for Shining Path. The rebels likened Spike to Agent Orange, the defoliant used by the Americans in Vietnam to flush out Vietcong by depriving them of food and cover. Reports of the Spike tests and their results reached mythical proportions. They left a widespread fear among the peasants that Spike would be used on a massive scale to kill not only coca plants but other crops as well in order to depopulate the valley. *El Diario* hailed its use as an example of the Peruvian government's "genocidal desperation" and "submission to Yankee imperialism whose real objective is the counterinsurgency battle." Fears about Spike were followed by the devastation of tens of thousands of hectares of coca and other crops by a mysterious soil fungus, which, university agronomists believed, either mutated naturally because of the saturation use of agricultural chemicals, or was introduced deliberately. Peasant claims that DEA helicopters released "dark clouds" above their plantations were not taken seriously until it was admitted in Washington that $17 million had been spent on developing biological agents to kill coca, poppy, and marijuana plantations. The United States denied dropping any such agent into the upper Huallaga valley.

U.S. antidrug efforts center on the UMOPAR police, with whom the Americans work closely on both intelligence and operational levels. Initial attempts to block the road transport of coca paste were crippled by corruption. Both road interdiction and the raiding of coca-processing laboratories grew increasingly futile as Shining Path gathered strength and sabotaged the Marginal Highway. Police trucks were no match over the trenches for the drug traffickers' motorbikes or land cruisers and were easily ambushed. By mid 1984 the guerrillas had already killed about twenty policemen in the valley and forced the police to retreat to the towns. Under the army's Brigadier General Julio Carbajal, UMOPAR was then taken off anti-drug operations and dragged into counterinsurgency. The traffickers and/or rebels kicked its garrisons out of Tocache and Uchiza the following year. Tocache was eventually recovered in an operation involving hundreds of policemen, including parachutists. UMOPAR did not return to Uchiza and, following Shining Path's attack in April 1989, its replacements were also withdrawn as the army took over.

In line with UMOPAR's need to depend on air transport for its operations, which also include the destruction of clandestine landing strips and the trapping of drug planes, by early 1989 it boasted nine serviceable U.S.-loaned helicopters. Once the Santa Lucía base opened and interdiction resumed, the emphasis continued mainly to be on raiding the drug laboratories. Police raided 151 laboratories in 1990, twice as many as in the last full year of operations in 1988. But they still failed to cut the air traffic: Just two aircraft were captured despite Peru's estimated 1,600 drug flights a year. In 1991, despite the assistance of U.S. radar AWACS planes and the intervention of Peruvian air force aircraft, efforts to throttle the drug flights proved little more effective. Meanwhile, the local population complained bitterly of abuses allegedly committed by both UMOPAR and the Americans helping them.

"The DEA agents harass the peasantry," said the mayor of Uchiza, Demetrio Díaz, who was installed after the army restored civil government there under Arciniega. "They burn peasants' coca as it dries, or hover above in helicopters to blow away the leaves, dropping tear gas. Dynamite is dropped on people's homes under the pretext that they are really cocaine laboratories." A statement by the coca growers' eradication defense front in October 1990 declared: "Uniformed UMOPAR personnel from the Santa Lucía base are entering the homes of our neighborhood [in the hamlets of Los Angeles and Santa Elena] without any judicial order, and in an overbearing manner; breaking doors and windows . . . they search everything and, on failing to find any crime, they take away the objects of the highest value which they come across, and the little money which we have, uttering threats and leaving us beaten up."

Not only are the Americans occasionally involved in armed skirmishes with the traffickers themselves, and not only are they loathed by the valley's inhabitants, but because of the protection offered to the coca growers by Shining Path they also run the gauntlet of the guerrillas. Valley residents further allege that at times the Americans have aided police attacks on guerrilla groups after UMOPAR or CORAH workers have suffered casualties at their hands. The U.S. embassy vigorously denies or plays down such incidents. But on the eve of the general elections in April 1990, Shining Path took the initiative and launched a gun attack on Santa Lucía which included the use of rocket-propelled grenades.

The base's helicopters, with U.S. pilots and DEA agents aboard, took off and blindly pounded the jungle on the other side of the river with grenades and M-60 machine-gun fire. According to one American official who spent the time ducking bullets in a trench, the rebels' attack lasted two hours. No casualties were reported in Santa Lucía, nor was it claimed that any bodies were found in the jungle (the guerrillas habitually take away their dead in order to protect the families of the victims from reprisals). The following week, a preemptive midnight strike was carried out by the Santa Lucía helicopters on suspected Shining Path positions in the surrounding hills. A year later, the rebels attacked the base again with similar results and, shortly afterward, dynamited PEAH installations farther south in Aucayacu after occupying the town for several hours.

The antagonism felt toward the United States for its role in promoting what even the Peruvian government prefers to term "repressive measures" against the drug trade rather than "interdiction" is such that the killing of a U.S. journalist in Uchiza in November 1989 was greeted almost with a shrug of the shoulders. Todd Smith of the *Tampa Tribune* was kidnapped while boarding a plane at Uchiza's airstrip. Four days later, the army reported that an unidentified corpse had been dumped near the town's main square. When a party of U.S. embassy officials arrived by helicopter, the body had been transferred to a clinic where it lay sprawled on a concrete floor in an outhouse. The hands were tied behind the back and the stick and rope with which Smith had been garrotted were still attached to his neck. The body was bloated and the ribs and nose broken, the face unrecognizable. After a lengthy silence, the man from the Narcotics Assistant Unit murmured, "Only the guerrillas would hang a guy like that."

Outside, as the group inspected the site where Smith had been abandoned, passersby turned their dark, silent faces the other way and quickened their pace. A woman in a food kiosk switched off her radio; what may have been an act of courtesy heightened the atmosphere of insouciant hostility. Her customer paid up and left. While the helicopter blades whirled around to beat the fall of dusk, blowing dirt over the bent, protesting palm trees, an army officer produced a notice found beside the body. Its red lettering ran (*sic*): "Thus die north american spies linked to the pentagon who are fulfilling an anti-subversive plan in Latin America, especially in Peru. Death to north american imperialism. Long live the PCP. Long live the People's War. Death to the genocidal George Bush." It was sealed by the hammer and sickle. The helicopter pulled away from the ground and headed back to Santa Lucía as the night haze slowly enveloped the endless plantations of coca below.

Although it was never fully confirmed whether Smith's killers were guerrillas or drug traffickers—who, some believed, may have rigged the notice as a red herring—the cold reaction and the confusion themselves characterize the deep social and political discontent generated by U.S. actions in the Huallaga valley. The umbrella antidrug accord signed by the United States and Peru in May 1991 represented a mutual commitment to fighting drugs through economic development and interdiction. Its follow-up agreements embraced both military and economic aid and contained a commitment by Peru to pursue free-market policies and involve the armed forces in the war against drugs.

Under what was the first substantial U.S. military-aid package to Peru since the late 1960s, when the Velasco regime swung the country's political axis toward the Soviet Union, the Peruvian security forces were to receive training, arms and ammunition, uniforms, and medical supplies to the tune of $40 million. The agreement stated, "In order to effectively support the attack on the narcotics threat and defend the sovereignty of Peru, the capabilities of the Peruvian Armed Forces must be enhanced and training intensified. The Peruvian Armed Forces must be able to assure and reinforce civilian government control over the most important coca-growing and trans-shipment areas, provide protection to police forces on counter-narcotics operations from guerrilla insurgents, and develop the capability to strike at drug-trafficking organizations." Drugs and guerrillas were successfully coupled.

Economic aid worth about $70 million was aimed at stimulating crop substitution and development by assisting the liberalization of the economy and the repairing of roads. The total of food and economic aid was about sixty-five percent more than the previous year. However, attempts at bilateral governmental economic aid in the valley have hitherto been thwarted by guerrilla violence. Shining Path's power to sabotage development projects—which it views as reformist and therefore counterrevolutionary—remains substantial. Fierce clashes are inevitable, although in mid-1991 there were signs that the coca growers were beginning to organize themselves better and even to trust the government's promises.

Despite the army's increasingly random killings in the Huallaga, which have continued under other generals since Arciniega, the guerrillas still retain sufficient influence in many communities to exclude the government's authorities. Mayors and other elected officials are absent from most of the rural districts (the Huallaga valley covers approximately 5,800 square miles; slightly bigger than Northern Ireland). Those elected authorities who are left in the towns are assassinated by the rebels. Local prosecutors and civic officials, who are caught in the crossfire of death threats, bribes, and extortion from the security forces, drug traffickers, and guerrillas, live in constant fear of their lives.

Manuel Espinoza, a reluctant mayor of Tingo María who followed a line of assassinated mayors, mayors who had abandoned office, and aldermen who had refused it, said in January 1989, "I am a taxi driver, I never imagined I would occupy this position. But the others did not want it. I have no power in the countryside. I do not know how long they [Shining Path] are going to let me live. The moment I receive a threatening letter, I will leave. I die here every day." He died in June that year when the guerrillas shot him in his office, presumably without a warning.

Guillermo López, an alderman and reporter in Tingo María with strongly suspected sympathies for Shining Path, said, also in January 1989, "Government here is now completely centralized. All the villages are in the hands of Shining Path. The police and army are more and more desperate and the DEA help them go after the guerrillas. I have been told the DEA want to make me disappear because I defend the peasants against the corrupt CORAH workers." The previous year, his home had been dynamited. In April, he was tortured and shot dead in front of his family by either soldiers or police. His claims regarding the DEA can probably be dismissed. However, such claims—made at a time when the Americans had a conspicuous presence in Tingo María, where they were still living in what by local standards is the luxury hotel—materialize into potent local myths which Shining Path take full advantage of, especially when events such as the death of López might appear to bear them out. The DEA is hated with a vengeance.

As U.S. antidrug funding in Peru grows every year, so too does Shining Path. Even if the guerrillas' relationship with the coca trade does not provide them with the vast income their opponents accuse them of enjoying, random repression has served only to forcibly displace the coca trade, both leaving behind discontent that swells the ranks of Shining Path and creating new areas for it to act as the coca growers' protector. Meanwhile, the state's drug-addicted economy and corrupt security forces make it unlikely the trade will disappear in the short or mid term. One way or the other, the traditional Indian currency of coca has metamorphosed through cocaine into the lifeblood of both government and revolutionaries. And while the smoking of *basuko*, or coca paste, is a rising problem among Lima's poor, the snorting of cocaine is a popular pastime among sections of the rich. Witnesses and participants tell of parties where silver bowls piled high with white cocaine powder have been passed among them. And where some of the country's highest political leaders were as high as they could be.

# 5

# Under a State of Terror

It was around ten o'clock on the night of Friday, May 13, 1988, as the pair of army trucks trundled along the dirt-track mountain road near the hamlet of Erusco high above the Pampas River valley in the department of Ayacucho. The road was pitted and pools of water glinted under the stars as the convoy bumped and splashed its way up and down the twists and turns that edged between rock face and ravine. The trucks were carrying food—cattle and swine—and medical supplies, as well as about twenty soldiers, to a military base in the town of Huancapi. As they neared the district of Cayara, they fired a few shots into the darkness, a customary gesture when passing areas believed to be infested with *terrucos*, slang for "terrorists."

Several of the troops were young conscripts from the coastal port of Chimbote; they had arrived in the emergency zone two months earlier. The commanding officer, Captain José Arbulú, was coming to the end of his six-month tour in the heart of the "red zone." He was shortly to be promoted and transferred to Lima where, with the help of his uncle, a former prime minister and minister of war, his prospects looked good.

The first truck had already entered the curve when the mines exploded.

The dynamite blew the second truck into the fresh mountain air; rocks and more dynamite, enclosed in milk and coffee tins, rained down from above. Figures in ponchos emerged on the edge of the cliff and opened up a barrage of fire at the soldiers as they spilled from the wreckage. A sergeant and private were killed by the initial explosion. Another private writhed in agony with a perforated abdomen. Captain Arbulú, whose right thigh had been torn apart and whose left leg had been shattered, died in a hail of machine-gun bullets loosed off at point-blank range. The rest of his men fought for forty-five minutes before hurling themselves down the bank to seek cover among its shrubs and hillocks.

As dynamite charges exploded in front and behind the first truck, which was still within the narrow curve, its occupants abandoned it, too. The guerrillas jeered at the troops, shouting "Long live Chairman Gonzalo!" and "Miserable dogs, we only want your FALs [Belgian assault rifles]!" Like their companions, the soldiers from the first truck opted also to escape down the bank. The rebels descended to the road, set fire to the second truck, broke up, and dispersed. According to official army reports, their arms haul included eleven assault rifles, eight rocket-propelled grenades, and about three thousand cartridges. The first truck made it to Huancapi, five miles away, at 1:30 A.M. At dawn, the bodies of the captain, a sergeant and private, along with the many badly wounded, were evacuated by truck and helicopter. One of the soldiers died in the hospital. There is evidence to suggest that the deaths of four others traveling with the convoy may have been hushed up.

The inhabitants of nearby Cayara, a large village of low mud huts with earthen floors, and roofs of wood and straw, were making the most of the fresh, sunny weather when the army helicopters and trucks started to arrive later that morning. Soldiers on horseback were among the ten patrols that entered the district. The Indian peasants had been up late the night before celebrating the Feast of the Virgin of the Incarnation of Fátima, dancing and drinking home-made *chicha* beer. But it was harvest time and no sooner did the sun rise than most were out and about, gathering in their corn, wheat, and barley. However, some had fled the district for fear of army reprisals on hearing the explosions the night before. By the time the army arrived, work was well under way as men, women, and children toiled on their plantations.

Fernandina Palomino, twenty-four years of age, later told reporters, "We were finishing the harvest. Little by little we had put it all together at the foot of the slope. My husband and I were carrying three sackfuls toward the village when the soldiers stopped us. 'Now you are going to see, you terrorist shit,' they said, taking us away. 'Don't cry,' my husband told me. 'We haven't done anything and they are not going to do anything to us.' They laughed and said to him, 'We are going to give you nothing but caresses,' and hit him on the head and back with a machete. Bleeding silently as he walked, he said to 'hurry along, my love, we will clarify everything with the gentlemen.' They made all the women and young children line up against a wall. The men were flung face downward to the ground. There was a long line and my husband was at the end.

"A bearded gringo was the leader. The soldier had been ordered to ransack the village and set fire to the teachers' homes. They raided the shops and took away alcohol and soft drinks. Houses were burned. At midday, the soldiers were walking around with axes, machetes, and hammers which they had stolen. They kept asking us about the *terrucos*, thinking that we, all the village, were *terrucos*, that we had attacked the army truck and killed the captain and soldiers.

"But that day me and my husband had been happy, dancing in the fiesta. We did not know anything about the *terrucos*. How was it possible that my husband could be a *senderista* if he was the municipal secretary of the Cayara council and had been on the Aprista committee in Huancapi? They did not want to listen, señor, but he was innocent. We women began to cry, begging for mercy from the officers. The gringo captain shouted, 'You'll cry more still, shits! Why did you kill the captain?' "

The troops, many of whose faces were hidden behind black balaclavas, were said to be mostly from a special force known as the lynxes. Witnesses said they demanded the return of twenty guns rather than eleven, indicating that the ambushed patrol had eventually surrendered and been totally disarmed. Despite being warned off with shots in the air, the women watched from a short distance as their fathers, husbands, brothers, and sons met their bloody end. The soldiers cut off branches of prickly pear cactus and ground them into the men's backs with their boots. According to the women, they proceeded to hack to death each of the prostrate bodies in turn with bayonets, machetes, picks, and axes. One was decapitated.

Fernandina Palomino said, "They cracked open my husband's head with a hammer and then with an ax they took out his brains. He died crying, my husband, and without protesting." The local prosecutor's evidence indicates that twenty men were killed. The women and children were finally chased away. The bodies, which were initially piled beneath a tree, were later hurled into a gully. One man survived, only to be taken away by soldiers the following day, along with an elderly woman who had given him shelter. They were never seen again.

First to fall victim to the soldiers had been a fifty-eight-year-old peasant who, according to a witness, stumbled drunkenly out of the church into their path at the entrance to Cayara. He was shot and his body thrown behind some cactus bushes. Inside the church a group of people were dismantling the tin-foil-decorated wooden platform on which the statuette of the Virgin of Fátima had been carried joyfully through the streets the day before. As befitted the customs of the fiesta, the group had been drinking homemade spirits and *chicha* beer since dawn and were almost oblivious to the sounds of the helicopters, never mind the first shots. As they moved outside into the courtyard, somebody struck up on a violin and they started to dance.

The appearance of the soldiers broke up the party. The men were forced into the church while the women were warned off with threats. The Virgin of Fátima bore silent witness to the interrogation, torture, and slaughtering of five more peasants. They were knifed, strangled, and shot. According to their widows, the church floor was turned into a "river of blood." Forbidden to approach the church that day, they returned on Sunday to find the bodies had been moved. They eventually discovered them away from the center of the village in an area known as Quimsahuaycco, and buried them as best they could without being seen by the soldiers. In all, at least twenty-eight people had died.

No sooner had the massacres ended than the cover-up began. The church's floor was scrubbed with bleach and its walls were whitewashed. And the bodies started to disappear. Eustacia Oré, who said her son had been taken away and killed after showing his identity papers, added, "The next day I found his body. I put clean clothes on him and flowers in his hand. When I came back, his body was gone." Other widows, dressed in black, with dark, parched, weather-beaten faces, breaking into uncontrollable sobs, told similar tales. Of how they had searched for their menfolk, found them, wrapped them up, and buried them only to discover that the bodies had later been removed from their graves.

Over the next few weeks, the soldiers were reportedly seen evacuating the corpses by mule, horse, helicopter, and truck as the news seeped out from fleeing villagers who had managed to evade the military checkpoints and make it to the city of Ayacucho. Those who admitted to the troops they were from Cayara were turned back.

Judicial authorities, senators, and journalists were refused access to the Cayara district for a fortnight in order that, as one soldier told a reporter, everything could "be put in its place." When a small group of civilian and police officials accompanied by Carlos Escobar, the local state prosecutor specially appointed to investigate human rights abuses, finally arrived at the behest of the army to inspect some graves, the graves were empty. There were only bloodstains, the skin of a hand, and pieces of skull and hair. A few days later, more empty graves were discovered.

The political-military commander of Ayacucho, Brigadier General José Valdivia, claimed that the bodies must have been dug up and carried off by the guerrillas. His version was that eighteen rebels had died in clashes with the army after they were hunted down following the truck attack, and that the guerrillas had carried off their dead despite the fact that the army by then controlled the whole district. Without the bodies it was impossible to prove who the victims were and how they had died; the hand skin was merely identified as that of a fifteen-year-old student, Eustaquio Oré. It was the general's word against the villagers'.

According to witnesses, four more peasants were shot by soldiers in the nearby hamlet of Mayopampa in the week following the military incursion. Traces of their graves were never discovered. The military claimed that, in spite of the rigid control they now exercised in the region, there had been an attack near there by a Shining Path column. No more details were forthcoming. A further six peasants were later reported disappeared after being detained by the army.

Unluckily for General Valdivia, whose web of contradictory statements won the blind support of the APRA senator who headed the government investigation of the killings, some bodies were found—albeit briefly—by Escobar, the local prosecutor. Jovita García, thirty years old, had been detained by soldiers on May 18–19 in Cayara after a list of suspected subversives, on which she did not appear, had been read out in the general's presence. She was arrested later and, along with two men who had featured on the list, taken up a mountain by soldiers at night. One of the men's wives followed the group, which slept in a hut before continuing its climb just before dawn. The woman then heard shots and fled.

When both wives led Escobar, accompanied by police, to the top of a barren peak called Pucutuccasa about 16,000 feet above sea level on August 10, he finally had a body. The two men were also identified. The occupants of a fourth grave were unknown and it was only superficially dug up. García's remains were taken down the mountain and formally identified; an autopsy was carried out. It showed that at the time of her death she was seven months pregnant and was bayoneted and suffered devastating head injuries. Bullet cartridges had been found nearby. The body corroborated the evidence of witnesses and implicated the military, including General Valdivia, in extrajudicial execution. At the same time, it undermined his denials of a wider army massacre.

General Valdivia promptly claimed that Jovita García was an army informer who had been killed by Shining Path for providing the list. Apart from again ignoring the fact of the army's saturation presence in the area, the claim was spurious because the guerrillas do not bury informers: They leave them in the open with notices over their bodies as a warning to others. It was all the more unlikely that the guerrillas would bury an informer next to two people who, according to the army's list —allegedly hers—were of their own kind. And even more illogical to suggest, as the general did, that Shining Path should have killed people accused of being guerrillas by the army.

The remaining bodies on Pucutuccasa had disappeared by the time the parliamentary commission arrived a fortnight later. And when, by casting doubt on its legitimacy, the APRA senator, Carlos Melgar, won his appeal for another exhumation and autopsy of Jovita García in the cemetery of Cangallo, she was no longer there either. Escobar had lost his proof.

It was now the turn of the witnesses. On December 14, Fernandina Palomino, who had watched her husband being killed with a hammer, was stabbed several times and finished off with a burst of submachine-gun fire when the truck she was traveling in was halted by troops near the village of Toccto. She left two young orphans. The mayor of Cayara, whose shop had been robbed and whose wife had been beaten up during the killings but who himself was absent from the village, was killed by the soldiers in the same incident. According to the remaining passengers, the truck driver was then tied to his vehicle before it was blown up. He had been in Cayara during the massacre. Several months later, Martha Crisóstomo, a niece of Jovita García, whose body she had identified, was shot in front of her family in the city of Ayacucho by men in military uniform and balaclavas.

Meanwhile, the time had come for the special prosecutor. Escobar, who had been investigating human rights abuses since 1987, said he regularly received threatening messages both from Shining Path and the military. During his investigation, he claimed his vehicle was sabotaged. His final report accused General Valdivia of bearing overall responsibility for the murder of Jovita García and the two men. He cited witnesses to the effect that during what the army had dubbed its Persecution Plan in the Cayara district it had massacred at least twenty-nine people and detained forty-five more who thereafter disappeared.

He was hounded out of Ayacucho by the gathering threats; they followed him to Lima and he fled Peru. On his return,

Escobar found he had been removed from his job; after a legal struggle he was reinstated in the judiciary but sent to the Amazon city of Iquitos, which amounted to internal exile. In the meantime, the witnesses' original statements were destroyed in a fire said to be caused by "terrorists" in Cangallo. The official copies, which were never released by the central state prosecutors' office in Lima, went missing. Some of the witnesses changed their evidence when interrogated in military barracks; they later said they were forced to do so under duress. The majority report of Melgar's parliamentary commission recommended legal proceedings against Escobar for supposedly exceeding his authority and it congratulated General Valdivia on his work.

In late 1989, Escobar fled again to the United States, where he was granted political asylum in September 1990. He claimed also to receive threats there. Brigadier General Valdivia was promoted and became commander of the key Second Military Region, which includes the department of Lima. The Cayara case was archived in February 1990.

Human rights groups acknowledge that the army probably did kill several people at Cayara who were either actual militants or had sympathies and links with Shining Path. Suspicion fell particularly on Martha Crisóstomo and the teachers. But the massacres, which were denounced by international human rights groups including Amnesty International and Americas Watch, were typical of the state's reponse to Shining Path's style of guerrilla war. Instead of endeavoring to fortify the country's judicial and political authorities in order to protect the population and win over its active support against the guerrillas, successive governments have preferred to leave what they call pacification mostly in the hands of the uncomprehending and underequipped security forces. The failure on the part of central government to take the political initiative against Shining Path and provide the police and military with bold, dogged, and effective civilian leadership has resulted in Peru acquiring one of the world's worst human rights records.

Left to its own devices, devoid of social, economic, and political vision, the military applies the only treatment it knows. Trained in antisubversive methods originally imported from the United States, in which in practice the military aspect dominates the economic, political, and psychosocial elements, it tends more to imitate the Argentinian model—based on the French—and acts like an occupation rather than a protection force, relying on indiscriminate killing to weed out the enemy from its midst. It fails to maintain a deep, continuous rural presence, preferring short operations; when patrols bump into Shining Path, it is usually because they have been ambushed. Terror is met with counterterror. In Ayacucho art and myth, the security forces have become identified with the *pishtacos/ nakaqs*. A peasant told anthropologists in 1987, "In Quinua four *nakaqs* were killed, and after cutting off their heads they were sent in homage to the chairman."

Cases such as that of Cayara are not infrequent, although rarely as well documented. According to the United Nations, more people in Peru were detained by security forces and consequently disappeared than in any other country each year between 1987 and 1990. The U.N.'s official—and conservative—figure was 884 people. Most of them vanished after being taken to military bases in the emergency zones, where torture and extrajudicial killings are reported as commonplace. Judges and state prosecutors are refused access to military detention centers. (These are also barred to the International Committee of the Red Cross, which between 1987 and 1989 was forced to close the Ayacucho office it had opened in early 1986.) No member of the military has ever been convicted of human rights abuses.

However, Sublieutenant Telmo Hurtado was sanctioned for "abuse of authority" when he apparently overstepped the mark in ordering the shooting and blowing up of about sixty people in Accomarca, Ayacucho, in August 1985. He is believed to have later been promoted. Asked why he killed innocent people, Hurtado told a Senate commission, "They have an ideological tendency. Those of you in Lima do not know what we have to live through here. One cannot trust a woman, old man, or a child. They begin to indoctrinate them from two, three, four years old, making them carry things and so on to different places. Little by little, by dint of tricks, of punishments, they win them over to their cause."

One of the armed forces' frankest proponents of the so-called dirty-war doctrine was General Luis Cisneros, the minister of war under the Belaúnde government, who oversaw the intervention of the armed forces. In late 1982, he said in a celebrated interview with a local magazine, "In order for the police forces to have success, they would have to begin to kill both *senderistas* and non-*senderistas*, because that is the only way they could be assured of success. Kill sixty people and at best there are three *senderistas*. . . . I believe it would be the worst alternative and that is why I am opposed, until it is strictly necessary, that the armed forces enter the fight." But by the time his words were published, the army had entered the struggle and assumed overall political control in five provinces of Ayacucho. The following two years were among the bloodiest of the decade as the military laid waste to whole communities where it believed the guerrillas lived or were helped and protected.

Even after the army had initiated its indiscriminate uprooting of Shining Path—Abimael Guzmán himself later acknowledged that those particular two years of "barbaric and ruthless genocide" had been "complex and difficult times"—the armed forces were still confused and divided by the insurgency. Serious accusations ricocheted publicly around Lima, at the highest of military levels, that the guerrillas were being assisted by generals in retirement. General Oscar Brush, Cisneros's successor as minister of war, postulated that "international communism" was to be found in all countries and that it was financed by drug trafficking and pornography.

But the declarations of General Julian Juliá, the Commander in Chief of the army in 1984, at least spoke volumes for official perception of the problem: "The demented action of a group of subversives will never separate us from the Western and Christian culture in which we have been trained." The implicit recognition that Shining Path sprung from roots alien to the official state came in the same breath as a vow to vindicate the state's imported Western and Christian character. The general's remark was a denial of the validity of the country's Indian culture; his foppish pride in Western tradition was an offense to the millions of Peruvians with customs and beliefs stretching back thousands of years before the arrival of the Europeans.

Such an attitude typifies many of the military, political, and industrial élite. In a country whose ills are blamed readily by the upper and whiter classes on an overpreponderance of Indian blood, it grants the purveyors and apologists of the dirty war an added moral foundation. In fighting an enemy who is mostly Indian, they feel they are fighting for a superior culture. The fear, ignorance, and frustration of the troops in the Andean emergency zones, who are mostly recruited from the coast, does the rest.

In an attempt to understand the soldiers' behavior during the events surrounding the Accomarca massacre, the Senate commission's majority report cited a series of psychological factors. These included an aggravated sense of local patriotism, an imperialistic desire for domination, frustration, fear of possible failure, resentment, the channeling of aggression toward a victim, genocidal aggression as a social security valve, a moral sense of pseudo-justice, fanatical intolerance, and revenge. Such forces only contribute to bringing about Guzmán's desired bloodbath. "The reactionaries are dreaming when they try to drown the revolution in blood," he said in the *El Diario* interview. "They should know that they are irrigating it."

The commission was also reminded of a Chinese proverb: "Kill one and terrorize ten thousand." A revolution that in its first three years had cost fewer than a couple of hundred lives collected more than 7,100 in the next two, according to the Senate's calculations. Official figures claimed that about thirty-five percent of the victims were civilians and around sixty-two percent subversives; the remaining fraction comprised members of the police and armed forces. Most of the victims listed as civilians were killed by Shining Path. Many of those described as subversives were in fact civilians. The overall total of victims is believed to have been at least ten percent higher, but information was restricted as well as twisted by the military and police.

The slaughter of eight journalists in the village of Uchuraccay highlighted the confusion, suspicion, and fear that came to dominate Ayacucho and eventually spread throughout the Andes, especially in the emergency zones under military control. The Peruvian journalists were stoned to death in January 1983 by peasants who, it was widely believed, had been put up to it by the security forces. They were making an unauthorized trip to investigate reports that peasants near the freezing uplands of Uchuraccay had killed seven guerrillas a few days earlier.

The peasants around Uchuraccay, who eke out a living mainly from the few beans and potatoes that the rocky soil can nourish, said the rebels regularly stole their food and animals as they crossed the peaks between the valleys. The friction had been heightened by the dynamiting of the nearest road as part of the guerrillas' strategy of developing self-sufficiency in the countryside in order to cut off food supplies to the towns and defend themselves from attack. As the tension grew and the peasants felt increasingly stranded—with the police and civil authorities abandoning their posts nearby—Shining Path had killed two peasants. In one case, according to a witness, a man was dynamited because he wanted to go to work on his *chacra*, or smallholding, instead of joining in the guerrillas' physical-training exercises. The peasants had attacked in revenge. According to the investigating commission led by Mario Vargas Llosa, they had lynched not just seven but twenty-four supposed rebels in the days preceding the arrival of the journalists. It was suggested that the killings may also have been fueled by an ancient rivalry with the communities in the valleys.

Amid President Belaúnde's congratulation of the peasants, who were being encouraged to take justice into their own hands by helicopter squads from the paramilitary police unit called the Sinchis (from a Quechua term for "warrior"), a tired group of journalists had emerged on the slopes of Uchuraccay. The little evidence available suggests the Indians mistook them for potentially dangerous outsiders, possibly guerrillas, and promptly unleashed a hail of stones before finishing them off with clubs and rocks. But the senior public prosecutor in Lima accused the security forces of deliberately inciting the peasants in order to scare all journalists out of the area. In the coming years the peasant witnesses were reported to have been systematically murdered by the security forces and Uchuraccay all but abandoned.

The Vargas Llosa commission's report concluded that the victims were treated with the kind of ritualistic Andean savagery meted out to people deemed to have made a pact with evil spirits. It cited how the journalists had been buried facedown and how the nature of the wounds corresponded to the Andean belief "that the sacrificed victim ought to be deprived of his eyes, so that he cannot recognize his killers, and of his tongue so that he cannot speak and betray them, and that his ankles ought to be broken so that he cannot return to bother those who took his life."

Because of this episode and the disappearance and death of three other journalists in Ayacucho, all at the hands of the military, reporting from the countryside has been cut to the bone. The victims also included a prominent environmental reporter who ran into a Shining Path column in the Apurímac department. Her death provoked particular outrage among the well-to-do in Lima, principally because she was white and considered one of their own and, ipso facto, nothing to do with the war.

The widow of Hugo Bustíos, a reporter for a leading Peruvian magazine who was shot and blown up by soldiers, said, "People are more scared of the army than of Shining Path. Hugo was killed because he wanted to publicize the army's atrocities and they thought he was a leader of the subversives. The army steals and rapes, but the marines are the worst of all, and the bloodiest are those from the aristocratic families—they think they are superior to all the rest, they do not know how to treat people."

Margarita Bustíos, who trades cochineal in the small town of Huanta, Ayacucho, added that most people collaborated with the guerrillas out of fear and that "only" a quarter of the population really supported them. "We are caught between two flames," she said. "If businesspeople do not pay Shining Path, they are killed or their goods are destroyed. We are told to limit trade beyond the town. But the army does not accept the danger we are in and bullies us to carry on as normal. Shining Path revolves around hunger and the atrocities. The more poverty and the more atrocities, the more support they have, especially from the young."

Torture is commonly used by the military and police to extract confessions, which are later used as the basis for prosecution. José Navarrete, a wealthy agricultural merchant in Huanta, was detained for suspected terrorism after he was denounced by a jealous neighbor. "The marines kept me blindfolded without food and water for fourteen days, hanging me up by my hands tied behind my back until my eyes were popping out," he said. "I was punched and half drowned. Eventually they decided I was not guilty and freed me. I was lucky —a prisoner accused of blowing up a bridge had his hand cut off with an ax in front of me. He confessed." Navarrete was also robbed of his strongbox. Other forms of torture that repeatedly have been denounced by international human rights groups include application of electric shocks to the genitals; burning with cigarettes; insertion of bottles into the anus; stabbing with knives; and tying of people to metal sheets before leaving them to toast in the sun. Many of the victims, who were also expected to denounce others as guerrillas, report that the military threatened to have them pushed out of a helicopter. Visiting representatives of human rights groups are liable to be ejected from the emergency zones. The Peruvian establishment views them as busybodies who distract the security forces and play into the hands of Shining Path. Carlos Melgar, the leader of the Cayara parliamentary commission, said Amnesty International was a bunch of "idiots and crooks."

The initial two years of random military repression in 1983 and 1984—which had been preceded by policy dithering on the part of the baffled and unprepared Belaúnde government as it struggled to work out how to counter the guerrillas—witnessed the failure of a brief attempt at sudden, kick-start economic development in Ayacucho. They also gave rise to the formal birth of Abimael Guzmán's People's Guerrilla Army. General Adrián Huamán, a Quechua-speaking Indian, followed the wholesale slaughters of his predecessor, General Clemente Noel, with an attempt to build trust between the troops and the villages.

"My strategy was to give protection to the population so they could produce, travel, have animals, sow seeds, and keep others from killing them," said General Huamán. "For them, Peru does not exist. They care nothing about senators; the police abuse them and the judges jail them because they have not got the cash to defend themselves. Meanwhile, Shining Path has killed off all the cattle thieves and promised a better future. The state has to protect the people. When I arrived, the time for bullets was over. I helped irrigation canals to be built, I won people's trust, spoke the same language and danced and laughed with them. Development plans were made and the politicians promised a large sum of money but it never came. The local development authorities helped themselves, not the communities—that is why Shining Path kills them. When I denounced the corruption, I was booted out."

However, mass graves continued to be uncovered and were blamed on Huamán. The consensus among military analysts is that, in effect, he gave the guerrillas a breathing space and then, feeling increasingly betrayed by the government and state, cracked down with random frustration on the villages. Guzmán, who had formed what he called the First Company of the First Division of the Red Army in December 1979, responded to the dirty war in kind. Shining Path's People's Guerrilla Army began to be created in March 1983. It amounted to the concerted militarization of the party on all levels, bringing the principal, regional, and local forces into play. This was the basis for the fanning out of the rebel actions in May 1984 beyond the departments of Ayacucho, Huancavelica, and Apurímac to other parts of the Andes and the jungle: Huánuco, San Martín, Pasco, Cajamarca, La Libertad, Junín, Puno, and Cuzco.

While the security forces tried to oblige the peasant communities in northern Ayacucho to form self-defense groups or *rondas*—and treated them brutally if they showed a lack of willingness—Shining Path responded by crushing the *rondas* with all the savagery it could muster. The rebels called their members *cabezas negras*, meaning "black heads," apparently because of their occasional use of balaclavas to hide their identities; the term also identified them with the blackness of the "Reaction" and, possibly, with the return of the mythical "damned," who were reputed to come by night and eat people's heads. There were relatively few direct clashes between the rebels and the soldiers or police. Instead, each side concentrated on punishing the people for whose hearts they were supposedly fighting. Where they were unable to win support by mere conviction, they both resorted to terror. In order to trick the peasants into revealing their sympathies, each side would assume the guise of the other and slaughter those who welcomed them. The communities found themselves in a no-man's-land where death came from within and every side.

As the bloodshed, fear, and fury gathered momentum, ancient rivalries burst into the open. Germán Medina, a doctor who became a left-wing congressman for Ayacucho and eventually fled the city after receiving threats against his life from the guerrillas as well as from government-linked paramilitary forces, said, "In some places, the formation of the *rondas* involved transferring communities from the higher areas to the valleys, acting as cushions to protect the military bases. With the soldiers following, they were obliged to comb the area for the *senderistas*. Anybody who did not take part was considered suspect.

"The creation of the *rondas* exacerbated intercommunity fights and brought old hatreds to the surface. These stem from the extermination of the Huari/Wari tribe by the Incas, who moved the survivors elsewhere and repopulated much of the region with other groups. The peasants try to take advantage of the *rondas* to settle scores, or just to gain general political ascendancy. But whole villages have disappeared, either through massacres or emigration, which is what the army wants because it leaves the *senderistas* with nowhere to hide and no one to feed them." The militia, which in some cases are suspected to be interested only in securing control over drug routes, welcome Shining Path deserters. The *ronderos* are a sharp thorn in the guerrillas' side and treated mercilessly.

One of Shining Path's earliest and most brutal massacres of militarized peasants came in April 1983. The guerrillas wreaked revenge on the villages of Santiago de Lucanamarca and Huancasancos, Ayacucho, where the peasants had recently attacked and killed several of their militants. The villagers, whose economy was being strangled by Shining Path's virtual ban on outside commerce, had been encouraged by a succession of clashes or possibly slaughters in which about sixty guerrillas died at the hands of the security forces after they had supposedly gained the help of neighboring communities. The rebels punished the two villages by shooting and axing to death up to eighty of their inhabitants, who tried in vain to defend themselves with stones.

One survivor said, "They put us in the corner of the square. Little by little they brought our brothers who had run away. They put them up against the church and then made them lie down with their hands on the back of their necks. They massacred every last one they brought there. They started with axes and finished off with an FAL." Many were killed in the puna, the high ground where they were grazing their vicuña, others in the collective farm. "Death to the traitors of the armed struggle," said the notes on the bodies.

This was the moment of "excess" that prompted Guzmán to ruminate later about an angle which only "has a certain degree of opening, and no more." But in the *El Diario* interview, he openly vindicated the use of terror. "Our problem was to deal a crushing blow to curb them, to make them understand . . . to make them understand that we were a tough nut to crack and that we were prepared to do anything, anything. When you undertake the insurrection and take up arms, you do not lower the banner; you hold it aloft and victorious until the triumph . . . regardless of the cost! Marx . . . Lenin . . . Chairman Mao Zedong have taught us what the price to pay is, what annihilating to preserve means, what it means to keep the banner up high, come what may."

However, it was the security forces' atrocities that caught the greater limelight. In 1984 the Peruvian government came under increasing domestic and international pressure to call a halt to the human rights abuses perpetrated by the military and police. Meanwhile, the number of bombings, blackouts, and assassinations soared in the capital in the period before the municipal and general elections in April 1985. APRA's Alan García was elected to the presidency, traditionally known after the Spanish conqueror as Pizarro's Chair, amid a wave of national euphoria despite the terrorist attacks. The runner-up in the first ballot, Alfonso Barrantes, withdrew from the second. The optimism surrounding García, whose prestige was enhanced by the support of some of the country's leading busi-nessmen—who were dubbed the Twelve Disciples—centered on his populistic promises to create a "different future." Inter-national creditors were to be defied; peasant massacres were to be investigated; the military was to be reined in, and there were to be no more human rights abuses.

Thinking that by playing upon APRA's own revolutionary roots it might be able to draw the sting out of Shining Path, the government attempted to initiate talks with the rebels. A senior APRA figure, Armando Villaneuva, was dispatched to Sweden in the hope of making contact with them. His approach was shunned. The guerrillas, whose election boycott was accom-panied by heavy terrorist intimidation, had severely disrupted voting in Ayacucho, Apurímac, and Huancavelica. They greeted García's triumph by attempting to shoot the president of the electoral commission, exploding their first car bomb (be-side the presidential palace), killing a newly elected congress-man, and dynamiting APRA offices.

Hopes of dialogue still flickered. After the army massacres at Accomarca and elsewhere in August 1985, García forced the resignations of the Commander in Chief of the armed forces as well as two other generals, while the parliamentary investigat-ing commission openly recommended dialogue with the rebels as well as an amnesty for those not involved in homicide. As with Belaúnde, whose seventy-two-hour surrender ultimatum on the eve of military intervention had been greeted with a Shining Path communiqué saying it was "sufficiently prepared to respond to whatever repressive action," such efforts were utterly futile. Guzmán's position is embodied in the Lenin quo-tation with which he closed a speech to the central committee in February 1982 and is the title of a Shining Path march sung to a Polish melody: "Other than power, all is illusion."

Throughout 1985 the country's jails grew more and more restless. Both ordinary prisoners and those accused or con-victed of terrorist offenses demanded better food and health treatment as well as faster trials. Prison guards were held hos-tage as deals were struck with the authorities to improve con-ditions. As part of García's appeasement approach—"state barbarity should not be the answer to *senderista* barbarity"—

The execution of the Inca Atahualpa by the Spaniards in 1533, by Huamán Poma

*Pishtacos* extracting the grease from bodies in folk art from Ayacucho (Nicario Jiménez)    JOHN THOMPSON

Guzmán in his days at the university in
Ayacucho, 1963

Augusta La Torre, his wife    CARETAS

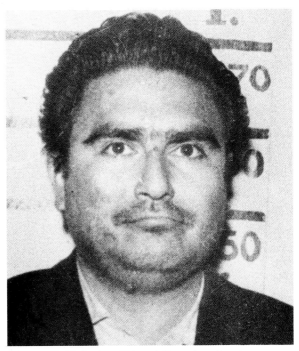

Shining Path's leader, Abimael Guzmán, when he was
detained by police in 1979    CARETAS

Guerrilla graffiti near
Tingo María, 1989

The rebels' flag hangs below
the belfry of a church at
Quinuapata, Ayacucho, during
an "armed strike" in 1983
VERA LENTZ

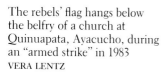

A man killed with a rock by Shining Path for being a *soplón*, or
informer, at Companía, Ayacucho, 1985     VERA LENTZ

Children harvest their crop of coca leaves near Tingo María, 1986
VERA LENTZ

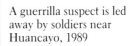

A guerrilla suspect is led away by soldiers near Huancayo, 1989

The widowed bride of one of thirty-four victims of an army massacre at Soccos, Ayacucho, at the moment their bodies are unearthed after being taken away during her wedding feast, 1983    VERA LENTZ

Women *ronderos* armed with sticks to defend themselves against guerrillas in Acosvinchos, 1985     VERA LENTZ

U.S. helicopters with American crewmen at Progreso in a combined drugs and counterinsurgency police operation, 1987     VERA LENTZ

The whites of his eyes show as a traveler is asked for his identity papers by police on the Ayacucho–Quinua road, 1985    VERA LENTZ

An armed *Sendero* guerrilla near Uchiza, 1987    VICTOR VARGAS

Rebels use a poster celebrating the anniversary of the prison massacres in order to indoctrinate recruits in the jungle near Uchiza, 1987    VICTOR VARGAS

Guerrillas near Uchiza undergo military training, 1987    VICTOR VARGAS

*Senderistas* on parade in Lima's Miguel Castro jail, where they controlled their cellblocks, 1991
VERA LENTZ

Detail of a Lima prison mural painted by the rebels, 1990
VERA LENTZ

Shining Path supporters in the London May Day parade, 1991

Picture taken from a September 13, 1992, Peruvian television broadcast showing Abimael Guzmán in jail following his capture in Lima on the previous day. While his arrest is a major political blow to Shining Path, most of the group's military leaders are still at large and analysts say that the revolution remains strong.    AFP PHOTO not only were the tortures, disappearances, and extrajudicial executions reduced, but an agreement was signed under which Shining Path's captured militants were given the status of "special prisoners." They were allowed to administer their own cellblocks. The agreement applied to the three Lima prisons that had been filled up by the transfer of rebels from the provinces after the Ayacucho jailbreak in March 1982 alerted the government to the insecurity of the provincial jails. Later, the policy was reversed.

Most of the Maoist prisoners were walled up in the sinister and crumbling confines of El Frontón, a penal colony built in 1917 on a rock-and-desert outcrop adrift of San Lorenzo Island, whose somber mass, often blurred by mist, rears up more than thirteen hundred feet above the Lima bay. The jail had played host to generations of political prisoners, including Fernando Belaúnde, Armando Villaneuva, and a throng of APRA congressmen, before being shut down under the second military government in what marked the beginning of the return to democracy. It was reopened in 1982 to house Peru's latest and more virulent brand of rebel.

In October 1985, three months after they had been granted special status, the Shining Path militants in Lurigancho jail were alleged to have resisted an arms search by the police and to have set fire to their cellblock, tying up and burning alive those who refused to participate. According to the prison authorities, who said they had been unable to enter the cellblock since about a year and a half earlier, thirty inmates died. *El Diario* claimed that the rebels were shot at by police, who then hurled dynamite and incendiary bombs made of liquid phosphate. No public investigation was carried out, and amid the obscurity and contradictions it was suspected that *El Diario's* version might be nearer the truth. Henceforth, the Shining Path prisoners claimed the authorities were looking for an excuse to exterminate them.

As García's relationship worsened with the armed forces, whose precious institutional pride was badly singed by his firing of the three generals and who felt that in being held to account for human rights abuses they were expected to fight a war with one hand tied behind their backs, García's peace commission resigned for lack of support. The rebels promptly shook the capital with a wave of bombings directed against restaurants, shopping centers, government offices, and banks; police assassinations were also stepped up. The president responded in February 1986 by imposing a night curfew in Lima, which lasted eighteen months, and placing it once again under a state of emergency whereby civil liberties were reduced, the armed forces patrolled the city, and tanks squatted on street corners.

While the military started to clamor for the death penalty on the grounds that it was impossible to "reeducate" Shining Path rebels by putting them in jail, the prisoners, with mounting fervor, accused the government of planning to orchestrate their massacre. The armed forces' calls for the death penalty won significant support from diverse political parties as well as the attorney general. The hardening attitude accompanied calls to transfer the prisoners to Miguel Castro Castro, a new high-security jail among the shantytowns of Canto Grande, in a bid to deprive them of the power and privileges they had acquired. At the same time, newspaper editorials reflected the erroneous belief that the jails were becoming Shining Path's central planning centers, a belief fueled by the extraordinarily disciplined regime that the prisoners adopted.

The jailed rebels consider prison a place of political action, a temporary inconvenience or work accident to be turned into political advantage. An article in *El Diario* arguing that they were prisoners of war said they were "combatants of the people's guerrilla army led by the PCP who, even while prisoners, maintain such a role and carry out three tasks. . . . [First,] combating: They have developed successive struggles to conquer and defend their rights. . . . [Second,] producing: The prisoners of war . . . make handicrafts. . . . [Third,] mobilizing: They carry out work of the masses, politicizing, mobilizing, and organizing their relatives, neutralizing the common prisoners; and, what is fundamental, [they] develop their own ideological, political, and organizing work. . . . In this way, the black dungeons of the reaction [are transformed] into shining trenches of combat." The government believed that the jails were being used as command centers for attacks in Lima.

Visitors to El Frontón and Lurigancho were struck by the

rebel inmates' orderliness and cleanliness; how no prison guard ventured into their cellblocks; how slogans were chanted while the prisoners stood in military squares or they marched up and down below portraits of Marx, Lenin, and Mao. They cooked their own food. Revolutionary songs were sung. There were indoctrination classes. The library at Lurigancho was stocked not just with Communist classics but with philosophical works and novels ranging from Mario Vargas Llosa's *War of the End of the World* to Robert Louis Stevenson's *Treasure Island* and Goethe's *The Sorrows of Young Werther*. The surreptitious usurpation of power within the prisons was a microcosm of what was happening in the rest of Peru. Likewise, the jails came to be seen by the government and military as pustular boils which it might be convenient to have surgically lanced.

In May 1986 the Shining Path prisoners in Lurigancho issued a statement in which they rejected claims that they were building tunnels. Such statements, they said, were part of the government's propaganda to inflame public opinion in preparation for its "new genocide plan." They criticized the prison authorities for not sticking to the deal of the previous year (it was signed four days after the rebels' assassination in Lima of the director of El Frontón) and claimed that the prison authorities were using ordinary inmates against them in order to provoke an incident that the guards could use as an excuse to intervene with firearms. By June the guards were staging strikes for better pay; with the consequent suspension of prison visits, the tension increased further. General Cisneros, retired, said the rebels' threat that their transfer to Canto Grande would take place only over their dead bodies should be taken seriously; that is, that an agreement should be signed and the transfer hurried along with. A journalist was tipped off by the prisoners at Lurigancho that "something" was about to happen.

The prison guards struck again at daybreak on June 18. It was the eve of the Seventeenth International Socialist Conference—the first time it was being held in Latin America—and missions from forty countries were in Lima. Twenty-two of the delegations represented their governments. Several prime ministers had canceled their presence because of security fears, but the former West German chancellor, Willy Brandt, helped to make it a high-profile occasion. Hundreds of journalists were present; it was Alan García's opportunity to shine on the world's stage and to win international support for his "can't pay, won't pay" policy on external debt. The day the guards renewed their strike, riots broke out in the three prisons simultaneously.

Police, guards, and the women's prison governor were effortlessly disarmed and taken hostage. The Shining Path inmates in El Frontón and Santa Bárbara handed over a list of twenty-six demands. These revolved mainly around the authorities' compliance with the previous agreement concerning prison conditions and a guarantee not to transfer them to Canto Grande. García, already reeling under a wave of police killings and bomb attacks in the capital, entrusted the armed forces with the task of restoring order if the resuscitated peace commission failed to persuade the prisoners to surrender. The military were to rescue the hostages and move the prisoners to Canto Grande. García is reputed to have accompanied the order with an untranslatable expletive.

There followed the biggest massacre in Peru since the army slaughtered thousands of members of the APRA party in the early 1930s. The peace commission, which had no negotiating power anyway, failed to interview the prison director in Lurigancho, much less talk to the mutinous inmates. Its members were unable to dissuade the women at Santa Bárbara. And when they arrived at El Frontón, navy commandos were already taking up positions on the island. State attorneys, judges, and the prison authorities were blocked by the security forces in their efforts to create real forms of dialogue—requested by the prisoners in El Frontón—and to delay armed intervention.

Army explosives and antitank shells blasted a hole in the cellblock wall in Lurigancho sometime after midnight. Soldiers tossed tear gas through the cavity and opened fire as the prisoners started to sing songs and shout slogans. After further army explosions, which wounded two policemen, police entered the cellblock. They initially shot about thirty prisoners, who were unarmed. The hostage was rescued and the rest of the inmates either were dragged out or surrendered with their hands on their heads. They were laid on the ground and shot too. In all, 124 prisoners were killed.

At Santa Bárbara, which was entrusted to the overall command of the air force, the police descended from the roof as well as entering from two other points with the help of dynamite. They were attacked by the women with homemade weapons and responded with gunfire. Three prisoners died and several were badly injured. The rest, who were all beaten up, were transferred temporarily to another jail.

Plastic explosives blew open a hole in the cellblock at El Frontón after three shells had failed to produce an effect shortly after nightfall. A second charge brought down part of the building and blocked the hole that had just been made. The inmates initiated an exchange of fire with the police and marines using the handful of weapons they had taken off their hostages, throwing homemade bombs and firing makeshift crossbows. They were greeted with tear gas and submachine guns. A few hours later, with the prisoners still unbowed within the pulverized building, which was said to be riddled with walls, tunnels, and trenches, a company of marines disembarked from San Lorenzo and relieved the police. Heavy machine guns, bazookas, and 81mm antitank guns were brought into play. The prisoners fought and sang as the roof and walls began to crumble around them at dawn amid a gigantic cloud of dust.

Nobody admits or knows for certain what happened next or how many prisoners died or how many were deliberately killed once they fell into the marines' hands. In the midafternoon, according to the navy, twenty-eight inmates surrendered. Except for the badly wounded, who were taken to the hospital, the survivors were removed to Canto Grande. Diverse witnesses reported that the jail was bombed from the air; that inmates were hauled out, tortured, and shot; that their bodies were tossed back into the rubble and blown up with grenades; that some were taken to San Lorenzo or other military installations and killed off there. According to a parliamentary investigation, after the surrender the marines demolished more of the cellblock in a deliberate attempt to crush and asphyxiate the rest. Prison doctors were refused entry and navy doctors ignored the wounded, tending only to the marines and police. The marines made next to no effort to look for bodies, alive or dead, beneath the debris. Ninety-six prisoners were killed, according to the armed forces, although the true figure is broadly accepted to be around 120. Hardly any were identified and the whereabouts of their graves remained a mystery.

President García, who congratulated the armed forces, was reported by a journalist with whom he had breakfasted two days before the killings to have asked in a rhetorical manner, in reference to the jails, "What would happen if we shot all the *senderistas?*" and to have answered, "Nothing, absolutely nothing." All that happened was that a police colonel and lieutenant were later sentenced to fifteen years and ten years for homicide and abuse of authority; eight other police were jailed for up to six months. No military personnel were convicted. García himself was accused by a special parliamentary commission in 1990 of breaking judicial as well as other regulations, abusing his authority, and bearing overall responsibility for the massacres. However, a deal was struck with President Fujimori despite Fujimori's electoral promises to curb human rights abuses. Fujimori was politically weak and needed APRA's support on other issues; the accusation was voted out of Congress by a narrow margin. On that night, forty bottles of whiskey were drunk as García threw open his home for an ecstatic celebration party.

By embittering friends and relatives, the prison massacres promptly widened Shining Path's support as well as providing the organization with martyrs. Tomás, a young activist whose brother-in-law was killed, said, "Before, I was just interested, but afterward I became more committed. They died for the poor. Someday, after I have finished my studies, I will get a gun and you will never see me again."

By 1991 there were about four hundred rebel captives at Canto Grande. Most of them are lower-middle-class, first- or second-generation Andean migrants. Once again, they had complete control of their cellblocks—including custody of the keys—which acted as a military and ideological training, informal communications, and cultural center. Sunday parades were held, plays performed, organized lectures given to visitors, and souvenirs ranging from fluffy teddy bears to plaster models of bloody assassinations sold to raise funds. Through a tactical alliance with the drug trafficker Reynaldo Rodríguez, the Godfather, whose money greased the wheels of prison life for guards and prisoners alike, the rebels not only secured considerable political control within the jail but also smuggled goods—probably the most innocent of which were swathes of red and black material which the women turned into a parade uniform and topped with green Mao caps. The complex power struggles inside the jail made it a microcosm of Peru.

In the women's block, portraits of Abimael Guzmán decorated in red and gold were to be found in the cells. Poems were posted up in praise of the "Red Sun," and murals of Mao and a genial-faced Guzmán enlivened the walls of the yard above the rickety cages of rabbits and pigeons. In stark contrast to the ordinary prisoners, the women are clean, well-organized, and welcoming. They are convinced the authorities are seeking any excuse to attack them and give credible evidence to support the claim. In the face of provocations, such as their cellblock being opened at night for ordinary prisoners armed with knives to enter and steal their chickens, they turn the other cheek and lose the chickens. "The police use the common prisoners to attack us in the hope we will defend ourselves and that they can then come in and kill us under the pretense that we are rioting," said María, a pretty girl with sparkling eyes whose legs were destroyed by a land mine as she tried to blow up an electricity pylon. "The war is going to cost millions of lives: The upper classes will not let go. But we know we will win. We are winning. If they do massacre us here, our blood will fertilize the revolution anyway." The prisoners maintain there are four ways they will leave the jail: legally; by liberation at the moment of insurrection; by escaping; or by "heroic resistance" in the face of "genocide."

García's initial public enthusiasm for the savage crushing of the prison revolts turned to bitter recriminations against the security forces as the full horror of the massacres dawned on the country. Still lacking any overall strategy other than to kill peasants more or less randomly and by so doing strike terror into the Andean communities, the military started to fall into deep decline. Its ignorance and desperation was characterized by the influential retired general Luis Cisneros. The general, an enthusiastic apologist for General Augusto Pinochet's savage, all-out war against Marxism in Chile, blamed subversion on European priests and suggested that Shining Path was funded by Amnesty International. More rationally, he complained that while Congress was pushing for military personnel to be tried in civil law courts, the judiciary was constantly liberating terrorists. Poor police work, depending largely on the extraction of confessions under torture, and inept or terrified judges and attorneys as well as an inadequate judicial structure meant that many rebels were released. The failure of the democratic system in turn encouraged the security forces to take the law into their own hands, at both a personal and institutional level. In Latin America, said Cisneros, "coups d'état have not ended, nor will they end."

The executive power of Peru's three armed forces, which each had a Cabinet minister, was severely weakened in October 1987. The individual ministers were replaced by a single minister of defense, and a unified command was established. García had already embarked on a major reform of the police forces. Although both moves were well overdue, they aggravated the security forces' deep institutional rivalries and absorbed much of their energies, distracting them from fighting Shining Path. The military's historic relationship with APRA was far worse than that with Belaúnde in that the military had persecuted the party ever since it started in Peru (APRA began life as a pan–Latin American movement, but its other branches had quickly withered away). The armed forces were now slowly squeezed of cash by the government while the police entered an era of relative prosperity. Angry at García because they felt he had double-crossed them over the prison massacres, the armed forces began to reduce their patrols against the guerrillas. They were unwilling to fight without political leadership that sheltered them from complaints of human rights abuses. García responded by slicing their budget still further. The military, which was anyway still more concerned with the supposed external threat from Ecuador and Chile, virtually withdrew to its barracks in the emergency zones.

Sixty percent of the approximately 120,000 members of the Peruvian armed forces are two-year conscripts who receive hardly anything in exchange for their labor except for food and barracks. University students are exempted from military service, and bribes also take care of it for the rich. Whereas the conscripts used to be dragged reluctantly into service, the economic crisis since the late 1970s has encouraged the poor to volunteer themselves in order not to starve. Since they are made to serve outside their home area, most of the conscripts in the mountains—who are pushed into the emergency zones after only a few months' training—come from the coastal towns and cities. The cultural and ethnic differences sharpen the fear and antagonism between the military and the local inhabitants. The officers, who in the navy mostly come from the upper socioeconomic classes and in the air force and army from the upper middle and middle classes, are even more alienated from the people in the zones influenced by Shining Path. Furthermore, the system of simultaneous one-year rotations for senior officers undermines stability, breaks continuity, and breeds corruption. No sooner have officers worked their way into their new posting than they become preoccupied with the next one. As retirement beckons, the feathering of nests casts war into the background.

When the cash dried up during the García government, so did the soldiers' uniforms, boots, and bullets. By the end of the 1980s the navy, army, and air force were left at only twenty-two percent, thirty-six percent, and forty-five percent, respectively, of their operative capacity. In order to preserve their boots— they are given a single pair annually—troops were said by military intelligence sources to resort to shoes made of rubber tires in the barracks. Occasionally, they were reported even to patrol barefooted. As for ammunition, one élite division was down to an average of just two bullets per soldier. In general, patrols in the emergency zones were kept small because there was not enough equipment to go around. Food was so scarce that the troops were forced to hunt, beg, and steal to survive. So desperate were they that weapons were sold to the guerrillas.

Terror of the war, rock-bottom morale, and the dreadful conditions brought about mass desertions. The level of troop desertion at the end of the decade in the guerrilla areas was running at between thirty and forty percent, according to military analysts. It was not known if some deserters joined ranks with the rebels but it is believed that a significant number abandoned ranks because they were enjoined to do so by Shining Path. More serious still was the growing number of officers deserting from 1987 on, when voluntary-retirement requests, which had been running at an average of one a day in the navy, were suspended. Later reopened, they were banned once more after nearly a quarter of the navy's officers resigned in 1990. During the first quarter alone of 1991, 550 army officers resigned. In the emergency zones, according to military sources, the officer desertion rate was between two and five percent and included professional people of military rank, such as doctors and lawyers, as well as officers under arms; scant effort was made to look for them. Both fear and abysmally low wages drove the officers away.

In 1988 a colonel of twenty years' service was paid the equivalent of about $80 a month. The poor wages removed the main incentive for joining the armed forces as a professional. Military vocation in Peru is almost nonexistent. Officer cadet lecturers remark on the total lack of background interest in weapons, tactics, and geopolitics. One foreign military attaché said, "The graduates want to stay in Lima; they do not want to get involved. The attitude and composition of the officer classes is clearly symptomatic of the complete lack of interest by the rich in what is going on in their country." In 1989 twice as many army cadets were said to have applied to join the army's management as they did to enlist in its artillery, infantry, or tank divisions. And the number of applicants for the air force officer-training college dropped by three quarters over the decade.

While the APRA government bled the military dry it reformed, partially unified, and invigorated the police forces. A crack anti-"narcoterrorist" unit, called the Directorate of Special Operations (DOES), and comprising about a thousand of the best policemen and former soldiers, was set up in 1988. It incorporated a similar paramilitary police force from the 1960s, the Sinchis, who were already operating in the emergency zones with the same reputation for brutality as the military. The DOES was trained by Sinchi officers with the help of the U.S. Special Forces, the Green Berets, at a police jungle base called Mazamari in the department of Junín. Urban training was carried out in the outskirts of Lima near Vitarte, on the strategic central highway, by a former member of the U.S. Special Weapons Assault Team as well as other Peruvian and foreign specialists, including the Israelis.

A Ministry of Interior source during the APRA government said, "The idea was to redefine the emergency zones as security zones, to reinstall or beef up police control in order to allow normal civilian life to return by creating the power to exercise democratic authority. No cases of human rights abuses have been reported against the DOES. They only killed people who were armed with a gun." He added that the armed forces, who claim that the internal defense of Peru is their responsibility, had opposed the DOES because they resented its privileged status. "The armed forces did not want to lose control of the emergency zones, which are a nice source of income for them. Their budget is kept very secret and for operations such as intelligence is entirely unaccountable."

While the police were strengthened—and the increasingly efficient antiterrorist detective squad, the Office Against Terrorism (DIRCOTE), was bolstered—the military also believed that APRA was buying arms for itself. At the same time, a paramilitary death squad with direct links to the APRA party and the Ministry of Interior started operations in October 1987 when two of its members died in a bungled bomb attack outside the offices of *El Diario*. Earlier in the year, the police arrests of APRA members and the seizure of a considerable quantity of weapons and explosives were quickly covered up by the government. Named after a prominent APRA member allegedly killed by Shining Path—the killing may have been a private or party vendetta—Comando Rodrigo Franco (the Rodrigo Franco Command) moved into the limelight by killing a lawyer who was defending Osmán Morote, a high-ranking member of Shining Path, on Independence Day in July 1988. The lawyer, Manuel Febres, was a member of the Association of Democratic Lawyers, an organization whose members specialize in defending alleged terrorists and that sympathizes with Shining Path.

The Rodrigo Franco Command initiated a national campaign of intimidation, bombings, and assassinations in which journalists, human rights workers, trade unionists, and left-wing politicians were among the targets. According to the Senate Special Commission on Violence and Pacification, the group killed at least eleven people in 1989. In one incident, its members tied two students back to back and blew them up with plastic explosives. The Rodrigo Franco Command announced that it was acting "to defend Peru and for each mayor, soldier, and policeman killed, a leader of Shining Path or those groups that support or protect it will die."

A young APRA member who said he had declined to participate explained, "The Rodrigo Franco Command was formed by high authorities in the government in order to defend APRA from any military coup and also to fight against Communist terrorism, to infiltrate institutions where Shining Path has a presence. You do not have to have a pistol in your hand to be a terrorist." He added, "They have groups in all the emergency zones and a large central office which, incidentally, is very close to where you live." (A few months afterward my telephone answering machine played back a message from them: The name "Franco" was spoken followed by bullet shots, a pause, and the words "The number you've got is . . ." The following month, March 1989, another message said, "I am telling you, OK?" Later that year, an alleged deserter of the Rodrigo Franco Command gave to a leading magazine, amid a welter of names and details, the address of its headquarters, which was where Alan García had run his presidential campaign. The house was one block away from my flat in the district of San Isidro, a fact that helped to confirm the validity of both witnesses and thereby established almost beyond doubt the official involvement of APRA.)

A parliamentary investigation by right- and left-wing politicians, whose work was constantly undermined by APRA, concluded that the Rodrigo Franco Command was linked to the minister of interior, Agustín Mantilla, and to some police generals. The privileged treatment given to the police, the existence of the death squad, the advances of Shining Path, and the fear that García might try to hang on to power beyond his presidential term—whose disastrous economic policies brought

about inflation of 2,178,434 percent over his five years in office
—all contributed to rumbles within the armed forces for a coup
d'état. The first such real threat had its guns spiked by forceful
United States diplomatic intervention. The police strength may
also have helped dissuade its leaders. The second plan crystallized when it was decided that APRA's candidate, Luis Alva,
might win the 1990 presidential election through an alliance
with the left-wing parties in a second-round runoff against
Mario Vargas Llosa. The coup plan, whose details were re-
vealed much later at length to a Lima magazine by a high-
ranking officer involved, was ditched because of the sudden
emergence of Alberto Fujimori, who, as a political unknown,
in turn provoked coup rumblings in the navy.

While the military mood darkened—the conspirators' agenda
resounded with admiration for General Pinochet, who had fur-
nished Chile with a prosperity that was the envy of the continent—there was a return to the bloody excesses of the
Belaúnde era. In the last two years of the 1980s, at least seven
thousand people were killed as the military and the rebels
fought for popular domination. As before, it was a question of
winning over minds where it proved impossible to conquer
hearts. Each side relied on terror to instill obedience: Exemplary savagery was employed to convince people where their
best chance of survival lay. Although Shining Path was responsible for the vast majority of the civilian killings, the military
shed any last misgivings about using the same tactics; and the
state and public opinion started not to care.

The Cayara massacre of May 1988 heralded the beginning of
a military crackdown that only relaxed in times when Shining
Path reduced its attacks, as in the first quarter of 1991 when it
prepared for a big offensive in April. Civilians continued to
bear the brunt of the war. The driving out of the special prosecutor, Carlos Escobar, and the execution of the witnesses happened even as Brigadier General Arciniega was burning down
villages suspected of harboring guerrillas in the upper Huallaga
valley. He alone claimed to have killed around a thousand rebels, many of whom were almost certainly innocent peasants
compromised by Shining Path's presence. Arciniega invoked
Saint Augustine in order to help articulate his position. He had

found the passage in an Argentinian military book on ethics and repression. Citing the saint, Arciniega said, "Man can only be made to see reason through love or through terror." He claimed it was "false that force is always irrational, since it constitutes the ultimate of reasons, and conforms to reason when it serves to reestablish order when there is no other suitable means." The general continued, "This use of force is similar to how, faced with the damage produced by the violence of a crime, the surgeon has to turn to the violence of the surgical method to avoid a greater malady. . . . Subversive violence destroys order; the surgeon's violence restores it."

Two days after the speech, made in September 1990 in the presence of President Fujimori, the political-military commander in Tingo María, Lieutenant Colonel Miguel Rojas, announced that eighty-five subversives had been killed while taking part in a large fiesta in honor of the Virgin de las Mercedes at the village of Merced de Locro. Soldiers had attacked on the ground and by helicopter, and it was alleged that the subversives were shot as they fled. A large arsenal of weapons was reported to be captured. The information was never independently verified but witnesses claimed the army had fired indiscriminately into their midst. Peru's main human rights group, APRODEH, said the operation had "all the characteristics of those 'punitive actions' carried out by the armed forces against villages in Ayacucho considered as 'social bases of subversion.' "

The following year human rights abuses continued unabated despite renewed government and army rhetoric. As a paramilitary group believed to be linked to the army picked off innocent civilians in Ayacucho, a secret document was leaked from the Armed Forces Joint Command. It stipulated that in "special intelligence operations" actions should normally be clandestine, using "legal or illegal procedures" and that "if the situation and the conditions permit it, eliminations will be carried out without leaving a trace." The document concluded, "Antisubversive operations that are executed on the basis of information provided by the Intelligence Detachments will be of a highly aggressive and offensive character, not forgetting that the best subversive is the dead subversive; therefore, no prisoners will be taken."

As the army went on the offensive in the valley of the river Ene, where Shining Path dominated large stretches of the jungle, no prisoners *were* taken. And in Lima, letter bombs blew off the arm of a human rights lawyer and killed a young journalist working for the MRTS-linked *Cambio* newspaper, as well as two other people, in separate incidents. Most sinister of all was the massacre of sixteen men, women, and children by up to ten men with submachine guns and silencers a few blocks from Congress in November 1991. The victims were mowed down during a fund-raising party, apparently for new drains. The killings had none of the hallmarks of Shining Path and by a broad consensus, they were believed to be the work of an "antiterrorist" command—although the exact motive remained a mystery that the police appeared little inclined to fathom. Despite there being a police station only thirty yards away, they arrived after the firemen, and the getaway vehicles, which were stolen from a ministry and President Fujimori's brother, were never found. Some of the victims were believed to have low-level links with Shining Path.

Meanwhile, in the province of Huanta in Ayacucho itself, those civilians who failed to participate in the peasant *rondas* that were being organized by the armed forces and taught to build guns were getting their heads blown off with dynamite. According to the notices laid beside their bodies, which accused them of being subversives, the method of execution was applied because they did not "know how to think." A nineteen-year-old peasant from the village of Runguyocc described what happened to those who did "know how to think." "Because we formed a *ronda*, my family was killed by the *terrucos* and our community destroyed," said Antonio Ccente. "They blew up one girl with dynamite. It is no longer safe for me to sleep inside. We have fought them with lances, slings and arrows, and homemade rifles, but they have FALs and Kalashnikovs." Not far from where he spoke, a donkey had recently exploded near a military parade, the dynamite hidden in bags of alfalfa.

Just as the church bells in Huanta began to peal for the Sunday service, Ccente glanced nervously across the square toward two young men who were staring at him. He mumbled excuses and fled. It was on the eve of the municipal elections in November 1989, when Shining Path's killing of about sixty mayors had prompted the resignations of more than three hundred candidates. The rebels were pursuing an election boycott. While the guerrillas stole identity documents so that people were unable to vote, the military detained those found without papers. While the guerrillas threatened to assassinate anybody found with a voting stamp, the military declared it would punish anybody caught without it. Peruvian voters traditionally have to dip their fingers in mauve dye as a precaution against their trying to vote more than once. In order to take the heat off the voters, who are fined if they fail to attend, it was decreed that such a nicety should be dropped. Shining Path had threatened to cut off the fingers.

# 6

# Enter the Church

In the same way that the armed forces initially had to struggle against claims from both within and outside its ranks that generals were in some manner involved with Shining Path, so too did the Catholic church have to stomach allegations that priests were implicated. There was a degree of substance, albeit fractional, to both charges. Each institution underwent revolutionary traumas during the 1960s. Under the left-wing military dictatorship of General Juan Velasco, which characterized the mood of revolution sweeping Latin America and the sense that only through violent, authoritarian measures could the continent be hauled out from underneath its grinding poverty and its states transformed into more equitable entities, the army was at the vanguard of radical nationalist and socialist reform. Even as Peru moved in the late 1970s toward a much more authentic, if still deeply flawed, democracy than prior to the Velasco regime—which ended in 1975—many army officers continued to embrace revolutionary change.

Among them was Major José Fernández Salvatecci, who led a clandestine organization called the Third of October Military Command, which wanted to continue the armed revolution where Velasco had left off. Salvatecci, who was suspended and persecuted but never court-martialed, was an army intelligence officer and boasted that its intelligence service was really his own. "There were dozens of colonels, majors, and captains in the organization," said Salvatecci, who fought with the Sandinistas in Nicaragua against the dictator Anastasio Somoza. "Some are still there and still sympathize with its original aims." He accuses others, such as General José Valdivia, who was implicated in the Cayara massacres, of having sacrificed their revolutionary sympathies for the sake of ambition and social status.

The organization tried unsuccessfully to convert into its political arm the Revolutionary Socialist party, which included men who became prominent politicians, including Enrique Bernales, who in 1988 assumed the presidency of the Senate Special Commission on Violence and Pacification. Salvatecci himself was a close friend of an allegedly important member of Shining Path, Elvia Zanabria, who was believed to be among Abimael Guzmán's personal entourage. Salvatecci was arrested as a suspected rebel at the same time as she was, on the occasion that police raided Abimael Guzmán's house in Monterrico in June 1990. He was later released.

While the military suffered severe internal traumas during the 1960s and 1970s, the other pillar of post-Columbian Peru, the church, also experienced profound change. The 1962–1965 Vatican II General Council, a meeting in Rome of the world's bishops which last took place in 1869–1870, launched the Catholic church into the modern age. Thereafter, the Eucharist was said in the language of the country in which it was celebrated, instead of in Latin, as part of a wider drive to make the Christian message more relevant to the real world. Christianity in Latin America was brought further down to earth at the bishops' conference in 1968 in Medellín, Colombia, when it was decided in the light of Vatican II that the church should commit itself to what became known at the next conference in Puebla, Mexico, as the "preferential option for the poor." This stemmed from a Marxist-style analysis of social and economic structures which, it was perceived, kept the rich in power and the poor oppressed. The church's aim was directly to address poverty and the systems that maintained it by making people aware of their human rights and their country's laws in order that they should stand up for themselves and slowly work, from the bottom, to bring about more just and democratic societies.

One of the principal architects of what he called liberation theology was a Peruvian priest, Gustavo Gutiérrez. He rejected the Latin American church's "ghetto" attitude, which pitched most of its energies into defending the faith, and wrote, "Liberation theology that is based on the commitment to abolishing the present situation of injustice and to building a new society must be substantiated by putting that commitment into practice; by the active and efficient participation in the fight that the exploited social classes have embarked on against their oppressors. . . . [A]ll political theologies, of hope, revolution, liberation, are not worth one authentic act of solidarity with the exploited social classes. They are not worth one act of faith, charity, and hope committed—in one way or another—to an active participation in liberating the human being from all that dehumanizes him and impedes him from living according to the will of God."

The creation of liberation theology also came about in the wake of the short-lived guerrilla activities of a Colombian priest, Camilo Torres. A leader of the National Liberation Army, Torres reconciled violent rebellion with Christian ethics and became a mythical figure after he was killed in 1966. Elsewhere, the Catholic church played a vital part in the Sandinista revolution in Nicaragua, which it initially supported, and was notorious for assisting the rebels in El Salvador. A conference of American generals in Mar del Plata, Argentina, declared in 1987 that liberation theology was an instrument of international communism, "reducing the figure of Jesus to a sort of social and political leader."

In Peru, liberation theology took root in Cajamarca, in the southern parts of the department of Cuzco, and in the department of Puno. It was enthusiastically adopted by foreign as well as national priests. (Nearly two thirds of Peru's two thousand Catholic priests are from abroad; poor wages and celibacy are blamed for the lack of local recruits.) There began a long and continuing battle between the church's progressive and conservative wings; the latter disliked what is considered the politicization of peasants and workers. The misgivings were shared by the main political parties, including APRA, and the business establishment in general. Toward the end of the first year that

Shining Path took up arms, newspaper reports started to blame the terrorism on foreign priests. A Canadian prelate bishop, Alban Quinn, denounced the reports from the pulpit in Sicuani, Cuzco, as a slanderous campaign instigated by those with landowning interests who were angered by the church's identification with the interests of the peasants who, he said, "today are more conscious of their rights and are organizing themselves in order to defend themselves."

The division in the Catholic church was exemplified by its differences in attitudes toward human rights abuses. Although the official position was to condemn them unequivocally, the ultra-conservatives uttered hardly a word of protest and in some cases, notably in Ayacucho, intervened to prevent denunciations against the security forces. In its first intervention over a human rights case, the church plunged its hand into a hornet's nest. In May 1981 four people were arrested by the police and accused of being subversives in, as it happened, Sicuani. They were severely beaten up and one of them, Edmundo Cox Beuzeville, a Lima student, was covered in a poncho to hide his broken arm and fractured shoulder and was filmed confessing his allegiance to Shining Path. Police alleged the prisoners gave away the whereabouts of eighty sticks of dynamite, but the police claim was never proved.

The Episcopal Commission of Social Action (CEAS) under the presidency of the bishop of Chimbote, Luis Bambarén, denounced the torture. Of Cox, the bishop said, "He may or may not be a terrorist; that is up to the judiciary." He added, "I reject torture. There are other ways of punishing. This is not to say that I am supporting terrorism." What caught public attention was that Cox was the nephew of a prominent auxiliary bishop of Lima, Augusto Beuzeville. As well as triggering off the reaction of CEAS, Beuzeville appealed to the minister of interior, José María de la Jara, to help his nephew. Cox subsequently received privileged treatment, the torture was proved, and he was released. Amid the church's complaints, President Belaúnde accused the bishop of Chimbote of double standards for having turned a blind eye to human rights abuses committed under the military regimes.

Cox, who was rearrested and released several times, was finally sentenced to twelve years in jail for terrorism in March

1988. Police claimed he had reached a significant rank on Shining Path's Lima metropolitan committee. Cox, whose grandfather was British, was educated at a Catholic college run by U.S. Maryknoll priests and came from a devout upper-class Catholic family. Most of his brothers, sisters, and cousins married people they met directly through their parish activities.

Ten years on, the arrest of a former nun who police had strong evidence to show was Abimael Guzmán's and Shining Path's accountant caused shockwaves in Lima. Nelly Evans, who carried a British passport through her great-grandfather, was married to a former Catholic priest from another élite Lima family, Carlos Alvarez Calderón. Evans had been a member of the Sisters of the Immaculate Heart of Mary and worked as a teacher in the shantytowns. On her return from studying in Virginia, she had made the most as a nun of her newfound freedoms under Vatican II and worked alongside left-wing clerical organizations that espoused a more pointed fusion between Marxism and Christianity. The friction between herself and her exclusive, upper-class convent, which reacted sluggishly to the Vatican II directives, brought about the renunciation of her vows. "It was as if because her community had failed to confront the changes, she overreacted and became ultraradicalized," said a priest who knew her at that time.

When she met her husband, Evans had already cast away her habit, as had several of her fellow nuns. Alvarez Calderón, whose brother Jorge became a highly respected member of the progressive wing of the church, turned his back on his vows too, and they married in the mid-1970s. Shortly after, police believe she became involved with a guerrilla group called the Revolutionary Vanguard (Vanguardia Revolucionaria), which was led by Julio César Mezzich, another upper-class and formerly dedicated Catholic. Revolutionary Vanguard, which was prevalent mainly in the department of Andahuaylas, later merged with Shining Path. Mezzich is believed to be one of the guerrillas' top military commanders. Evans went on to become an activist in the national teachers' union, which is notorious for the rebels' infiltration. Her husband, whose allegiance to Shining Path was unclear, grew sick. They parted in the 1980s.

"When freedom arrives, it is like a dam bursting. Water escapes everywhere," said Monseñor Beuzeville. "There were excesses after Vatican II and Medellín. Some small sectors in the church radicalized themselves; nuns and priests left. They wanted to fight for the poor but in a more radical manner. Some get too close to the misery and poverty. They understand why people turn to violence, and if their Christian faith is not strong enough, they are tempted to sympathize." The religious dedication felt by those who wanted to be at the service of others, he added, could become perverted by anger and, on a more psychological level, by feelings of rejection: "They may not see the tyranny which they join, or they may swallow the line that every revolution has its cost." In the case of his nephew, Monseñor Beuzeville said Cox had lived for the poor and may have become embittered by his torture and by the abuses suffered by the peasants. Radical left-wing sympathies were among the reasons why a succession of national and foreign priests abandoned the church in Peru during the 1970s, when the church's traditional wing started to reassert itself.

Citing chapter five of the Epistle of St. James, Monseñor Beuzeville added that the example set by Jesus Christ and his disciples in protesting against injustice should be understood and imitated in the context of "the fundamental law of Christianity—love." The text reads:

> Come now, ye rich; weep and lament over the woes which are coming upon you. Your wealth hath wasted away and your garments are become moth-eaten, your gold and silver are rusted, and the rust thereof shall be in witness against you, and it shall feed upon your flesh like as fire. Ye have laid up treasure against the last days. Behold, the wage of the laborers who reaped your fields crieth out, being withholden by you, and the cries of the harvesters have come "unto the ears of the Lord of Hosts." Ye have abandoned yourselves on earth to luxury and pleasure, ye have fattened your hearts "for the day of slaughter."

Throughout the first decade of Shining Path's insurgency, the Catholic church was in the forefront of the defense against abuses of human rights by the police and armed forces. It also condemned the state of Peruvian democracy, defended work-ers' rights to strike, and blamed terrorism on the poverty brought about by historic social and economic repression. This brought it into open clashes with the government as well as the security forces, who claimed that the church's denunciations of human rights abuses played into the hands of the rebels by weakening the state through damaging its public image. At the same time, they bitterly resented that, like secular human rights groups, the church appeared to defend the human rights of terrorists while ignoring those of police and troops. After the prison massacres, the church was refused permission by the military to take medical aid to the survivors at El Frontón. Monseñor Beuzeville commented, "A navy officer asked me, 'What about our four wounded marines?' I pointed out that they had their own priest and doctors, while the prisoners had no one. It was like talking to a brick wall. He kept on protesting his Catholicism but he did not think the church should get involved."

Despite the Catholic church's official condemnations of Shining Path, and its eventual acceptance that dialogue was out of the question because the rebels were ideologically op-posed to it, the church continued to be a target not just for verbal criticism but also for physical attacks by the security forces and the Rodrigo Franco Command. Predictably, the aggression centered mainly on the departments of Cuzco and Puno. After his bishopric was dynamited in the town of Juli, Puno, Monseñor Alberto Koenigsknecht and his assistants re-ceived death threats in a letter, of which the bishop said in September 1981, "The message indicates a marked disagree-ment with the pastoral work of the church in favor of the poor. . . . [T]he authors of the violence may be those who do not accept the norms outlined at Vatican Council II, Medellín, and Puebla." The bishop was not referring to Shining Path.

Such attacks became a regular feature of the church's life in Puno. The bishops complained of police raids and even the torture of parish priests accused of participation in a guerrilla attack on a police station in the town of Umachiri in September 1982. While President Belaúnde and his Cabinet ranted against false priests—especially foreign ones—who turned their flocks against the government, Cardinal Juan Landázuri was forced to come out and deny that anyone in the church was involved in terrorism. His cause was not helped by the three-week detention of an elderly French priest, Jean-Marie Mondet, who police had some evidence to suggest was indeed linked to Shining Path. Mondet was rearrested much later and fled the country once released.

In August 1983 the prelate of Sicuani, Albano Quinn, was locked out of his church and given a fortnight to leave the province after he was accused of carrying out "subversive indoctrination." The order was overturned by the Ministry of Interior, and the local police subprefect was fired. Shortly after, Monseñor Koenigsknecht claimed there had been an assassination attempt against him. The following year, which opened with the president of the Episcopal Commission of Social Action, Monseñor Luis Bambarén, describing as "murderers" those who "from an economic model like that of the International Monetary Fund condemn the people to slow death and unemployment," a French former nun, Anne-Marie Gavarret, was accused of taking part in the killing of a landowner near Cajamarca. Her capture was given banner-headline treatment; her innocence and release were scarcely reported. In November a priest was falsely arrested as a terrorist by the Sinchis in the province of Calca, Cuzco.

Under the APRA government, priests' homes were bombed in the Puno department and the church's radio station there, Radio Onda Azul, was dynamited. While the church denounced paramilitary violence stemming from the authorities' distrust of popular organizations, a police subprefect and APRA member in Puno claimed that Shining Path was "harvesting what the church was sowed." Death threats dressed up crudely to look as though they were from the guerrillas were delivered to the church as well as to other authorities sympathetic to the peasant communities' fight for their land, which had been gobbled up by APRA-controlled agricultural cooperatives. The church was convinced that the Rodrigo Franco Command was involved. In Ayacucho, members of the Episcopal Commission of Social Action and an Irish priest, Charles Gallagher, were arrested by police under the accusation of being terrorists during the command of General Valdivia; in the coastal port of Chimbote, Monseñor Bambarén survived an assassination attempt, which was also attributed to the APRA paramilitaries.

While the progressive wing of the church was constantly subject to government and police or military aggression on the grounds that it assisted Shining Path, it was also viewed as a serious threat by the rebels. In encouraging poor peasants and workers to fight for their social and legal rights, to organize themselves and to become owners of what it called their own "human destiny," the church in the southern Andes, Cajamarca, and parts of the department of Lima acted as a powerful block to Shining Path's advance. The priests who applied the principles of liberation theology were a direct recruitment threat to the rebels in that they worked with and espoused the aspirations of the very sections of society that Shining Path wanted for itself.

By contrast, the conservative wing was a pushover. Alienated from the people, thin in the countryside, only passively interested in human rights and the economic advancement of the poor, the church has traditionally been identified with the landowners, the rich, and the status quo. (In the *pishtaco* myth, human grease is used by the *pishtaco*s in the manufacture of church bells to make their peal louder and thereby summon congregations from farther afield.) Ayacucho was considered the Catholic heart of the Peruvian Andes. Yet the church's grip was profoundly undermined by the opening of the university and was effortlessly shrugged off in the rural areas by the atheist rebels. After centuries of domination, the peasants' Christian evangelization was proved to be as flimsy as gossamer.

Unlike the progressive Catholic sectors, the ultraconservative Ayacucho bishopric retreated into itself as the security forces moved in for the massacre. Further Gutiérrez said, "Ayacucho is a weak point in the Peruvian church in terms of the bishops, probably because they want to preserve certain customs and privileges and fear losing them by being stronger and more energetic in the face of the repressive violence." In failing to defend the population or recognize the roots of subversion, the church hierarchy in Ayacucho divorced itself from the poor and contributed to the power vacuum filled by Shining Path.

It also unconsciously contributed to the martyrdom of a

young guerrilla who because of her classic Indian good looks, proud bearing, and visionary zeal had captured the hearts and minds of people in Ayacucho. Edith Lagos, who had been arrested and released after dynamite attacks in the city, was killed in a shoot-out with police in September 1982 before the revolution's real bloodshed had begun and when Shining Path enjoyed widespread, open support in the area. More than thirty thousand people attended her funeral procession. So great was the popular clamor that the archbishop of Huamanga, Federico Richter, celebrated the mass himself in an ostentatious show of Christian forgiveness and reconciliation that was never to be in such evidence again. Once outside the church, Lagos's coffin was draped with the red hammer-and-sickle flag and swept away by the multitude for burial. The ceremony helped turn her into a legend that could only have served to galvanize recruitment.

The traditional relationship between the armed forces and the church in Peru, as in other Latin American countries, is symbolized by the regular spectacle of priests blessing weapons and military installations. Little has changed since the Inca Atahualpa hurled away the missal and the Spanish Dominican priest gave his blessing for the slaughter of Atahualpa's troops in Cajamarca square. Military chaplains, whose existence as an institution is anathema to the progressive Catholics, help to inspire in the armed forces the sense that they are fighting in the name of the Lord.

Rebel graffiti up and down the country articulates the tenor of Shining Path's plans for the church: Slogans gleefully announce the revolution will have it for "dessert." Abimael Guzmán told El Diario: "Religion is a social phenomenon that stems from exploitation and will die out as exploitation is swept away and a new society emerges." While insisting he is respectful of people's religiosity—and thereby setting the stage for such outbreaks as at the Lagos funeral—he accuses the church hierarchy of acting as a "reactionary shield" that represses "the people's struggle" and adapts tardily to historic change. "It seeks to survive," said Guzmán. "This is why the church held the Second Vatican Council, at which it sought conditions that would enable it first to defend the old order, as it has always done, and then to adapt and accommodate itself to serve new exploiters." He claims that since "half of the world's Catholics are in Latin America . . . they [the church leaders] seek to use the five hundredth anniversary of the discovery of the Americas to launch a so-called movement of 'new evangelization' . . . [T]his plan should be seen as part of a world campaign and plan that is tied to relations with the Soviet Union on the thousandth anniversary of its conversion to Christianity, or the links to Chinese revisionism, the church's actions in Poland, in the Ukraine, etc."

According to Guzmán, Pope John Paul II's visits to Latin America in February 1985 and May 1988 formed part of the same campaign, and in the case of Peru were linked to bolstering its government in its war against Shining Path. Guzmán complained, "He [ the pope] has even called on us to put down our arms while he blesses the weapons of genocide." On the pope's initial visit—the first ever by a pontiff—the rebels triggered an electricity blackout to coincide with his arrival at Lima's airport. The dynamiting of power pylons extinguished the landing lights just before his plane touched down. The pope exhorted people against following "those who claim that social injustices can disappear only through class hatred or the recourse to violence and other anti-Christian means." In Ayacucho he called for dialogue and stated, "Evil is never the road to good."

On the eve of the pope's return to Peru, a bomb was deactivated where he was due to attend a bishops' seminar and, along the papal route in Lima, naval infantry arrested two Shining Path rebels who were disguised as police and armed with submachine guns. The visit was brief. It was controlled by the ultraconservatives within the church, and the pope's public speeches touched only on religious doctrine. While the pope and his bishops pondered the Eucharist behind closed doors, General Valdivia and his troops initiated the massacres and cover-up at Cayara. The coincidence of the two events sharpened the impression that the mainstream church was living in a different world, that it was twiddling its thumbs while the country burned.

Shining Path's attacks on the Catholic church were stepped

up over the decade. Cathedrals, churches, and seminaries were intermittently dynamited, burned, or car-bombed, causing several people to be injured. The hammer-and-sickle flag was hung from or painted on steeples. One bomb was deactivated at a church shortly before the daughter of the army's chief of intelligence was due to walk up the aisle to take her wedding vows. A police chaplain, Víctor Acuña, was gunned down as he celebrated mass in Ayacucho in December 1987, while another priest, Teodoro Santos, was shot as he tried to intervene during a guerrilla attack on a police station near Jauja, in the department of Junín, in June 1989. A nun, María Agustina, who attempted to stop the rebels massacring peasants accused of being police collaborators in a jungle hamlet called La Florida, also in Junín, was machine-gunned in the head in September 1990 after praying aloud and blessing each of the victims as they died. The following year an Australian nun was killed in the same area, apparently because of her involvement in social work, which was also the reason for the assassination of a provincial director of the Catholic church's national charity, Cáritas, again in Junín. And in August 1991 an Italian and two Polish priests were shot dead in the department of Ancash.

Catholic priests are constantly threatened by the rebels. In order to stay alive, many of them obey guerrilla dictates, such as to suspend mass on days that Shining Path decrees general strikes, or to keep a low profile in village processions. The rebels resent the church's existence as a rival power structure in small communities. They permit its religious teaching but not its social, development, or political work. A foreign Jesuit priest working in Junín, Lima's strategic hinterland, where a large proportion of its basic foods are produced and which is also home to many of the country's biggest mines, said in April 1989 that his work had been reduced to helping the sick and defending human rights. "Hardly anyone comes to mass anymore, because they are scared," he said, "although what Shining Path dislikes the most is the church's organization of secular activities and development aid. They want total domination." An adult training school supported by the church had been burned down at nearby Jarpa the previous September. Later in the year, a similar fate befell a large church-backed rural education center in Ayaviri, Puno, which provided farming, engineering, and health training. Its destruction was a terrible blow to the peasants but, for the guerrillas, it represented a victory over antirevolutionary reformism.

Shining Path's attempts to penetrate Puno have been thwarted by the strength of the progressive Catholic bishoprics, which have allied with the peasant communities in their bid to wrest back their land from the big agricultural cooperatives. This has fortified the peasants' Christian faith and turned it into a potent moral and political force. The department, whose population is mainly spread around Lake Titicaca and up a bleak, freezing river valley towered over by snowcapped mountains, provides the rebels with a corridor to western Bolivia, where there are regular reports of Shining Path columns. However, the guerrillas in Puno have found it hard to develop a significant presence outside that corridor. After setbacks in 1985–1986, the guerrillas decided that military action had been premature in outpacing its development of a political support base. While the rebels teach the peasants that they will only conquer their lands through taking up arms and expelling the legal, radical left-wing parties as well as the church, the priests inveigh against subversive violence and encourage the peasantry to organize itself and to win its land battle through pacific means, among which they include land "reoccupations."

Although police and civil authorities are being scared off by the rebels' threats and killings in Puno, the fact that the church has stood its ground and has continued to set a positive example to the Indians has lessened the rot. And the guerrillas there have hitherto not dared to kill the priests, apparently for fear of creating popular martyrs. However, according to Father Hilario Huanca, of Ayaviri, whose baroque, twin-towered church dominates the square and whose pews brim with the brown bowler hats perched on top of the women's pigtails, Shining Path has infiltrated the church instead. Children from its district youth groups are kidnapped and indoctrinated. "Boys and girls as young as twelve years old are being grabbed in the streets and taken away for a week," he said in August 1989. "They are told they will be killed if they fail to cooperate afterward. Sendero has the names on our lists and is picking on group leaders. It is a battle between the children's faith, their trust in us and our power to protect them—and their fear of Sendero." An army general in Puno, whose provinces are only slowly falling under states of emergency, claimed that Shining Path knew the Catholic church was "the only organization that really has influence in the countryside." Benito Gutiérrez, an Aymara Indian and union leader of the peasant communities, warned that "if the church were destroyed, the peasants would lose a powerful instrument of support and perhaps look to Sendero instead."

Shining Path has adopted similar tactics with the church in the shantytowns that sprawl around Lima and are inhabited mostly by first- or second-generation Andean migrants. Father Robert Gloisten, the North American vicar of San Juan de Lurigancho, a parched and yawning desert valley whose reed huts climb up the hills on every side, squeezing the last square yard out of the barren scrub, celebrates mass in tiny reed chapels in the knowledge that at least one or two of his flock are linked to Shining Path. Nearby graffiti'd slogans proclaim: "Long live the New Power." The valley has one million inhabitants and three police stations; the rest have closed because of rebel attacks. Police dare not patrol off the main road, and at dusk retreat from that, too. Except at the lower end of the valley, there are no government authorities.

Father Robert, a stout, white-haired American with spectacles and spatula fingertips, is building up parishes in the valley's poorest zones. As he raised the chalice from the trapezoidal rock that was his altar, blessing the sacrament in both Quechua and Spanish, shots rang out somewhere in the rare, nighttime drizzle. Dogs barked and crickets paused in their song; but elsewhere, Andean brass-and-wind orchestras played on in the unpaved, boulder-strewn lanes. Men, women, and children were playing and dancing around the *yunsa*, a willow tree planted and hung with children's presents as part of an Andean Carnival festival in which the men take turns hacking the *yunsa* with an ax. He who fells it, amid much drunkenness and fighting over whose turn it is, wins the honor of hosting the festival the following year. And as the *yunsa* falls, the gifts rain down upon the children.

While the crowds conducted their own sacrificial celebration of nature's death and rebirth, Father Robert offered up the body and blood of Jesus Christ "who died and on the third day rose again from the dead" and whose sacrifice and resurrection ensured the "salvation" of man. A collection among the sixty worshipers brought in a pile of banknotes worth under three dollars. Prayers were offered up to God via a microphone passed from hand to hand. Another shot went off. "Let us create a new community," said Father Robert in his sermon, as if echoing the nearby graffiti. After some singing accompanied by a drum, a *charango* guitar, and a *giro* gourd instrument, about a dozen worshipers lined up for communion.

"The *senderistas* want to divide and break up the church for political reasons," said the secretary of the chapel committee, Hugo Quiroz, afterward. "They want to manipulate the masses. That is why they encourage their traditional beliefs. They do not like it that it is we who get projects done for the community." A younger committee member explained how he had come to take Catholicism seriously: "I have received evidence of God's love several times. God has brought me things in life, like college."

Presents from trees, God giving his body and blood, God's gifts: "Poverty is a cultural as well as a material state," said Father Robert. "The poor have a terrible sense of not being worth anything. People look for God to value them. They want everything given. I deliberately leave them to organize themselves, because the parish community will get stronger that way. Sometimes I do not appear for mass at all, just so that they will take it on themselves to read the liturgy. It is important always to remember that the more you give of yourself, the more you get out of it. Why did God create the world? Because he wanted people to love him." The officially planned districts in his parish, which were granted electricity and running water but left mostly to their own devices, have a slovenly attitude toward community work and develop slowly. Where the land has been invaded by settlers—often led by *senderistas* —the communities are purposeful and highly organized; they grow much faster.

"Shining Path is very strong here, it has infiltrated all the popular organizations," said Father Robert. "The church has to build itself up from the people so that, if I am forced to leave, it will survive." He tries to expel those he believes are rebel sympathizers from his confirmation and youth groups. "Shining Path recruits from the classes," he said. "They make people accessories to conspiracies and acts of violence, then say that they must help them by painting graffiti and distributing leaflets, until eventually they are fully compromised. If someone refuses, he is threatened either with being killed or with being denounced to the police as a *senderista*. People do not dare go to the police for fear of being killed by the *senderistas*, and at the same time cannot trust that some police themselves are not *senderistas* or in the hands of the *senderistas*."

As Father Robert drove his Volkswagen Beetle slowly down to the main road for an overnight visit to the city center, armed teenagers sprinted up the lane. More teenagers with guns and flashing knives stood around rocks placed across the road. "They're *senderistas*," he muttered, put his head and foot down, and swerved diagonally away onto the asphalt streak toward the mouth of the valley. "Martyrdom touches you, you do not look for it." The following week at midday at least a hundred guerrillas marched down from the hill waving red flags. A group of waiting vehicles drove most of them off toward Lima.

A few hundred miles east the other side of the Andes, in dense mountain forest and plunging ravines, another American priest was driven to arms in his bid to save the last of the Asháninka Indians from the clutches of the guerrillas. Father Mariano Gagnon, a tough, chain-smoking Franciscan with a strong love of whiskey, had devoted his life to an isolated mission in the valley of the river Ene. The Cutivireni mission became the communal hub of about a quarter of the Asháninka population, which at seventy thousand is the largest Indian group left in the Peruvian Amazon. Instead of trying to break all their customs, such as polygamy and female breast nudity, Father Mariano saw himself as their social and cultural buffer against the outside world. He strove to protect them from the encroaching settlers, whom he excluded from his parish, and from the drug traffickers, whose attempts to persuade the Indians to grow coca he fought off by threatening to leave the mission if the Indians did so. But the priest was powerless to prevent the traffickers from using the airstrip.

The mission, with its school, workshops, and hospital, was burned to the ground in May 1984 by armed men who Father Mariano believed were drug traffickers. The cursing priest wept over the ashes. By the time he had rebuilt the mission four years later, Shining Path guerrillas had arrived in the valley. Rumors of their proselytizing among the settlers began to circulate. In June 1989 the rebels paid their first visit to Cutivireni and asked for food, tools, and other objects. Father Mariano complied, as he did several times, for fear of violent reprisals. The guerrillas upped their demands: They wanted him to recruit young Asháninkas for indoctrination. He refused and, a little later, took a holiday.

While Father Mariano was away, a U.S. helicopter landed at the mission with Drug Enforcement Administration agents during a series of cocaine-laboratory raids and illicit-airstrip bombings in the Ene valley. The presence stiffened the Asháninkas' resistance to Shining Path and, on the day of the municipal elections in November, they pulled down the rebels' red hammer-and-sickle flag and replaced it with the national one. Shining Path's response was savage and horrifying. A column of sixty guerrillas armed with submachine guns and assault rifles pillaged and burned the mission before shooting three of the Indian mission leaders. Among them was the head schoolteacher, Mario Zumaeta, who was crucified, castrated, and disemboweled. His remains were stuffed with stones and tossed into the river.

A minority of mission Asháninkas now publicly supported the rebels. Allegedly, an Indian evangelical priest from a nearby community also sided with Shining Path. In retaliation for the rebels' slaughter of a shaman and two boys, an Asháninka group ambushed and killed a guerrilla group with bows and arrows. As the mission's seven hundred inhabitants fled into the jungle, other groups began to turn their back on them for fear of antagonizing Shining Path. In February 1990 the guerrillas massacred fifteen of the mission Indians in their camp. The residents eventually broke up into small groups and dispersed. Meanwhile, Peruvian police and U.S. antidrug personnel bombed the Cutivireni landing strip.

Under Shining Path's sentence of death, Father Mariano returned in a U.S. helicopter (which was based at Mazamari, where U.S. Special Forces officers were training Peruvian paramilitary police); the remnants of his community gathered around him. Father Mariano decided to arm the natives with shotguns and seek to fortify a hill. Hearing that guerrillas were approaching, the priest organized two ambush parties and lay in wait with a gun and two hand grenades. Shining Path fell foul of the other party, and three guerrillas were killed. The Asháninkas persuaded Father Mariano they should flee to another mountain. After a grueling five-day trek in which their numbers halved to about 230 as the rest gave up and melted away, and during which they fed themselves mainly on worms, the priest radioed his position and was airlifted out. His Franciscan superior, Father Félix Saiz, ordered him back to Lima.

"These people believe in me, they see me as their last hope," said Father Mariano in the capital as he consulted Father Félix and waited for transport to return to the Indians. "I do not know if I can protect them. They need arms to defend themselves from Shining Path. Little by little they are joining the rebels out of terror because they have no choice." His relations with the U.S. embassy had soured because the DEA was more interested in fighting drugs than in saving the Asháninkas from the guerrillas, which also would have sucked the United States directly into the war. The embassy turned down his request for weapons.

When he finally succeeded in returning to the mountain, Father Mariano found his Asháninkas' camp deserted and partially destroyed. A Peruvian helicopter flew him to their last refuge, a rocky riverbank wedged between steep, cloud-clustered jungle on either side. Shining Path, which now controlled most of the Asháninka communities and could mobilize at least a thousand people among them, had attacked their mountain retreat. Several of the mission Asháninkas died and, although they managed to kill about twenty guerrillas in return, the survivors were heavily outnumbered and fled.

Starving and armed with eighteen shotguns and some hand

grenades brought to them by Father Mariano, they planned to escape to the land of the Machiguenga Indians 125 miles away in the lower jungle. Since only the fit would make it, they were going to kill their younger children. Instead, Father Mariano persuaded them to trek back to the mountain, from where he organized a mass air exodus to a Dominican mission among the Machiguengas. A private Peruvian pilot braved the wrecked landing strip and the fickle Andean weather to make forty-two rescue flights in the space of two days. The 169 refugees who made it to the Dominicans were given new territory upriver. Father Mariano, who had spent thirty-three years with them, returned to Lima and, eventually, the United States. Shining Path controlled the Ene.

During the following year, hundreds of people died in the Ene as terrible bloodshed ensued. The rebels imposed a reign of fear over the colonists and Asháninkas, while the army encouraged the formation of *rondas*. Dissidents and those who tried to escape the "People's Republic" were savagely killed. One peasant who had fled after being dragooned into one of Shining Path's local forces said, "I saw how they killed an entire family because they caught them when they were trying to escape. One of the murderers grabbed a child and cut his neck with a knife. Then, he held him up by his feet and let the blood flow out until the body ceased to tremble."

In the Convent of Los Descalzos in Lima, Father Félix, with a smell of alcohol on his breath, said of Father Mariano, "It might have been better if the natives had been without him so that they were not grouped together like sheep ready for the wolves to devour. But Father Mariano gave his all. Intertribal rivalry and the drug trafficking left him with no space in which to move. In other areas our missionaries have been able to avoid such clashes. They refuse to stop celebrating mass but they do help wounded *senderistas*. One priest was asked to hand over a truck. He said no, but was powerless when they stole it. And when he realized the teenagers were being recruited, he closed down the school. But he has not been threatened. The main objective is to save lives and not to fight political battles. Perhaps Father Mariano will return to the area when it has been cleansed by the security forces."

A fervent believer in what he calls "nonresistance" by the church, Father Félix was alarmed by Father Mariano's stand. At the same time, Father Félix rejects liberation theology on the grounds that it is Marxist and countenances violence. "By espousing violence, liberation theology as an idea helped to nourish Shining Path," he said. "There are Catholic priests who are in favor of the movement, just like with other guerrilla movements in Latin America. Liberation theology has divided the church."

In attempting to keep his flock separate from the outside world and in partially respecting its cultural integrity—he was, after all, there to evangelize—Father Mariano held out against modernity in a social and political as well as economic sense. He was an old-fashioned Franciscan; his heart lay more in preserving the Indians' idyllic native way of life than in changing, and inspiring them to change, the society from which he wanted to protect them. When Shining Path arrived, his Asháninkas were as defenseless as children. Grouped together, they were stripped even of the forest in which they could hide and ambush, where their semi-nomadic hunting-and-gathering existence gave them a precarious but authentic security. As Father Félix had put it, they were sheep for the wolves.

New impetus for the conservative wing of the Catholic church came with the election of Cardenal Alfonso López Trujillo, the Archbishop of Medellín, as secretary general of the Latin American bishops' conference in 1972. His election was followed by papal appointments of bishops of the more traditional mold; consequently, the Puebla document was milder than that of Medellín. Meanwhile, the hermetic and radically traditionalist organization Opus Dei (some of whose lay preachers take an oath of celibacy) and a conservative Peruvian group called the Sodalitium de la Vida Cristiana grew in influence. In 1989 Peru's key ecclesiastical position, the archbishopric of Lima, was given to Augusto Vargas, a conservative and Jesuit. He replaced a moderate and conciliating predecessor.

The identification of the traditional sectors of the church with a right-wing political establishment was blatant during the electoral campaign of Mario Vargas Llosa. The Lima head of Vargas Llosa's Freedom Movement, Rafael Rey, was an eminent—and celibate—Opus Dei member. In response to anti-Catholic leaflets from extremist Protestant evangelical groups identified with Alberto Fujimori, the archbishop convoked an extraordinary procession of Lima's most venerated effigy, the Lord of Miracles. It is usually brought out and paraded only during its own festival and in times of war or national catastrophe. When Vargas Llosa, ironically himself an agnostic, had decided to resign from the second round of the election in the face of Fujimori's success, the archbishop jumped into a car with darkened windows, furtively raced to his house, and talked him out of it (then lied about his action). The church's ultra-conservatives had their wings clipped the following year when neither the archbishop nor the auxiliary bishop being groomed for stardom by Opus Dei, Juan Luis Cipriani, were reelected to the presidencies of their respective episcopal commissions.

While skepticism about the chances of transforming Peru into an equitable country and vanquishing Shining Path without an all-out random bloodbath generally increased during the 1980s among the more conservative members of the Catholic church and the traditionally wealthy secular sectors, so, too, did the consensus in much of the rest of society that the ultra-conservative elements were to blame for Shining Path's existence in the first place and that the fight against the rebels had to be linked with the protection of human rights and the drive to legitimize government by opening up the state and economy to the millions of marginalized Peruvians. The advocates of liberation theology felt their social analysis had been vindicated, and pointed to their success in containing Shining Path in Puno as concrete evidence of what could be achieved by encouraging people to organize themselves, learn their rights, and take their own destinies in hand.

The Protestant churches agreed. At around the same time that the progressive wing of the Catholic church realized how skin-deep Christianity really was in Latin America, the Protestants, fractional presence in Peru until 1965, started to make inroads. The active adult congregations or the churches comprising the national Evangelical Council of Peru grew to about 2.5 percent of the population by 1980 and leaped to five percent by 1990. The Assemblies of God, Peruvian Evangelical

Church, Christian and Missionary Alliance, Baptist, Methodist, Presbyterian, and Pentecostal churches are among the council's members. At the start of the 1990s a further 450,000 people were estimated to belong to sects such as the Mormons, Jehovah's Witnesses, and Seventh-Day Adventists.

Pedro Merino, the Evangelical Council's general secretary, said, "The country is not evangelized. People are nominally Catholic but not so in practice. They call themselves Catholic because they are baptized, but most are Catholic just three times in their lives—at their baptism, marriage, and funeral." Fewer than ten percent of Peruvians go to Sunday mass. The Anglican bishop of Peru and Bolivia, Alan Winstanley, said, "The Catholic church has not gone out looking for people. We have more of a missionary approach and a greater evangelistic emphasis."

Although the Protestants already felt a growing kinship with the progressive Catholics—for their more modern and ecumenical attitudes—Shining Path's war has brought about a more profound narrowing of the gap. The Protestants have taken a stronger social and political stance that also stresses the structural violence suffered by the poor. They too strive to inform people of their legal and constitutional rights. In late 1989 a national human rights commission was set up. Pastors began to be taught their human rights so that they in turn could teach them to their congregations and spread not just the word of God but that of Habeas Corpus as well.

In a declaration in April 1990 on the causes of violence in Peru, the Evangelical Council's Department of Action and Social Services criticized institutionalized exploitation, injustice, and socioeconomic inequality. The first of seven forms of violence it condemned was racism, a word missing from most Peruvian political and Catholic discourse. It attacked not only terrorism but also "the marginalization of indigenous peoples, their cultures, and their languages" and Peru's "social stratification based on socioeconomic inequality where power and privileges are in the hands of the few and where, consciously or unconsciously, the poor are marginalized and exploited."

The document accused the arms of the state of lacking the will to change. It added, "Grand masses of citizens have come clamoring for a more just social order. . . . Regrettably, we are today rediscovering this fact because of the destructive work of subversion. . . . The existing gap between expectations and opportunities that are unjustly distributed makes insurgency a reality . . . because, when many words have been poured out, for some there is no other recourse than violent and clandestine action." As a "methodological instrument" of action and protest, violence is, however, rejected. The churches sought "a more active participation in material development."

As in the case of the Catholics, it is development and charity as well as the challenge to their authority at which the guerrillas take umbrage. In May 1991 they killed a Canadian evangelical pastor, Norman Tattersall, in front of the Lima headquarters of the U.S.-based Protestant aid organization World Vision. According to the Evangelical Council, Shining Path, the security forces, and also the *rondas* had by then killed more than 350 pastoral leaders. It was believed that eighty percent died at the hands of the rebels; the rest were killed by the security forces as terrorist suspects. Caleb Meza, the Indian director of the council's social department, said, "It is clear that in the emergency zones the only social force that stays is that of religion. The only thing that cannot be taken away from people is their religious formation, and whereas the response from the Catholic church has been timid in many areas, the Protestant evangelicals, especially the Pentecostals, have been aggressive."

The Pentecostals' religious and sectarian fundamentalism, with its millenarian, apocalyptic concept of the world, tallies with elements of Andean culture and fulfills the psychological needs of the poorest and most alienated sectors of Peruvian society. Its heavy emphasis on a dualistic vision of the universe strikes a historic social, religious, and mythical chord. The Pentecostals believe history has a finite end in which Good will conquer Evil and God will vanquish the Devil. Although such absolute moral opposites are absent from the traditional Andean religious view, they nevertheless fall in line with the myth of the next *pachacuti*, which is to mark a tumultuous but beneficial reversal of order, the end of one age and the beginning of another. Caleb Meza said, "The Pentecostals believe Shining Path is a satanic phenomenon and that direct divine intervention is near at hand."

Clashes between the rebels and the evangelicals arise because the latter are usually among the leaders of the peasant communities. Despite the cultural confrontation, typified by their stern stand against drinking alcohol and chewing coca, the Indian evangelicals are respected because of their honesty and upright moral behavior. When the guerrillas apply pressure on community leaders to cede authority to their own commissars, attend indoctrination sessions, participate in attacks, and stop their Christian worship and teaching, the Pentecostals are intransigent in the face of the threats. "The next time the rebels come to the village, the Pentecostals are still there, exercising their civil and religious functions," said Meza. "Their dogmatic belief that they will go to heaven if killed maddens Shining Path. They often die singing and praying publicly, converting death into a victory. The guerrillas can kill the body but not the spirit. The deaths have a strong pedagogic effect on the community. It is one of the reasons why the evangelical churches, especially the Pentecostals, have multiplied in strength."

Testimonies recorded by the Evangelical Council from the heart of the emergency zones bear witness to the burning, self-sacrificial nature of the Protestant evangelicals' faith, which hinges on people's conviction of divine reward. One Pentecostal leader from the village of Santa Rosa in Ayacucho, who was identified only by his initials, VVA, for the sake of security, said he had handed over his life to the Lord Jesus Christ because he had been cured of an illness. Recovering from gunfire wounds sustained when a Shining Path column attacked his church, he declared, "I promise to serve the Lord when I am healed of this wound. . . . I will not leave Him. That is why now with the pain, I say 'Lord, how have I sinned before you that you punish me?' . . . The pain has calmed down a little recently. . . . [T]he Lord pardoned me, the Lord is with me, he does not leave me. . . . There are nights he says to me 'Son, how are you?' and passes His hand over me. There are times when in my vision I see the Lord, the Lord is with us, Glory to the Lord!"

VVA was injured after the guerrillas dynamited his church when the congregation refused to stop praying. The rebels killed "six brothers and sisters and one Catholic." Bible and hymn book in hand, his son bleeding "like a knifed chicken," he was shot in front of the pulpit by somebody he knew to have been baptized as an evangelical. " 'Lord,' I said, 'help me. Deliver me to God outright!' " He added that the guerrillas had attacked them because they would not attend indoctrination sessions. "We serve the living God, we cannot go somewhere else, we do not want to serve two patrons," VVA said he had told the rebels on a previous occasion, going on to warn them that they were in the hands of the devil.

The rebels, he added, had argued that the evangelicals were being exploited by the gringos who brought them their leaflets and Bibles. "If it had been written by the gringos," he answered them, "it [the Bible] would not have received the blessing of my God. I in my body received the will of God, I receive the mercy of God . . . for my faith, for believing the Lord Jesus Christ died on the cross for my sins, for your sin, and how can you say, 'The gringos brought the Bible,' it is not like that, the Bible is not just anything, it has been inspired by the Holy Ghost."

Shortly after the military forced his village to form a *ronda* and swelled its numbers by making other communities move there, they received more visits from the guerrillas. "They came to the church but did not enter because we padlocked it and we prayed to the Lord and they did not shoot; they just banged and went away. Another day, they came to kill the authorities, they wanted to kill our brother who is mayor, but they clashed with us." The testimony included no further details. In areas where *rondas* are prevalent and the Pentecostal churches are strong, Shining Path has met some of its toughest challenges.

The guerrillas, who initially restricted themselves to burning Bibles and ransacking chapels, grew more vicious in their attempts to break the evangelicals' will and influence. Pastoral leaders were regularly subjected to cruel and torturous deaths while being taunted with the failure of their God to come to their rescue. As more martyrs were born, so did the conviction that the Last Judgment was at hand. A Presbyterian from Cuzco, Eugenio T. C., whose parents were singled out and hanged by the rebels because they were known to be evangelicals and refused to participate in an attack on troops, said, "If God permits this violence, it is because the Word of God is being fulfilled in these final times."

Of the sects, the Mormons, members of the Church of Jesus Christ of Latter-Day Saints, are perceived by Shining Path as the purest apostles of U.S. imperialism. Their gleaming chapels, their spruce and sanctimonious missionaries in crisp white shirts and dark gray slacks, entice congregations with their basketball pitches, charity, and the chance to study in the modern Promised Land: the United States. Although most of the North American Mormons were withdrawn from the Andes because of the threat posed by Shining Path, Peruvian and Latin American members of the church continue to operate. Several have been killed. Their chapels have been dynamited by both Shining Path and MRTA.

"The attacks have had a tremendous impact," said a U.S. Mormon and embassy official. "The churches are bombed because somehow they are associated with the United States." The Mormons pay no respect to indigenous culture; they seek instead to impose their own. Ties are handed out in reward for achievements, as if to signify that the happy recipient is no longer one of the great unwashed. Emphasis is placed on upward mobility, middle-class values, and noninvolvement in sociopolitical issues. (Ironically, the diplomat in the U.S. embassy in Lima specifically responsible for analyzing Shining Path from 1989 to 1991 was himself a Mormon.)

In contrast to the Mormons as well as the more orthodox Protestant evangelical churches and the traditional Catholics, the radical, progressive Catholics actively embrace indigenous religious beliefs. Prayers are offered up during mass to Pachamama, the Aymara and Quechua earth goddess. "The Christian message has to be acculturate," said Gustavo Gutiérrez. "The incarnation of God takes many forms." The integration not just of indigenous cultural forms but also of local theological beliefs has further strengthened the Catholic church in areas such as Puno and has been another factor in containing the rebels' physical and ideological expansion. The fusion of biblical and Andean historical and cultural traditions has similarly been the secret of success for the authoritarian Ezequiel Ataucusi, whose Israelite sect has proved a headache for Shining Path in diverting potential recruits and establishing colonies in Lima and the jungle—several in Junín and Huánuco—in areas that the Maoists consider their domain. In 1990 the Evangelical Association of the Israelite Mission of the New Universal Pact claimed to have eighty-five temples and 230,000 members. A central feature of the Israelites' practice is animal sacrifice (they use sheep and cattle).

The willingness of the more fundamentalist Protestant evangelicals to die for God is matched only by the guerrillas' willingness to die for the revolution. Taking to an extreme the concept that the more one gives, the more one receives, each side is prepared to make the ultimate personal sacrifice. The shared readiness to give their lives for a cause also led each side to win converts from the other, not just because it was seen to be stronger but because it was felt to demand a greater sacrifice and commitment. In defense of his decision to stay with Shining Path, a baptized Pentecostal told VVA, "I have signed up with my blood." Similarly, according to Caleb Meza of the Evangelical Council, many rebels—including Shining Path military commanders—have abandoned the movement, assumed an evangelical faith, and changed their names because they identified with Christ's example of offering up his own life to God in order to save others. "They hope thereby to save themselves," said Meza. "It is as if people on both sides are betting on an ideology. They want to follow someone."

The secular, organizational power of the Protestant evangelical churches became strikingly clear during the presidential and congressional elections in 1990. It was the evangelical churches that not only motivated people in the emergency zones to defy Shining Path's call for an election boycott but directly helped sweep to power the previously unknown Alberto Fujimori. The short, unobtrusive, and Catholic agronomist who campaigned on the back of a tractor tilled the electoral fields with calls for honesty, work, and faith.

Although the totem of "faith" soon evolved into "technology," Fujimori courted the evangelicals with such diligence that they flexed all their muscle, sending the word antlike from community to community up and down the country, to push him into the runoff against Mario Vargas Llosa (whom he trounced, thanks to the support of APRA and the left-wing parties). Despite Fujimori's subsequent and cynical abandonment of the Protestant evangelicals, his election proved that they were a powerful new force to be reckoned with in Peruvian politics.

The victory caught the Catholic church, the political establishment, and Shining Path all by surprise. Right-wingers claimed that guerrillas had decided to support Fujimori's presidential bid in order to undermine Peru's stability, while the guerrillas saw their terror-backed electoral boycott reap a much meaner harvest than anticipated. By expressing and fulfilling the needs and aspirations of the most marginalized sectors of society, the evangelical, and particularly the Pentecostal, churches enjoyed such support that they were able to make a powerful contribution to bolting together Peruvian democracy at the very moment when it could have been torn asunder by Shining Path.

# 7

# Peru in the Time of Cholera

Every week, more railings or walls go up around the florid, poker-faced homes in the prosperous residential districts of Lima. Iron spikes, electrified wire, or broken glass run along their rims. As the watchmen doze outside or army jeeps creep around the neighborhood, the encroaching war is buried amid the clink of whiskey glasses and the splash of swimming pools. Rather than facing up to the apocalyptic challenge of Shining Path, most upper-class Peruvians, including those whose families have shaped the country's history or milked it of its riches, prefer to turn their heads the other way. The relentless economic decline, provoked by corruption, the foreign debt burden, obsolete labor laws, and a quarter of a century's overweeningly bureaucratic domination by state and government-protected monopolies, is being aggravated further by the cost of the insurgency. With business confidence and investment drying up anyway because of the inept and fickle policies of successive governments, which culminated with Alan García's attempted nationalization of the banks and his unilateral freeze on debt payments—thereby cutting off Peru from fresh as well as current public loans—capital and human flight scarred the country. Industrialists were more inclined to shut down their factories and flee the country than struggle to create a fairer society or accept smaller profit margins. (Whereas in a developed economy businessmen may be content with a profit of fifteen percent, in Peru few are interested in a return of less than fifty percent.)

Bereft of credit to buy seeds and fertilizer, and fleeing the violence in the Andes where the government offered no protection, peasants abandoned their terraced plantations and poured into Lima. In turn, the wealthier sectors, as well as young professionals looking for better employment opportunities, migrated overseas, mostly to the United States and Canada. Capital flight was estimated to average $600 million annually during the 1980s, about one sixth of total exports. Human flight between 1985 and 1990 surged to about 400,000—the equivalent of about half the public sector—according to official figures and conservative projections. Slowly but surely, the whites are being pushed out in what is a social revolution.

To the south of Miami, where in the downtown area Spanish is the principal language because of the torrent of Latin American immigrants, the coastal suburb of Key Biscayne became known, after a formerly elegant beach resort near Lima, as Little Ancón. Meanwhile, its Peruvian namesake was swamped by Indian migrants from the shantytowns, the shacks adorned with red Shining Path graffiti, that were springing up on all sides. The yachts were leaving the bay, the street vendors displacing the bicycle rickshaws along the promenade, and the sea growing smelly and dirty from the sewage that Ancón's dilapidated and overloaded drainage system was powerless to combat.

Those members of the upper classes who do not physically escape the twin afflictions of economic decline and terrorism are inclined to build a screen between themselves and reality. The screen may be their garden walls and darkened car windshields, their heavy consumption of alcohol and cocaine, or, in the case of devoted Christians, the adoption of a more personal relationship with God—a response triggered, according to the progressive theologians, by fear of making a more outward commitment to society. So strong is the pancongregational growth of the "charismatic" movement, which develops an inward-looking response to God and emphasizes spontaneous prayer, clapping, and hallelujah shouting, that it has taken root among Catholic groups in some of the wealthiest of districts.

Liturgical dancing, in which members of the congregation give interpretative dances of the Lord's Prayer, is a regular part of such worship. Meanwhile, such was the renewed demand to join the church between 1989 and 1991 that three seminaries were reopened.

By 1990, a decade of recession in the formal economy had brought the gross national product back down to pre-1975 levels. Since then, the population had increased by about fifty percent. The economic abyss was bridged by the entrepreneurial vigor of the black market, street vendors, and land invaders; the sociopolitical chasm was engorged with the totalitarian bloodlust of Shining Path. The armed revolution thrived on the starvation of the poor, whose numbers multiplied in Lima with the arrival of economic and war refugees fleeing the Andes —Shining Path militants among them.

The rebels' violence, which had probably cost closer to 30,000 lives than to the officially calculated 22,000 by July 1991, pummeled the formal economy into a slow and agonizing submission. The military, judiciary, and political institutions, which were already fragile, insecure, and unhealthily divided among themselves, failed to protect the archaic economic and political engine that kept them going. Still less did they try seriously to renovate it, although President Alberto Fujimori broke his electoral promises and applied a radical economic "shock" program along the lines favored by the International Monetary Fund. He embarked on a bold series of structural, free-market economic and land reforms that amounted to the beginnings of a full assault on the stagnant, socialist apparatus implanted by General Velasco. Meanwhile, as most sectors of the formal economy rusted away with neglect, the guerrillas systematically hastened its demise.

Guerrilla violence, from the day that the small group of Shining Path rebels burned the ballot boxes on the eve of the general elections in May 1980 until the close of 1990, cost Peru more than $20 billion. The economic damage represented the equivalent of eighty percent of Peru's external debt and seventy-five percent of its annual gross domestic product. The guerrillas reduced the country's energy and transport infrastructure, which was already hopelessly underdeveloped, to a shambles. More than fourteen hundred electricity pylons were blown up with dynamite in urban areas, coastal valleys, and the rugged, frozen wastes of mountain passes, where the insurgents often rode on horseback to lay their loads of dynamite.

Pointing to the line of black crosses marking the bombed-out pylons in the department of Huancavelica, Electroperu's operations director, Anibal Tomecich, shrugged and said, "They've won the war there. That transmission line has been bombed so many times it is past repair." Despite huge concrete skirts spiked with broken glass and topped with razor-edged wire, and despite the construction of live electric cages charged by induction—which have killed cattle, pigs, and children—the guerrillas still manage to destroy the pylons. Only the introduction of land mines has in any way checked the attacks on the crucial transmission line to Lima from the Mantaro valley in the department of Junín.

The many millions of Peruvians who live either in the Indian communities in the mountains and jungle or in the urban shantytowns fail to notice the blackouts. Either they are without electricity supplies anyway or they are subjected to severe rationing because of the country's inadequate generating capacity. However, sixty-six workdays were lost in 1990 alone, thereby wrecking productivity, provoking labor cutbacks, and damaging industrial machinery. The chaos was compounded by failing computers, inoperative gas pumps, and seized-up traffic lights that paralyzed intersections. Water supplies ran dry as pumps gave up the ghost (although somehow Lima's exclusive sauna baths survived for the rich and obese to pamper themselves into an accommodating sweat). Inhabitants of apartment blocks were forced to collect water in buckets from below and, since the elevators were jammed, climb endlessly up and down the steps. Preparations began in San Isidro to build its own thermo-electric plant. A Shining Path central committee document in May 1990 said that aside from causing economic damage, the power-cuts tactic "affected the masses hugely because whoever sees the blackout knows what is the cause and the masses see how the Peruvian state . . . attends first to the needs of the grand bourgeoisie and postpones those of the people."

When the guerrillas relaxed their pylon bombing the following year—mangled pylons were replaced with flimsy towers, which Shining Path tended to ignore—Peru was struck by a cholera epidemic. Aided by the appalling hygiene brought about by the state's inability to maintain the existing water and sewage systems, much less build new ones for the burgeoning shantytowns—García's aggressive policies on debt had forfeited Peru major development credit—the disease spread rapidly throughout Peru before contaminating neighboring countries and the rest of the continent. By mid-July 1991, 2,288 people, almost exclusively from the poorest areas, had died of it in Peru; more than 231,000 had been infected. The ease with which the disease swept through the country highlighted the state's failure to have fended for the nation by investing in its infrastructure, a task made all the tougher by Shining Path's inimical drain on its scant resources. Cholera symbolized Peru's social, economic, and even psychological malaise. The disease bred on the country's hunger and rottenness. And like the war it partnered, cholera victimized mostly those whom the state had long ago abandoned.

Around the packed streets in downtown Lima near the increasingly anomalous features of the presidential palace and Congress, the nauseating smell of urine, rotting fruit, and burning garbage thickened the air. Most of the lower windows of the Ministry of Finance had been smashed by rocks. As manhole covers were stolen for scrap—causing children to fall in and materialize several miles away in the river Rimac, drowned in sewage—gaping holes opened up in the roads where water and sewage pipes had burst underneath. Sewage seeped into the water. Traffic grew ever more congested, not because there were more cars or even buses to relieve the chronic pressure on Lima's battered and choked public transport, but because the street vendors had expanded from the pavements into the inside lanes.

In response to the failure of the state to incorporate the sea of mostly Indian migrants into the formal economy, the migrants had taken the initiative and created a market of their own. Carts and wooden stalls bearing everything from fuzzless tennis ,balls to plugs, custard apples, books, and cookers blocked out the shops. Eating was informal, too. Barbecued beef hearts and marinated fish were consumed at fly-ridden sidestalls instead of in restaurants which were rarely much cleaner; eating utensils were washed in buckets of water, hands went unwashed, and people urinated and defecated in the streets and parks. Even before the arrival of cholera, dysentery was common. All around, the old, downtown colonial mansions crumbled to pieces while passersby turned a blind eye to assaults, street urchins sniffed glue, and hordes of moneychangers parried with the greenback, the only commodity everybody trusted.

Shining Path thrives on Peru's apocalyptic decline. It is symptom, cause, and beneficiary. The guerrillas seek to sharpen the polarity between the rich and poor by aggravating economic hardship and stimulating the mutual socioracial resentment and prejudice. The legal left is cursed as revisionist because it holds back open rebellion, because it seeks to close the gap rather than widen it into a social explosion. The aim of the guerrillas' sabotage of the country's energy and transport infrastructures as well as factories, mines, research stations, agricultural cooperatives, and other commercial or production centers is to destroy the economy and, with it, the state. Anything that induces the workers' or peasants' ties or loyalty to the existing order, even just a community medical post, is regarded as antirevolutionary and therefore likely to be dynamited or firebombed.

With the object of encircling the towns and cities from the countryside, and cutting them off from its products, whether food for domestic consumption or metals for export, Shining Path has blown up bridges, roads, and railways. Public transport has been further crippled by the bombing of state and private buses in Lima and, in the rural regions, of other commercial vehicles whose drivers disregard its general strike decrees. In areas under its control, travelers and traders are forced to pay war contributions, thereby boosting business costs. The guerrillas' attempts to develop self-sufficient local economies have met with strong resistance. However, since they have no compunction about resorting to the cruelest exemplary violence, peasants either agree or flee. The net result is the same: less agriculture.

The foodbasket of Lima is the Mantaro valley in the department of Junín. It produces a third of the capital's vegetables, half of its corn, and most of Peru's potatoes. Junín is also the conduit from the jungle for a third of Lima's tropical fruit and for the bulk of the agricultural produce coming out of the central Andes. The department is a traditional provider of up to a fifth of the wool fiber used in the textile industry and a significant producer of meat and dairy products.

Shining Path dominates Junín. The guerrillas' flag flies above hundreds of villages where mayors and governors have been killed, have resigned under rebel threats, or have simply abandoned their posts. Slogans are daubed over churches and burnt-out municipal ruins. A senior police official in the departmental capital, Huancayo, a six-hour drive from Lima, admitted that only a tenth of the district authorities remained. "We are all being threatened that we will be murdered if we do not resign," he said in April 1989. "The subversives say they have a thousand eyes, a thousand ears, and it's true. They have infiltrated everywhere." The APRA official, Flavio Llerena, asked to remain anonymous because of security fears. But Shining Path gunned him down six months later.

Although it is hard to quantify the damage done directly to agricultural production in Junín by the rebels' presence, the net effect of the guerrillas' control, the intrinsic economic decline, and the migration of economic and war refugees between 1988 and 1989 was, according to the Agriculture Ministry, a seven percent decline in the vicuña herds, a halving in the acreage of yellow-corn production (for animals), an eighteen percent cut in white corn, and a thirty percent drop in potato plantations. Shining Path's biggest sabotage was the dismembering of a major agricultural cooperative, SAIS Cahuide, in November 1989. It blew up the buildings, trucks, and dairy equipment, and when there was too little time to divide up the pedigreed animals, and since anyway it was difficult to hide them, the guerrillas slaughtered the stock. Hundreds of sheep, cattle, and alpacas were burned to death or had their throats slit. The cold-blooded magnitude of the attack was typical of countless others carried out in the name of scientific socialism. Meanwhile, owners of private, middle-sized farms are being forced either to abandon their plantations or to pay hefty sums of money to the rebels.

So dogged is Shining Path's determination to wreck the state's productive apparatus that its targets have included agricultural research and development institutes such as the world-renowned International Potato Center and the National Semen Bank. Although the refrigerators stacked with bull semen survived the blasts of dynamite, the laboratory equipment next door was destroyed and the national insemination program crippled for months afterward. Scores of pedigreed cattle have been shot in the head at research stations. Foreign aid projects considered part of a "low-intensity war" strategy against Shining Path are also on the rebels' eradication list. The insurgents seek to drive them out of the country through terror and, where necessary, death. Some overseas aid workers have been assassinated. As a result, most foreigners involved in aid programs have been withdrawn from the Andes; many have left Peru. Their local employees in the emergency zones are also under intense pressure to withdraw.

Tourism, whose foreign earnings grew by 560 percent in the 1970s, giving it a ranking alongside zinc and fish meal (after cocaine paste and copper), was another economic sector that Shining Path specifically designated for sabotage. Its task was effortlessly achieved. In 1991 Peru's external image was so blackened by war, cholera, common crime, and its dilapidated and unreliable national air services, that tourism returned to the levels of the early 1970s. The rebels unsheathed their intentions in June 1986 when they bombed the tourist train to the Inca ruins of Machu Picchu, Peru's quintessential tourist attraction. Seven passengers were killed and forty wounded. Although the attack was not repeated, a series of direct assassinations, as well as bombings of luxury restaurants, served to deter both individual backpackers and organized tours from coming to Peru.

The victims were assassinated in zones and circumstances off the beaten track which with any foresight they would have avoided. With the exception of the bombing of the train, which was meant as a warning that signaled the rebels' determination to destroy the industry, tourists have not been hunted down. However, Shining Path has no qualms about killing a few in order to scare off the many. In an internal document dating from 1991, Abimael Guzmán wrote of the need to pulverize tourism in the Ancash department by sabotage and to resort to "liquidation" if necessary. With the "annihilation of one tourist, a lesson is taught," said Guzmán. "If it is not understood by one [annihilation], then another. But it is not our rule to wipe out all of them." Excluding the train victims, by that time nine had been killed: three from England, two each from France and West Germany, and one each from New Zealand and Australia.

Nearly half of Peru's legal export earnings derive from mining. A quarter are earned in Junín and the neighboring department of Pasco—which is also heavily influenced by Shining Path—by the mining of metals such as zinc, lead, silver, and copper. The mines have been sabotaged hundreds of times, causing millions of dollars of damage. The guerrillas regularly blow up the railway lines that convey the minerals to the capital. Dozens of miners, company officials, and union leaders have been assassinated, and the rebels have infiltrated the unions. Engineers are unwilling to work in the region despite the private armies of security guards and specially contracted police.

Together with the economic crisis and energy problems, exploration has ground to a halt, at least four hundred of the small mines—about ninety percent—have closed down, and, according to the vice president of the National Mining and Petroleum Society, Augusto Baertl, in March 1991 the larger mines were "on the road to extinction." Nearly a third of them were applying to the government for permission to close or to reduce drastically their work forces. The antiquated state mining giant, Centromin, had lost about $115 million because of sabotage, was running at a monthly loss of around $4.5 million, and sought to lay off eight thousand workers. Mining officials were worried that unemployed miners, finding themselves homeless after being displaced from the isolated mountain encampments, would be recruited with ease by Shining Path and help to make the rebels' sabotage more efficient still.

Baertl said, "The immediate intervention of the military is needed, but there is no political decision. The soldiers earn nothing and there is not even enough money to buy fuel, bullets, and tires. The terrorists are easily identifiable but the army is paralyzed." Mining-union leaders maintain that although they reject the rebels in the face of death threats, they are treated as terrorists and threatened by the security and paramilitary forces. The killing of the general secretary of the National Mining Federation, Saúl Cantoral, in February 1989 was made to look as if it were the work of Shining Path. However, it was later believed to have been carried out by the Rodrigo Franco Command.

Exploration of the huge oil and gas deposits believed to lie along the eastern Andes has also been jeopardized by the guerrillas. In December 1990 about 180 rebels meticulously destroyed a prospecting camp belonging to subcontractors of Mobil Oil in the Huallaga valley. They firebombed and dynamited all its equipment, including the computers that stored the seismographic results gathered since prospecting had started six months earlier. The attack came after a series of visits over the year, during which Shining Path delegates had been appointed. The subcontractors, who believed they had found a modus vivendi with the guerrillas, may have acceded to requests for money.

Before Shining Path devastated the Barranca camp, a small group of rebels arrived and forced the camp's helicopters to airlift guerrilla reinforcements to the surrounding area from diverse parts of the jungle. Although the army knew of their presence, it failed to lift a finger, possibly at the camp's request. Having occupied Barranca for ten days, ripped up seismic lines, given lectures to the hundreds of workers, celebrated Abimael Guzmán's birthday, and killed five people—including a drunken prostitute who was shot dead and thrown in the river after reputedly performing a striptease to prove she had greater drawing power than the guerrillas—they razed the camp and escaped in the helicopters (which were later recovered). The damage was estimated at nearly $3 million and, although Mobil Oil planned to continue operations, the attack hardened the position of Shell, which was negotiating the exploitation of gas deposits in the jungle of the Cuzco department.

Shining Path's timing was such that the Mobil Oil sabotage coincided with high-profile talks between the Peruvian government and international creditors in Washington in December 1990. But as well as warning off foreign investors, it simultaneously exploited national controversy over Mobil Oil's contract. Several left-wing congressmen and the MRTA guerrillas —who have close historic connections with APRA and the legal left—claimed the contract sold out and defrauded Peruvian interests. While others spoke, Shining Path acted. Its attack swept the carpet from under the feet of the "revisionists," who had remained with no other political option than to claim the attack had been deliberately organized by Mobil Oil with the intention of escaping its contractual obligations. This contradicted the left's original argument that the contract was overly favorable. Meanwhile, the Huallaga's political-military commander, an army general, was removed from his post. The recriminations were angrier than the outrage against the attack itself. With acute political acumen, the Maoists had at one stroke seriously aggravated the divisions among the armed forces, the government, big business, and Congress and embarrassed them all internationally.

The increasing frustration with civilian government is shared by the manufacturing sector, whose main base is Lima and which is losing hundreds of millions of dollars a year in production because of energy shortages and boycotts inspired by Shining Path. Until 1988 the rebels manifested themselves by staging sabotage attacks from outside the factories. Since then, said Gabriel Ferrer, the National Society of Industries' (NSI) vice president, Shining Path has built up cells within the factories and challenged the power of the unions. Union leaders and senior staff are being assassinated. "Workers and executives are terrorized," said Ferrer. "The unions are losing their influence and executives are resigning. Sabotage is being replaced by boycotts: They are not interested in salary or labor claims. It is as if the terrorists are installing themselves in readiness for destruction at a later stage."

Most of the factories with serious Shining Path infiltration are grouped around the entry points of the three road arteries that connect Lima to the rest of the country. Similarly, the shantytowns in the areas where the central highway from the Andes and the Pan-American highway from the north and south join the city are also the main foci for the rebels' penetration. When electricity supplies are cut, the factories are forced to depend on diesel-fueled generators, whose output is three to four times more expensive than the energy supplied by the hydroelectric plants that provide almost all the power for the national grid.

Steep energy bills and the cost of sabotage, insurance, and security measures have added at least seven percent to factory sale prices in Lima's main industrial zones, according to the NSI. A further cost is the $20,000 to $50,000 a month that, said Ferrer, many businesses pay to Shining Path (and MRTA) in order for their installations and executives not to be attacked. "There is very little industrial expansion," he added. "Everyone is trying to defend their investments from terrorism and economic uncertainty. Peru's political circumstances would justify a military government. Parliament plays into the terrorists' hands by weak antiterrorist legislation."

The agreement on the need for greater military intervention against Shining Path—implying a wider, more indiscriminate, and brutal repression and, if democracy is unable to stomach that, a military government—is deepening in the business sectors. But so, too, are their own divisions. Battling against President Fujimori's free-market measures of March 1991, which drastically reduced import tariffs, endeavored to break up the industrial monopolies of the élite, and, all for the sake of lower prices and greater efficiency, were expected to bankrupt many businesses, the president of the NSI, Salvador Majluf, declared that it would be better to shut down mining than industry. He spluttered, "Not a single mine is competitive. The mines are totally obsolete, they are as inefficient as the wall opposite. . . . What has happened is that industries have been created and the economy revolves around those industries, efficient or not efficient. But in Peru there is nothing efficient: not mining, not fishing, not industry, not the government, not the municipalities . . ."

Such desperation and division in the business sector, looking for military force and the subversion of democracy in order to enable it to reassert itself, is precisely what Shining Path seeks and anticipates. An article in *El Diario* in March 1991 reveled in what it characterized as the economic indecisiveness of the "grand bourgeoisie" and its resorting to the army and private security forces to defend its mines and industry; all of which, *El Diario* asserted, was inevitable given the "historic bankruptcy" of the state's social base resting on an alliance of the "grand bourgeoisie" and the "feudal landowning class" (*sic*: the state-organized agricultural cooperatives), both "at the service of imperialism, principally North American."

The article claimed that Fujimori's lurch toward the free market was a bolstering of "bureaucratic capitalism" and symptomatic of the state's greater dependency on the armed forces to quell the "people's war" fueled by the consequent "hunger and misery of the masses." It feasted on the sour arguments between the different business interest groups as they readied themselves to survive the cold blast of foreign competition, and concluded that by giving powerful positions to men closely linked to United States governmental and financial sectors, Fujimori was handing over the reins of the Peruvian state to the imperialist giant in the north.

The most prominent such figure was an internationally lauded economist, Hernando de Soto, whose book *The Other Path* was heralded by then President Ronald Reagan as a blueprint for change in the Third World and who also won effusive praise from President George Bush. De Soto, whose concrete, technical vision of a genuine democracy and free market in Peru—incorporating the informal sector, of whose pragmatism and ingenuity he is an enthusiastic admirer—is detested by the traditional business sectors, which have long thrived on special government privileges and protective bureaucracy. Envy of his international stature and cross-party political influence is mixed with fear of the social, political, and economic revolution that de Soto espouses. De Soto, whom Shining Path views as Bush's personal lackey, was the principal mover of negotiations to reintegrate Peru into the international financial community. But more important, he was behind Peru's negotiations with the United States for the 1991 antidrug agreement. It was upon this that Peru's financial reintegration hinged.

If any one issue divides the country more than any other, it is coca. The abundance of dollars entering the economy from the coca trade brought down the dollar to half its technical value once markets were liberalized. While the government laps up the dollars cheaply for foreign creditors and the informal sector converts them into contraband, the exporters—especially the mining sector—are crippled by the dollar's poor return, which coincides with sky-high domestic costs. On the other hand, boosting imports in order to raise the dollar is viscerally unpopular with the local industrialists.

All productive sectors of the formal economy agree on one point: that they are in effect being held to ransom by the group they believe to be the drug traffickers' fairy godmother: Shining Path. But they are pitted against elements of the government and financial system, the military, the police, the informals, and the 300,000 people associated with the coca trade, all of whom in some way or another are dependent on foreign drug use for at least part of their livelihood. Protecting the coca growers thereby enables Shining Path to cavort with some of its principal enemies. The internal divisions of the state, which are aided and provoked by the very nature of that bond, ensure that the state is shooting itself in the foot in the battle against the Maoists.

The pressure brought to bear on the unions by the rebels in their determination to subvert them to their will has trapped the trade unions between Shining Path and the government. The country's main union conglomerate, the General Confederation of Peruvian Workers (CGTP), lost a third of its membership because of the drop in formal employment caused by the economic crash in 1988 once Peru's reserves could no longer sustain García's big spending. The CGTP's reduced power base, comprising 1.1 million people in early 1991 and founded mainly on the public-sector and peasant unions, weakened the confederation just when it was coming under greater attack from both sides.

CGTP leaders argue that the state has used Shining Path as a stick with which to beat the union movement over the head. Union representatives are regularly detained, the organizations are accused of being infiltrated by the rebels, and police trump up evidence on which to accuse their leaders of terrorism. In one celebrated case during a general strike, telephone cables were made out to be bomb fuses. Protest marches are brutally crushed, sometimes at the cost of lives; strikers hit back with brick-throwing and tire-burning in an upward-climbing spiral of violence. Whereas under the military governments the arrest of a union or popular leader caused national uproar, such detentions have turned into an almost daily occurrence and are virtually ignored.

Even superficial government efforts to secure union consensus almost ceased under President Fujimori. Pablo Checa, the CGTP's assistant secretary general, said in March 1991, "We have resisted the *senderistas* with our lives but [to judge] by its authoritarian manner it is as if the Fujimori government wants to prove them right. People start saying that democracy is not worth anything. The more people lose work and the less organizational help and protest channels they have, the more the situation favors Sendero." However, in Fujimori's initial period of government the expectations of change and improvement dampened grass-roots union protest.

The government's increasingly reckless treatment of the unions is particularly galling to the CGTP because, as Checa states, it believes it has risked its neck in standing up to the guerrillas and blocking their drive to infiltrate its ranks. After failing to take over power from the inside—Shining Path activists lost their attempt to be reelected to positions of leadership in several Lima factories where they had secured high union status toward the end of the 1980s—they opted to control the unions by force. In doing so, they demonstrated their true contempt for the unions, which are regarded as revisionist and simply another bureaucratic mechanism to prop up the decrepit state. Shining Path is interested in the unions' fight for better pay and conditions only insofar as the struggle coincides with its own purposes in taking it closer to power.

Mining strikes especially are aggravated and then usurped by Shining Path, which has employed what it calls armed strikes to ensure that production, commerce, and transport are paralyzed. Key people who defy an armed strike decree do so in the knowledge that they are crossing the party and are liable to be "liquidated." They often are. The deaths generate a psychosis of terror in which dissident workers fear they or their family will be attacked at any time. The tactic, which is used irregularly in workplaces, towns, and departments with varying success, almost invariably brings transport to a halt. The point is pressed home by the firebombing of buses whose drivers fail to comply. Meanwhile, threats are received constantly by union officials, who are enjoined to place their work forces on production slow-downs.

The shrinking union federations are bitter that not only have governments taken advantage of their vulnerability but that the mining companies and industrialists have tended to respond to the violence either by shutting down operations or by adopting a harsher attitude to legitimate union claims and protests. Pablo Checa said, "The business sector has not presented any proposal for beating Sendero except by military measures. There is no effort to promote democracy, investment, and better conditions in order to pull the carpet from underneath Sendero. On the contrary, it does not even raise its voice against high government taxes, never mind Sendero's requests for money."

Shining Path is also producing ruptures in Peru's educational system. Its ideology is disseminated through universities and schools by lecturers, teachers, and students. The same methods used by Abimael Guzmán in the National University of San Cristóbal de Huamanga to elbow his way into the university infrastructure are employed elsewhere with varying success. In San Cristóbal de Huamanga itself, heavy police and military repression, combined with strong leadership by senior academics, has curbed the rebels' influence within the university confines. However, the insurgents have a grip on several other campuses, including the university in Huancayo in the department of Junín, the National University of San Marcos in Lima—South America's oldest university—and the National University of Engineering, also in the capital. Several university lecturers have been killed by Shining Path and the Rodrigo Franco Command.

Red-painted slogans run along the buildings' parapets, the image of Chairman Gonzalo graces the walls, and, in Huancayo, chalk writing on a blackboard by the university gate justifies at some length the latest killings of students accused of being police spies. The hammer-and-sickle flag flies above the water tower. A Shining Path activist at San Marcos, who was studying business administration, said, "Students grow more conscious every day of the revolution. We carry out tasks such as painting walls [with slogans] in the working-class districts." Raids by the security forces regularly uncover weapons on the campuses. Miguel Gutiérrez, a history lecturer and vice rector of San Marcos, openly sympathizes with Shining Path and has been arrested several times. Ironically, one of Abimael Guzmán's half brothers, Arsenio, is a philosophy lecturer at the same university. He shuns attention, apparently out of fear of all sides.

The state's hegemony over the schools is also crumbling under the guerrillas' influence. Shining Path's penetration conforms to the policy stated in party documents: "Children have to be made to participate actively in the people's war. . . . [T]hey can comply with diverse tasks through which to understand the need to transform the world, they are the future. . . . [I]t is essential to change their ideology and that they adopt that of the proletariat." Many Andean schools are daubed in rebel graffiti. Teenage cells from Shining Path's Secondary School Revolutionary Front have been captured by police; they organize lectures by outside militants, which teachers are also expected to attend.

"We don't erase the graffiti because we don't have guarantees," said Pedro Huatuco, the director of a school near Huancayo. "They say perfectly clearly: 'He who erases them will be liquidated.' There are no police here to protect us." Pupils' lives are threatened if they do not collaborate. By late 1989 a quarter of the schools in Huatuco's area were reported to be heavily infiltrated. In September, death threats and the assassination of two teachers in Huancayo sparked off the resignations of a dozen others nearby. In the first four months of 1991 eight teachers were killed in the adjacent province of Concepción and two hundred resigned because of alleged death threats by Shining Path; however, they were also under pressure from the army, which considered them actual or potential rebel supporters. Many teachers disappeared, apparently after army detention, and in the town of Tarapoto, in the San Martín department, the teachers' union claimed that four were tossed out of an army helicopter; only one of them survived to tell the tale.

The Huancayo victims were singled out by Shining Path because they taught the "pre-military" course, which is compulsory in state schools. The course embraces basic military training and is part of the state's constant attempt to bolster a sense of unity, civic awareness, and national pride. Government and armed forces television advertisements endeavor to stimulate the same qualities. The national anthem is played at midday and midnight on all radio and television stations. On Independence Day, every household must fly the Peruvian flag by law. Military and police parades accompanied by political authorities take place every Sunday. At moments of crisis, the president tends to materialize in front of his palace to oversee the goose-stepping, sword-waving presidential guard in an effort to remind the country who is in charge. The gesture remains only a gesture. When the armed forces decide to unseat a palace incumbent, the presidential guard, little inclined to martyrdom, is powerless.

Despite calls for national unity to confront Shining Path, the state has splintered. There is no real cross-party consensus. Congress, the judiciary, the executive, and the security forces are still not only struggling among themselves to agree upon a common strategy; they blame the counterinsurgency quagmire on each other's inadequacies. The failure of the armed forces and police to bury their institutional hatchets in order to tackle the guerrillas reflects the fact that Peru's militaristic patriotism is little more than a pompous façade. They are divided by class prejudice engendered by the different social backgrounds prevalent in each of the forces. A Western military attaché noted wryly, "The naval officers would be at home in a European officers' mess while the army officers, one suspects, would feel more at ease halfway between the sergeants' and the corporals'." Police officers enjoy the lowest social status of all.

Historic, institutional chauvinism on the part of the security forces has been aggravated rather than diminished by the existence of Shining Path and the economic crisis. The greater demand on their already faltering budgets has greatly undermined their operational capacity and triggered bitter competition for funds. The resentment and mistrust inhibits the sharing of intelligence as well as operational coordination.

Air force helicopters are liable to be withheld from the army because the latter has not paid its bills or lacks the cash up front. Under President García, the army was said to be so jealous of a large police consignment of Israeli half-track armored personnel carriers that it forced the police to hand them over in return for a batch of similar vehicles of its own; these were of a later design but so poorly maintained as to be useless. And when Shining Path attacked the police station in Uchiza in March 1989 the army at nearby Tingo María remained inexplicably in its barracks as the police begged for help over the radio. The ensuing slaughter brought about the resignation of Prime Minister Armando Villanueva and allowed the army to wrest control from the police in Uchiza, thereby winning access to coca-derived municipal funds, drug protection money, and the trafficking itself.

Such internecine rivalry and corruption are a gift for Shining Path, whose ruthless single-mindedness and dogged adherence to mid- and long-term strategies cut a swath through the squabbling egoism of the state and security forces. The tone was set at the start of the 1980s, when the intelligence archives of the Ministry of Interior vanished on the eve of Fernando Belaúnde taking over government. The archives, which contained a considerable quantity of information relating to Shining Path— including its areas of operation in Ayacucho and the month the insurrection would commence—disappeared just as the civilian authorities were assuming the reigns of power.

It is widely believed that the military government was too

ashamed to admit that it was handing over a country with a subversive movement that had been spawned under its very nose. Avoiding a loss of face was a higher priority than contributing to national security. The fragility of Peru's born-again democracy also played into the rebels' hands: The Belaúnde government dared not create a fuss over the archives for fear of giving the armed forces an excuse to stay in power.

By 1991 Shining Path had seen to it that the tension between the armed forces and civilian government—particularly Congress and the judiciary—was keener still. The military was internally but unsecretively discussing the possibility of a civilian-military government in which it would control several ministries and thereby acquire greater resources and overall coordination in tackling the guerrillas. Such a move would provoke severe clashes with Congress, possibly leading to its paralysis and dissolution. Meanwhile, despite the growing awareness in some military sectors of the need to develop a nonauthoritarian counterinsurgency strategy along the lines of the British during the Malayan uprising, official abuses of human rights continued to flourish. New offices of the International Committee of the Red Cross blossomed in the emergency zones to provide medical support for the victims of violence, whether protagonists or innocents, from both sides.

While the military's morale sagged lower and its external defenses started to suffer—its institutional distaste for the job in hand and lack of preparation were summed up by one navy officer posted to the Amazonian port of Pucallpa: "I'm used to commanding submarines, not chasing terrorists around the jungle"—corruption and low pay corroded the police forces. Whether indulging in petty blackmail of errant car drivers, robbing bus passengers, or stealing from homes, the police came to be loathed and distrusted by the civilian population. Police pay strikes broke out; their wives led street protests, which were dispersed with clubs and tear gas by their husbands' colleagues. In March 1991 a policeman committed suicide because his wage had not been raised as promised and he was unable to cover his domestic costs. "The wage is dirt. I am fed up with working all month to receive this," shouted Diógenes Alvarez, shaking his paycheck, to one of his four daughters before he went inside their reed-built home and shot himself. In June, Minister of Interior Victor Malca, a retired army general, announced that five hundred police had been fired during the year for "immorality" and poor discipline.

The same month, amid almost daily reports of policemen shooting people on the slightest pretext and robbing anybody they could, an innocent student was filmed in Lima being bundled into the trunk of a police car only to materialize a few hours later in the morgue. Two weeks later, police who were either drunk or high on cocaine opened fire on a scheduled civilian flight, apparently because the pilot refused to undergo further revision of the cargo, which would inevitably entail extortion. The bullets ripped through the cockpit, and the aircraft crashed to the ground near Bellavista, in the department of San Martín. Seventeen people were killed. The Ministry of Interior announced that the police forces would once again be reorganized. Its eighty thousand members were subjected to psychological tests. Meanwhile, one of the policemen involved in the student's killing had already escaped police custody.

Ill-equipped and underpaid, the main bulk of the police scarcely tackled street crime, never mind Shining Path. While elements within the Ministry of Interior, and many officers, concentrated on taking their cut from the cocaine trade—or even, it was alleged, from the budget of the U.S. Drug Enforcement Administration—police stations collapsed like playing cards up and down the country. At the same time as police were paying their superiors in order to be sent to the Huallaga valley in the hope of earning coca protection money, others were retreating in the face of Shining Path's relentless, terror-sheathed advance. According to Malca, by March 1991 about 520 police stations had been abandoned. A police general explained, "They run away to avoid the threats. Either that, or they simply do not want the problems of work, arrests, and interrogations when there is no money in it for them. There is a lack of leaders in the police force; a kind of mystique is what is needed."

Just as the army general Adrián Huamán had attempted in

Ayacucho in 1983, a police general in the Ancash department made a concerted and successful effort in 1990 to grant the population security and to win their support and confidence rather than treat them as enemies in occupied territory. The policy reaped dividends as General Héctor Jhon Caro mingled with the Indian villagers, communicating through a Quechua-speaking colonel, dispensing medical aid and schoolbooks, dancing *huaynos* and drinking *chicha*. He claimed to have organized fifty *rondas*.

"We won them over onto our side," said General Jhon Caro. "When the *senderistas* came, the villagers would shout and whistle warnings, ring the church bell, and hurl stones until they were driven out to another village, where the same thing would happen until eventually the *senderistas* would be captured or killed. If people are with Sendero, it is out of fear. The state may be decadent and decrepit but the people prefer it to a bloody one." Nevertheless, the provinces of Bolognesi and Recuay were declared under a state of emergency that year. The decision angered the general, who ascribed it to ulterior political motives and added, "There are those in the armed forces and police who think that whoever fights more is praised more. Everybody wants applause. There is a mutual jealousy between the forces instead of the realization that we are up against a common enemy that takes advantage of the split."

Shining Path's most capable and dedicated foe is the plain-clothes, specialist antiterrorist police squad, DIRCOTE. For most of the 1980s it was starved of resources and riddled with Shining Path infiltrators. Computers were only acquired in 1988 and even then, because of security fears, DIRCOTE did not dare let outsiders teach it how to use them. However, under the auspices of President García's last minister of interior, Agustín Mantilla, who handed out wads of dollars of dubious origin (probably coca) as rewards to successful detectives, it was streamlined and its most sensitive work reserved for the most trusted men. Security improved and tough surveillance succeeded in tracking down Abimael Guzmán's safe house in Monterrico in June 1990. DIRCOTE proceeded to disarticulate the rebels' propaganda section later in the same year, raided several more safe houses closely linked to important Shining

Path members, and captured what were alleged to be the movement's main computer archives in January 1991. Videos and cassettes recording party ceremonies and central-committee meetings were also uncovered.

Although most of the information was kept secret, President Fujimori went on television to present a video showing Guzmán celebrating what appeared to be an initiation ceremony in which men and women in gray uniforms reminiscent of Maoist revolutionary China drank and danced with a slightly gauche and self-conscious mixture of gaiety and solemnity. The video was among several that, according to Shining Path activists, were to have been used as part of a national and international publicity campaign. It was the first proper picture of Guzmán to have surfaced since his arrest twelve years earlier. Bearded and bespectacled, knock-kneed and rather drunk, he clicked his fingers and danced to the music of *Zorba the Greek* beneath a glass chandelier. Fujimori hailed the video as proof that Guzmán was "flesh and bone."

The attempt to break his semilegendary status and demonstrate that Guzmán was indeed vulnerable corresponded to the government's pressing need at that time to show it was making advances against Shining Path. The defeatist minister of interior, army general Adolfo Alvarado, was being hauled painfully over the coals by Congress, and Fujimori was being mauled by the media and politicians for having failed to develop a coherent antisubversive strategy. But despite triggering off a rigorous process of self-criticism inside Shining Path regarding its internal security—which had grown lax and overconfident largely through little need to exercise it properly—the move backfired.

*El Diario* trumpeted the "people's jubilation . . . on knowing the physical figure of the greatest living Communist" and put his video picture on the front page. The man who the state had long claimed was either sick or dead was not only alive but dancing-fit. According to sympathizers of the rebels, the fact that their leader lived well was a reason for pride rather than resentment. They were thrilled that President Fujimori rather than DIRCOTE presented the video because, they argued, it granted Guzmán equal status. As the months passed and

DIRCOTE admitted it had finally lost Guzmán's scent, the myth surrounding him simply regenerated itself. The party machine had received a severe blow and the operational freedom of its nerve center was heavily curtailed, although its security precautions were aided by the advent in Peru of cellular telephones. Once again, Guzmán had vanished into thin air. DIRCOTE's spectacular success had been undermined by the government's shortsightedness and political opportunism.

DIRCOTE's bitterness was deepened by the little fruit its efforts bore in the judiciary. Of the seventeen people arrested by the police as a result of the evidence uncovered—several insurgents were allegedly identified in the videos—only one was held in jail. She was Nelly Evans, the former nun. All the rest were released on the grounds that there was insufficient evidence to convict them of terrorism. They included teachers, lawyers, a doctor, the son of a general from the Velasco era, a well-known folk musician, and a newspaper columnist who had worked alongside two former presidential candidates in the Lima municipality. Despite the fact that several were probably innocent of direct links with Shining Path, the release of the others illustrated the inefficiency of the police as well as the legal loopholes that sharp-edged lawyers of the Democratic Lawyers Association, whose fifteen to twenty members are sympathetic to the rebels, use to good advantage against the state.

While the courts blame the police and prosecuting lawyers for failing to produce sufficient evidence to support their charges, the police curse the lawyers and judges for, as they see it, not applying the law and letting the insurgents go. The police also claim that legal reforms are needed to expand the definitions of terrorism; they believe the judiciary is infiltrated by Shining Path sympathizers. In its defense, the judiciary accuses the police of considering a case proved merely on the strength of claimed "confidential information" that someone is a member of the proscribed movement. The reality is that, even though there probably is rebel infiltration, neither the police, nor the prosecuting lawyers, nor the judges have the resources to carry out their jobs. They lack transport, forensic laboratories, security, personnel, and computers. During the video saga, the police denounced one woman implicated as being of unknown abode. It transpired that she was already in prison.

Between October 1989 and March 1991 in the Lima department the defendants in only forty-four terrorist cases were found guilty in the Superior Court. The defendants in seventy-four cases were acquitted. Hundreds of people were implicated in cases that never passed the prosecuting lawyers and the next, preliminary layer of investigation at the Palace of Justice, an imposing Greco-Roman building with Doric columns built in imitation of its Brussels homologue, whose cracked marble corridors are crowded with families and candy sellers and which was built without women's cells because at the time it was not believed that women committed crimes. The long-winded, chaotic, and bureaucratic legal process, which does not involve juries, yields abundant opportunities for officials to be bribed or threatened and enables the defense lawyers to procrastinate almost interminably. So poorly paid are the prosecuting lawyers that it is not uncommon for them to stage unofficial strikes and slow-downs.

The president of the Superior Court in Lima, Luis Almenara, said in April 1991, "Successfully prosecuting terrorists is restricted by the lack of case law, fear, and the lack of protection for the judges. It is easiest for them to say there are not enough proofs and wash their hands of the matter. Everybody receives threats, both anonymously and from the defendants in court. There are not enough police to protect us." Two months later, his home came under gunfire and in July bombs went off inside the Palace of Justice. When Osmán Morote, the most senior member of Shining Path in captivity, was sentenced, he warned his judges, "This trial has had the peculiarity of its political nature being recognized by the genocidal and corpse-hiding government; but as my master, Professor Abimael Guzmán, taught me to live on the basis of my principles and not by circumstantial factors, I will accept the sentence that is imposed since it will prove that the pressures of the government party have been ceded to. When it is the people's turn to judge all that is happening, we will not be in the same place, since I assure you that you will be in my position and there will be no other prosecutor than your own deeds, that is if you reach the year 2000."

The judiciary is weakened not only by the terror it confronts but also by the rapid rotation of its officials, as against the years of experience built up by the rebels' defense lawyers. In 1991 the Superior Court resorted to drawing lots to appoint the two judges responsible for the preliminary investigations of terrorist cases. "It was the most impartial way," said Almenara. "It avoided fear, idleness, and the corruption affecting the designation of them by vote."

Peru's judiciary, security forces, government institutions, and economy are gradually being crippled by the rebels, recession, corruption, and cocaine. As each takes its toll, cholera and other diseases such as malaria and dengue fever continue to spread and to suck away the state's resistance, aggravating discontent: At the height of the cholera epidemic, the entire health sector went on a four-month pay strike. But in the country's unions, left-wing parties, and churches, Shining Path confronts genuine challenges to its hegemony. They each represent a threat to its inside political flank. Nevertheless, each front has been weakened by a plethora of factors whose common denominator is the government's or military's suspicion that in some way they cater to the guerrillas' cause. Although Shining Path's advance has been delayed most notably where the trio have worked together, as in Puno and Cajamarca, the rebels are slowly making inroads there, too. But the greatest threat to their influence is Peru's other guerrilla group, the Túpac Amaru Revolutionary Movement (MRTA). The Maoists themselves admit, if not explicitly then in their dark, revisionist curses and accusations, that MRTA is an instrument of the state whose primary purpose is to impede the course of history and, ipso facto, the people's revolution and the triumph of the Shining Path.

MRTA derives from a complex web of army, left-wing, and APRA factions some of whose seeds were sown by Major José Fernandez Salvatecci's Third of October Military Command, the clandestine, nationalist-socialist military movement that emerged briefly at the end of the 1970s and sought a return to the policies and dictatorial government of General Juan Velasco. When the dust settled in 1980 after the restoration of democracy under President Belaúnde, Shining Path had materialized as an armed revolutionary force and plunged the legal Peruvian left into a political limbo in which it has remained ever since. The international collapse of communism in the late 1980s deepened that limbo, from which the left, in Peru and throughout the world, is still struggling to escape. Meanwhile, MRTA was formed to plug the political gap between the legal left and Shining Path. It was created to keep alive the spirit and save the "prestige" of armed, anti-imperialist revolution and to siphon off potential Shining Path recruits. Most importantly, however, MRTA was launched in order to offer the legal left a ready path of insurrection were people to opt for it in the case of a military coup provoked by Shining Path. The object was to break the polarity between the Maoists and the government, thereby undermining Shining Path's potential claims to legitimacy as being the sole liberation movement in the event of a coup.

The MRTA guerrillas invoke the leadership and struggles of Manco Inca, Juan Santos Atahualpa, and Túpac Amaru II as well as most other rebel movements in Peruvian history, including those of the 1960s. It falls into the tradition of the Cuban revolution, Che Guevara in Bolivia, and the Sandinistas in Nicaragua. Initial flirtations with the possibility of an eventual "understanding" with Shining Path were brought to a halt after Guzmán learned of contacts between MRTA and the Maoists' Lima metropolitan committee. He is said to have had his dissident underlings assassinated. The man who after lengthy infighting emerged as MRTA's commander in chief, Victor Polay, was captured in February 1989 while sleeping in the government-run tourist hotel in Huancayo. He told a court tribunal, "Shining Path has done much damage to the Peruvian revolution because with its methods it has lost it prestige. It is not revolutionary to kill popular leaders, engineers who go into the countryside for development works, or to kill the policeman on the corner. The revolution has to be the work of the organized people, with their vanguard formed by popular leaders, the progressive sectors of the Catholic church, and patriotic members of the armed forces." Polay, whose father was a founding member of APRA, was a leading young Aprista and formerly a close friend of Alan García; they shared a flat in Madrid.

Although its first action was a Lima bank raid in May 1982 in which one of the attackers was killed, MRTA moved into full swing in the second half of 1984. Bombing targets included the U.S. embassy, Kentucky Fried Chicken restaurants, department stores, and political or government offices; radio and television stations were occupied and forced to broadcast communiqués; attempts were made to sabotage the general elections; and food was stolen and redistributed in the shanty-towns. The first personal violence was the cutting out of the tongue of an informer. The first assassination was of a police-man outside the Colombian embassy during an attack in soli-darity with the guerrillas of the Colombian April 19 Movement (M-19), with whom it formed an alliance along with an insignif-icant Ecuadorian group, Alfaro Lives, Dammit! Cells were es-tablished in several departmental capitals, especially Tarapoto in the central Huallaga valley.

A brief military truce with García, marking MRTA's approval of the president's aggressive "anti-imperialist" stance, ended after the guerrillas decided he was not fulfilling his word. Throughout García's term of government, the movement in-creased in strength; its push into the Huallaga mirrored that of Shining Path. Fully armed and uniformed—in contrast to the Maoists—MRTA guerrilla battalions suddenly bloomed in the Huallaga valley, blocking off Shining Path's northern advance and, to the same end, entering into a tacit agreement with the army. An MRTA leader in Tarapoto said in February 1988: "Shining Path was not only a threat to the zone, but is to the whole country. . . . If we do not rise up now, who will stop them later? No one. . . . Our rising up impedes Shining Path from advancing in the zone and trips them up on a national level." Nevertheless, the Maoists have given MRTA a bloody nose almost whenever their paths have crossed. In 1991 MRTA was under increasing pressure around Tarapoto and Juanjui, a zone where MRTA had dug roots since announcing its arrival in a blast of television publicity amid a wave of attacks on police stations in November 1987.

At the same time as its military activities expanded, amid several important arrests and internal divisions, MRTA was regularly suspected to be holding secret talks with the García government. It indulged in car bombings, kidnappings, extortion, and the killing of relatively small numbers of police, soldiers, and civilians (totaling around eighty between 1989 and 1990); the ransom-kidnap victims included a good friend of García's, whose release was preceded by his appearing on a video designed to undermine the electoral campaign of García's foe, Mario Vargas Llosa. But even as MRTA adopted a tougher line, rumors of its negotiating with APRA failed to go away despite some harsh military repression. "APRA bases have always sympathized with MRTA," said APRA senator Javier Valle Riestra. "We have revolutionary roots." Sources close to President Fujimori maintained that MRTA had weapons links with the APRA death squad, the Rodrigo Franco Command. Both movements shared common strategic objectives: to tackle Shining Path on its own ground and to combat a military government in the event of a coup. Just before Fujimori took office, forty-eight MRTA prisoners, including Polay, escaped from the Canto Grande high-security jail in circumstances that left little doubt of the government's complicity. A well-built tunnel was still unfinished and it appeared that, in order to save time, some escapees may have left by the front gate.

Denounced by erstwhile friends and sympathizers on the Senate Special Commission on Violence and Pacification as "pseudorevolutionary adventurers" lacking ideological consistency, by late 1990 MRTA found itself bereft of its Colombian and Ecuadorian allies. Those guerrillas had handed over their arms and returned to the democratic fold in March 1990 and February 1991, respectively. Shining Path's existence, which had given rise to MRTA in the first place, was primarily responsible for MRTA flying in the face of the worldwide winds of change. MRTA militants totaled about a thousand people, according to official estimates by the security forces. Approximately sixty percent were under arms and, mainly through kidnapping and charging protection money from the cocaine traffickers, they had acquired a considerable number of sub-machine guns. MRTA's militancy brings closer the very event which it was created to confront were it to occur: a rupture in democratic, civilian government.

Shining Path's frustration with MRTA was evident in the principal article in *El Diario* in March 1991 which claimed that MRTA was being used to diminish Shining Path's impact. "The government's propagandist campaign to cover up its biggest crisis," said the article, "caused it to inflate MRTA, a group put together and financed by social-imperialism." The article accused MRTA of stealing the credit for some of Shining Path's recent actions and thereby boosting the government's presentation of MRTA as the state's "true and greatest danger." *El Diario* claimed that Shining Path was the author of a string of attacks—including the launching of an antitank missile against the United States embassy and the blowing up of a statue of John F. Kennedy in protest over the Gulf War—which the Peruvian government maintained were carried out by MRTA. In the light of the state's acknowledged pursuit of a psychological war, the government's attempts to play down Shining Path's strength publicly, to restrain news releases of its actions —and in this respect successfully to secure the cooperation of most of the press and media—and to resort to disinformation such as distributing fake leaflets about the Maoists' internal divisions, the rebels' claims probably have substance.

The systematic dismantling of the state continued to be at the heart of the rebels' campaigns. Abimael Guzmán's fifth military plan, "Developing Bases in Order to Conquer Power," was launched in August 1989 and by the end of the year had officially borne 23,090 actions. It sought to boost the number of people's committees operating openly and centered on the boy-cott of the municipal and general elections while endeavoring to move the war into the phase of overall political and military "strategic equilibrium" between the two sides. A key element in the latter respect was to push harder for the transformation of guerrilla groups into platoons, companies, and battalions, particularly in the Huallaga valley. In July 1989 hundreds of guerrillas attacked the Madre Mía army barracks and, according to them, killed thirty-nine soldiers. Shining Path claims it gave at least twenty-five wounded soldiers medical treatment. The army never gave a convincing version of its own. The attack, in which, according to the party, some rebels ran and blew themselves up kamikaze-style to break through the gates, marked the emergence of Shining Path's capacity to marshal large forces and take on the armed forces directly as well as in ambushes.

The Peruvian government's estimates of the number of armed Shining Path militants—party members—in 1991 varied between three thousand and five thousand. The security forces said the guerrillas had created several battalions in the jungle areas along the east of the Andes, where they relied on the river routes for transport. They had established a strong military presence in the valley of the Ene River and pushed through to the coast in the north of the Arequipa department. DIRCOTE claimed that the guerrillas had the support of 22,000 people who provided food and logistical aid. Separate security sources estimated the figure was twice as high. By February 1990 the Maoists claimed they had twenty-four support bases, comprising hundreds of popular committees, in five zones corresponding to regional committees. These five regional committees were in Ayacucho, Huancavelica, and Apurímac; Junín, Huánuco, and Cerro de Pasco; the Huallaga valley; northern Puno; and the mountains of Ancash and La Libertad. Shining Path's sixth zone was the metropolitan area of Lima, where instead of using popular committees it operated through a network of specialized local movements.

By the time the death toll had reached at least 22,000 in May 1991, when Shining Path was claiming it had arrived at the stage of strategic equilibrium, the guerrillas were the dominating political influence in about forty percent of Peru. More than fifty-five percent of the population was living under a state of emergency: Civil and democratic liberties were severely curtailed and the military officially wielded overall local government control (with the exception of the capital). Shining Path wrecked the 1989–1990 municipal and general elections in many areas of the Andes and the upper jungle. About sixty mayors and mayoral candidates were killed by the guerrillas before the municipal elections, and around five hundred municipal candidates resigned in terror. Voting was suspended in many rural districts because no candidates remained. In many others, the election was a farce. Either only one candidate ran or mayors were elected with a handful of votes—and, in at least one case, the elected candidate had been assassinated before the ballot. Rebel strike decrees paralyzed the central Andes despite the massive deployment of police and troops. In support of Shining Path's campaign to impede voters' participation, placards in Lima attached to dead dogs were found saying, "Those dogs who vote will die like this." Official figures showed that nearly sixty percent of registered voters either spoiled their ballot papers or, despite heavy fines, failed to turn up (this compared to thirty-six percent in the 1986 municipal elections). In only eight out of the twenty-four departments (including Huancavelica, where the figures were probably a cover-up) was absenteeism less than forty percent; in Ayacucho it was eighty-five percent.

The 1990 general elections suffered a similar fate. Several congressional candidates were killed in a campaign of car bombings, industrial sabotage, and strike decrees. Voting was centralized in towns as far as possible in order to facilitate security, for which almost all army and police forces were mobilized. Amid the power blackouts generated by the bombing of electricity pylons, hillsides around Lima were illuminated by burning torches in the shape of the hammer and sickle. Official statistics indicated that thirty-five percent of the registered voters spoiled their votes or stayed away from the ballot boxes in the first round; the figure dropped to twenty-eight percent in the second. This was up from twenty-one percent in the 1985 general election and was higher than both the first- and second-round votes for the initial front runner, Mario Vargas Llosa (who secured the support of just twenty-one percent of registered voters in the first round and twenty-seven percent in the second). Absenteeism alone in the departments of Ayacucho, Huancavelica, and Apurímac doubled; the average figure for those departments and Junín, Pasco, Huánuco, San Martín, and Amazonas over both rounds was thirty-seven percent. In the same areas, the percentage of spoiled or blank ballot papers averaged twenty-five percent of those actually cast, even without allowing for some dubious anomalies almost certainly the product of an electoral cover-up, such as the recording of zero percent for spoiled votes in the second round in San Martín (in the first round it was thirteen percent). Because of these problems and the triumph of the hitherto unknown Alberto Fujimori, who captured the support of forty-five percent of registered voters, so gloomy were the upper classes and sectors of the armed forces, mainly the navy, that Peru came very close to a military coup.

Meanwhile, according to an opinion poll conducted in June 1991 by Apoyo, a leading right-wing think tank, seventeen percent of those interviewed in Lima "considered subversion justifiable." The figure had increased throughout the 1980s. Seven percent said they had a "favorable" opinion of Shining Path; if half of those who did not answer the question were added on —in the supposition that they might want to hide their sympathies—the figure came to twelve percent. Seventeen percent of the lowest of the four socioeconomic classes had a "favorable" opinion of Abimael Guzmán. And while eight percent overall said they believed Shining Path would win, the number who thought it would be defeated had dropped from forty-four percent in 1987, and thirty-six percent in 1990, to just twenty-five percent.

Despite the bloodbath that would follow a military takeover, Shining Path views a coup as an historical inevitability that need not be rushed and will ultimately advance its cause by polarizing the country. The armed forces, who according to some independent observers have already killed more civilians than the insurgents, could be relied upon to act without even the relative human rights constraints on which they blame their lack of success so far, and to initiate massacres that would indeed be of genocidal proportions. But Shining Path is anxious that the moment not come until it is ready to milk it of its honey. The rebels' spokesman in Stockholm, Enrique, said, "The party has the capacity to shut all the roads to Lima and cut all its electricity, but that would provoke the armed forces to repress the masses before they are ready. If you want to hunt a bear, you cannot just shoot it in the arm or leg, because then it is capable of whatever wildness. You have to wait to get close to give it the fatal bullet. The party is conscious of the genocide that must necessarily come, and it is politically, ideologically, and militarily left to pay the cost. The genocide is going to bring about greater incorporation of the masses." For Guzmán such a genocide—the party estimates that up to one million people could be killed before it takes power—should contribute to the achievement of strategic equilibrium.

The single-mindedness, adaptability, and ferocious ideological conviction of Shining Path, swept along by historic racial, cultural, social, and economic resentment and alienation, contrasts with the vapid posturing of an impoverished and divided state which has shown itself incapable of mustering the governmental and social willpower to confront the menace in its midst. A deep, concerted, national effort looks well-nigh impossible, although reconciliation with the international financial community by Fujimori could lead, with agonizing slowness, to a sounder economy. However, not only might it be too late, but foreign investors will not be attracted until Shining Path is no longer a threat (in September 1991, Business Risks International, a U.S. security consultancy, rated Peru the riskiest country in the world for investment). And Peru is not a nation, anyway. It is a country racked by a political and economic infrastructure that is rooted in prejudices inherited from colonial times and that, in effect, discriminates against the vast, Indian-blooded majority in favor of Europeans' descendants. The historic lack of interest by the economic élite in sharing its wealth and developing the rural areas except to suit its own exploitative agricultural or mining purposes is reflected there by the flimsy presence of state government, which offers but a pathetic target to Shining Path.

The Peruvian state's appalling lack of resources and administrative efficiency, and above all its failure to have whipped up popular will to fight the guerrillas tooth and nail at every level of society, renders bleak the prospect of the survival of democratic government. Opinion polls show that increasing disillusionment with the poorly instituted, traditional political parties among the bulk of the population—which although it mostly rejects Shining Path has little love for the state either, and is subject to the guerrillas' greater power to terrorize—goes hand in hand with a growing demand for a military regime, mainly among the wealthier, and powerful, business sectors. Meanwhile, it is Shining Path that continues to sustain the initiative and, in much of the country, to enjoy a greater political support base than the security forces, which have turned their back on civilian government.

Miguel Angel Rodríguez Rivas, Abimael Guzmán's intellectual guru while the latter was a student at the National University of San Agustín in Arequipa, depicted Shining Path as the "unconscious protest of Andean civilization which has suffered five centuries of repression by an official state founded on European civilization." For Rivas, the movement embodies a tradition of historic hope and struggle: "Guzmán is not the creator of Sendero Luminoso. No, Sendero Luminoso has created Guzmán. It is more than just an ideology, it is a hope, perhaps a mystical one, for a better world. Sendero Luminoso's triumph will be its death, it would have no more reason to exist." Recognition of the guerrillas' immortal commitment was central to a speech made privately by Alan García to young APRA members in Ayacucho in May 1988: "Mistaken or not, criminal or not, the *senderista* has what we do not have: mystique and self-surrender. . . . They are people who deserve our respect and my personal admiration because they are, like it or not, militants. Fanatics, they say. I believe they have mystique and it is part of our self-criticism, comrades, to know we must recognize that he who, subordinated or not, delivers himself to death, gives his life, has mystique."

A similar note of doom in the face of such a motivated and indomitable enemy was struck by García's most successful minister of interior, Agustín Mantilla, in February 1991: "The gravest problem [as opposed to Sendero's actual number of armed militants] is in the political force which is expanding all over the country and in a determined moment and under certain circumstances can be converted or is going to convert necessarily into a military force. Sendero's structure is a structure initially political but developed, guided, and directed toward a military apparatus. All cells, which begin as political, end up necessarily as military cells. . . . I believe that the first thing we have to realize is that we are living in a war, facing a ferocious war that is destroying our democratic system. . . . There is a loss of moral value, there is a loss of combativeness by the security forces, there is a withdrawal of the whole state apparatus, but it is because the state and the country observe that its ruling classes have not reached a capacity for consensus." Mantilla acknowledged that Shining Path could win.

Although a military coup looked improbable given the international political climate in the early 1990s, with Western-style democracy continuing slowly to gather strength throughout Latin America—and the legal left less of an electoral threat, leaving the military without a bait—democracy was no longer the primary issue in bilateral relations with the imperialist bogey of the north, the United States. Many might argue that in reality it never was. But officially it had been substituted, where relevant, by the war against drugs. In effect, this allowed the United States to guard against its old and real Latin American foe, Communist insurgency. An article in the Spanish edition of the U.S. *Military Review*, the official armed forces magazine, in May 1987 argued that the drug war could be used by the United States to regain its "moral superiority" and undermine "the religious groups and academics who have tirelessly supported insurgency in Latin America," thereby securing special military funding from Congress. This would be used "to launch a coordinated offensive effort" in the region. The article added, "The recent [antidrug] operation in Bolivia is a first step. Instead of responding defensively to each insurgency according to the individual case, we could take concerted action with our allies."

The open militarization of the drug war—in April 1991 fifty-six U.S. military advisers were flown into Bolivia; in Colombia, President César Gaviria was driven to calling for fewer helicopters and more trade—coincided with a bald admission by Melvyn Levitsky, the U.S. assistant secretary for international narcotics matters, that, as far as the United States was concerned, democracy now ranked second fiddle to fighting drugs. Levitsky's declaration in April 1991 was made via satellite to a press conference at the U.S. embassy in Lima. The sweetener came the next day, when the U.S. ambassador, Anthony Quainton, announced—for the first time—that the United States might pardon some of Peru's bilateral public debt. Quainton's statement fell in line with President George Bush's ten-year Initiative for the Americas, which was launched in 1990 and aims to break down trade barriers between the United States and Latin America as part of a move toward creating an integrated, U.S.-dominated economic bloc from Alaska to Tierra del Fuego.

Amid such a plan, in which the U.S. war against drugs has all the appearance of being the backbone of its military corollary, Peruvian democracy might no longer be sacrosanct. If a military government is finally provoked into being by Shining Path, it might not be blocked if it takes on the drug trade unequivocally and cooperates economically. Support for a military-controlled Peruvian government in its efforts to stifle the Maoist guerrillas, whose tentacles are spreading beyond the frontiers, could be provided not only under the traditional banner of defending international democracy but also on the "morally superior" grounds of fighting cocaine.

# 8

# A World to Win

In the same way that Peru became the pariah of Latin America because of its outbreak of cholera, which promptly spread to neighboring countries, so, too, did it come to be ill-regarded for the threat posed by Shining Path. Reports of the Maoists' presence in Bolivian provinces bordering Peru north of Lake Titicaca grew persistently during the late 1980s. They reflected the guerrillas' difficult struggle to push a corridor through from the Cuzco department across the top of the lake in the department of Puno. Documents seized by the Peruvian antiterrorist police, DIRCOTE, show that in December 1987 Bolivia's Committee of Support to the Revolution in Peru (CSRP), which hitherto had comprised a small group of peasants, was invited to a national conference of the Marxist-Leninist faction of the Bolivian Communist party. There, the CSRP secured the support of the Maoists and at their behest crossed the frontier in January 1988 conveying the Bolivian Maoists' offer of unconditional cooperation to Shining Path and their invitation to a member of the local Puno committee, "César," to travel to Bolivia for the treatment of a leg wound.

There followed a period of intense political activity which in August 1989 was to climax with a bomb attack on the visiting U.S. secretary of state, George Shultz. While the CSRP and the Bolivian Maoists swapped delegates, the doctrinal work of César was boosted by fresh orders from Puno, which included initiating an investigation of the zone north of Lake Titicaca, slogan painting, and researching the possibilities for arms and munitions purchases. The CSRP opened a branch in La Paz and the Maoist party faction started to promote the "two-line struggle" in order to strengthen its position and radicalize the Bolivian Communist party's Marxist-Leninist group. According to Peruvian police, Workers' Day on May 1 saw the CSRP issue a leaflet in support of Shining Path and the party Maoists disseminate internally a copy of Shining Path's joint declaration with a branch of the Communist Party of Spain by way of a discussion document. Thereafter, the CSRP encouraged "people's schools," rallies, and propaganda.

Shultz's motorcade was struck on its way from the airport to the center of La Paz during a twelve-day tour of Latin America when he was believed mainly to be attempting to drum up pressure against the Sandinista regime in Nicaragua. The remote-controlled dynamite device damaged four cars, but nobody was hurt. The attack coincided with a statement from the Bolivian Workers Center, the country's largest union confederation, saying that Shultz was trying "to involve the Bolivian government in an antidrug policy that constitutes no more than a pretext for legalizing the presence of North American troops in national territory" and would lead to "intervention in all the countries in the Andean area." Shultz was declared "persona non grata." While the CIA maintained that drug traffickers were probably responsible for the bombing—a claim that supported the U.S. case for stronger action to be taken against what it depicted as the growing threat posed by drug trafficking—two subversive groups insisted that it had been their work. One of them called itself the Armed Forces of National Liberation, Zárate Willka, taking its name after an Indian peasant leader at the end of the last century.

It was Zárate Willka's first appearance. The second came the day after the Peruvian naval attaché in La Paz, Captain Juan Vega Llona, was gunned down near his embassy in December the same year. The assassination was claimed by an unknown group called the Revolutionary Worker Movement, which left notices beside the body saying: "As part of the peoples of the world, today we express our armed word against the imperialists, who day by day attempt bloodily to crush the just struggles of the masses. Faced with these bloodthirsty hyenas, today we are carrying out justice, annihilating a butcher, murderer of the people. . . . Long Live the Peoples of the World." Vega Llona had been involved in the prison massacre at El Frontón; the Revolutionary Worker Movement was clearly a Shining Path front. The following day, a bomb blew up in the Congress building, causing extensive damage. The deputies, who responded by singing the national anthem, suspected it to be the work of a former general. However, joint responsibility was claimed by the Revolutionary Worker Movement and Zárate Willka; the groups issued a document entitled "Death to Parliament" encouraging the development of the "armed struggle."

A Shining Path column carrying walkie-talkies had been reported the previous September by a group of tourists on a mountain trek, deep into Bolivia in the province of Achacachi. The tourists were stopped and politely searched; somebody felt obliged to relinquish a pair of thick socks. That month, the armed forces denounced the systematic robbery of weapons from army bases in the frontier zone. In March 1989 Eudoro Galindo, a senatorial candidate for the governing party, claimed that groups linked to Shining Path were recruiting Bolivian children. Before the May general election, which eventually brought Jaime Paz Zamora to the presidency, twenty bombs exploded almost simultaneously in the offices of the main political parties around the city of El Alto on the high plateau above the valley of La Paz. The attacks, which were suspected to have been carried out by Zárate Willka, bore the hallmarks of Shining Path. In May itself, Zárate Willka claimed responsibility for the killing of two U.S. Mormon missionaries.

Reports were by now filtering regularly through to the Bolivian media of strangers in the village of Ulla Ulla, the presence there of unusually burdened mules, and even of an airplane and helicopters making illicit landings at the Peruvian village of Rosaspata. These flights apparently came from the other side of the border. Hours after the arrival of one helicopter at Rosaspata in April, the village was taken over by forty Shining Path guerrillas and the mayor was assassinated; the helicopter was reported not to have taken off until the evening. Despite regular claims that Shining Path was using Bolivia to rest and obtain supplies and medical treatment, the government and security forces rejected the possibility.

Just as had happened in Peru, the government was unwilling to admit Shining Path's presence, even though it might be a very small one, for political reasons. It feared a weakening in its position during a delicate moment in the country's consolidation of democracy. The claims were labeled alarmist and the security forces said that the fact that they could not find the rebels proved they did not exist; they tended to dismiss them as drug traffickers. Meanwhile, gold-mining cooperatives were raided by guerrilla columns armed with machetes and machine guns, unclaimed bodies were appearing, and the peasants in the areas of Achacachi, Puerto Acosta, and Sorata were reported to be turning silent and hostile to the authorities and outsiders. "Nobody speaks of that group [Shining Path] expressly, but it is obvious that the peasants there have a unique respect for them," said a Bolivian journalist in June 1989. At the same time, Zárate Willka was said to have issued death threats to government authorities in El Alto. Meanwhile, there was evidence that Bolivians had joined Shining Path columns in Peru.

An operation launched in June 1989 by police and soldiers to hunt down the rebels was reported to have detected traces of Shining Path in Blanca Flor, a village in the department of Pando. However, the peasants complained that the finding was a pretext for militarization in order to persecute peasant leaders who had denounced government corruption. In September a left-wing deputy, Miguel Urioste, announced: "The militarist ideology of the guerrilla group Shining Path is penetrating the peasants' organization." That month, General Fred Woerner, chief of the United States Southern Command in Panama, dismissed the guerrilla threat in Bolivia and rejected the possibility of sending U.S. troops to fight in the antidrug war (Bolivia produces forty percent of the world's coca leaf, as opposed to Peru's sixty percent). General Woerner said that although there would be joint military exercises and engineering projects, such as lengthening the Potosí airstrip, "it should only be assistance, not the military presence of forces from my country." Shining

Path was already claiming that the United States had ulterior motives and was mainly concerned with developing a military presence to repress revolution; this line was echoed by Zárate Willka's initial statements.

In December the Bolivian army officially confirmed that groups of Shining Path guerrillas were entering national territory, although it insisted their local aims were "pacific" rather than military and revolved around securing logistical and medical support. The army began to bolster its forces in the frontier zones. Possibly because of the increased military presence or because the rebels redeployed their forces for the Peruvian general elections, reports of their activity died away until June 1990 when the outgoing president, Alan García, suddenly declared that the Maoists were deserting and escaping to Bolivia and Ecuador because the government was "about to win the war." Two weeks later, the Bolivian minister of defense, Héctor Ormachea, demanded further border reinforcements and said that according to army intelligence there were constant outbreaks of national terrorist groups with possible links to Shining Path.

Those intelligence reports were still off the mark. On June 9, according to documents confiscated by Peruvian police, Shining Path's Puno committee had signed a pact with Bolivia's Committee of Support to the Revolution in Peru (CSRP). In the agreement, the CSRP was said by the police to have formally used the name of Zárate Willka, which indicated that the two had been linked all along. However, it remained unclear what had become of the Maoist faction of the Bolivian Communist party. Police did not reveal details of the agreement except for the names of its Bolivian signatories, that it was an undertaking to swap militants—and, they said, it was denominated a "Pact of Blood."

Two Peruvian members of Shining Path were captured in Ulla Ulla in August 1989 after they were apparently denounced by local inhabitants. One was shot dead as he allegedly tried to escape. The following February, in the wake of the Bolivian security forces being reported by the Peruvian police to claim that Shining Path was influential among extreme left-wing groups in the departments of La Paz, Pando, and Oruro, government authorities received death threats in the La Paz provinces of Camacho and Munecas. At the same time, a column of thirty guerrillas identifying itself as Shining Path was reported to have held up a truck and a bus, requested collaboration money, and distributed political leaflets near Ulla Ulla in the La Paz department. A Bolivian alleged to be a member of the group was arrested. A national deputy for La Paz, Wálter Alvaro, said the rebels were making regular incursions and sought to pay for food: "They buy animals, vanish, and appear at night. . . . [S]ometimes there are three, or four, or two of them; they want the peasants to organize themselves." He added that the guerrillas blew up Christian statues on the grounds that they came "not from Bolivia but from abroad."

Shining Path was among those suspected by Bolivian police to be responsible for a rash of bombs discovered in La Paz during March and April 1990. Anonymous calls were received by the police at the rate of one a day; although many proved to be false alarms, several were real. The campaign, which the government said was designed to provoke tension and destabilize democracy, coincided with the arrival of fifty-six U.S. military advisers assigned to the antidrug war. Meanwhile, even before the bomb incidents, an article in *El Diario* said, "The reactionary press [in Peru] is blocking information coming from the southern zone of the country but it is not able to hide the Maoist drive that is extending into Bolivia."

Shortly after, Bolivian troops were put on full alert and aircraft carried out reconnaissance flights after a clash between guerrillas and police in the Peruvian frontier village of San Ignacio. Two rebels and one policeman were reportedly killed. While the Peruvian government made the unlikely claim that the clash might have been with MRTA, the Bolivian armed forces insisted that, in what was suspected to be a connected incident on their side of the border, those involved were simply Peruvian game hunters stalking vicuña. A few days later, the civilian police prefect for the department of La Paz, Fernando Cajías, claimed that the hammer-and-sickle flag could be seen flying on the other side of the border just opposite the Ulla Ulla province, about 185 miles north of the capital.

Two thirds of the 475-mile Bolivian-Peruvian border north of

Lake Titicaca is lowland jungle that is virtually impassable, except downstream by the river Tambopata where it flows unhelpfully northeastward into the Amazon basin. However, the Andean stretch, with its high mountain passes and marshy lakeside plains, may be inhospitable but can be crossed and is impossible to police. Bolivia shares much of Peru's history as well as its ethnic and socioeconomic problems. Migration to the towns from the countryside increased during the 1980s as agriculture fell into decline and huge numbers of miners were laid off. El Alto became Bolivia's third-largest city, drawing many Aymara migrants. The country is haunted both by debt and drug trafficking.

Anti-U.S. feeling was inflamed by the arrival of the American troops who came to train and equip two light infantry battalions, including one from the Manchego Battalion, which triumphed over Che Guevara. The Bolivian troops were to participate directly in drug-interdiction operations in the Beni department. They were to fight the traffickers and not the coca growers themselves. As well as 112 U.S. antidrug advisers, nearly 450 more U.S. military personnel were to participate in military exercises and in engineering and medical programs. General Woerner's promise that there would not be a U.S. "military presence" started to look distinctly watery. Peasants and miners called strikes and blocked roads in their campaign for the U.S. soldiers to be expelled. "The government has declared war on the peasant sector and on the people, and the peasants will respond to the death," said one peasant leader, Secundino Montevilla. In June, the Permanent Defense Council of the Producers of Coca Leaf in the Andean Countries, with Peruvian and Bolivian representatives, declared: "For the United States, these agreements signed under the pretext of the fight against drugs are part of the policy of low-intensity war that seeks to destroy the peasant and popular organizations. . . . [T]he North American government is trying to tighten its imperialist grip." Such a scenario could not have delighted Shining Path more. It seemed to vindicate the group's strategies as well as to bear out all its political analyses and enthusiastic predictions of U.S. intervention.

Meanwhile, in late June an army intelligence source said,

"Not only is Bolivian territory being used for provisions and recuperation by Peruvian subversive groups, but it is known that in some parts of the country they are carrying out philosophical indoctrination and military training as part of the formation of . . . the Committee of Support to the Peruvian Revolution." A week later, two electricity pylons were dynamited in El Alto and the town of Cochabamba. It was the first time such attacks had occurred in Bolivia. A group calling itself the Túpac Katari Guerrilla Army claimed responsibility, saying it would continue the attacks in protest at "five hundred years of oppression."

North of Peru the country that for most of the 1980s was a haven of tranquility after ushering in the return of democracy to South America was starting to grow nervous of the guerrillas' advance. Ecuador, whose long-standing border dispute with Peru exploded briefly into war in 1981, had stamped down hard on its home-grown rebel movement, the small and ineffective pro-Cuban Alfaro Lives, Dammit! The group, which had done little except rob a few banks and kidnap a businessman (with the help of M-19 from Colombia), formally handed over its minuscule arms stores to the Catholic church in February 1991. Just beforehand, three electricity pylons were blown up north of the Quito capital during a national strike. It was the first sabotage of that kind. Three months later the Peruvian minister of interior, Victor Malca, claimed that Shining Path was allied not only with Zárate Willka but also possibly with a faction within Alfaro Lives, Dammit! Malca added, "They have said that they have laid down their weapons, but there is a little group within them that seems to be linked with Sendero and operates in the mountains of Piura, by Huancabamba." A former leader of the Ecuadoran rebels, Marco Troya, denied the claim, saying, "If, OK, we respect Shining Path, we are not in agreement with its methods." A source close to Shining Path said the party was expanding into Bolivia and Ecuador because it needed "to avoid being surrounded."

Abimael Guzmán has always viewed Shining Path's revolution in Peru within an international context. He perceives it to be "serving the advance of the world revolution" by proving "the invincibility and vitality of Marxism, of Marxism-Leninism-Maoism, principally Maoism." During a speech in 1989 celebrating the fortieth anniversary of the People's Republic of China, he declared, "The seizure of power will have far-reaching consequences because we are in a key part of Latin America at a time when this continent, in comparison with Asia and Africa, is undergoing the most severe economic, political, and ideological crisis, a general crisis with no solution in sight in the coming years. . . . [W]hile countries are growing at a rate of more than nine percent a year in Asia, at three percent in Africa and the Middle East, the growth rate for Latin America is one percent and this in turn should be measured against the continent's high population growth rate." Guzmán denounced the true purpose of the United States' greater military presence in the Andes as being counterrevolutionary. He added, "Yankee aggression, whether it be direct or indirect, is bringing about a war of national liberation."

Although the rebels clearly posed a security threat in Bolivia, and conceivably in Ecuador, their cause was less likely to prosper than in Peru because of the greater rapport between the rural populations and local authorities, stronger peasant organizations, and more successful agrarian reforms, which had maintained the peasants' commitment to their land and stemmed urban migration. Both countries, despite their populistic and militaristic tendencies, were relatively stable. However, according to senior Bolivian Ministry of Defense sources in June 1991, a tacit agreement had been reached in the border zone between government authorities and Shining Path under which the guerrillas would not be confronted so long as they restricted themselves to pacific activities. Were that to be true, it would be a gift to Guzmán. He seeks world revolution and is conscientiously working to bring it about. Some kind of pro–Shining Path Bolivian apparatus has been built and the rebels have proved that, once they have passed the embryo stage in a new location, they will flex their muscles as elsewhere when the moment is right.

Guzmán is ideologically committed to the autonomous nature of "democratic revolution" abroad. The response from most other South American governments to the possible threat ranges from dismissal to paranoia. Their armed forces do not understand what Shining Path is or how it operates. The Maoists are variously perceived as common criminals, drug traffickers, subversives who will one day turn into a legitimate political party, or subversives who clearly do not wish to seize power because if that were the case they would have already done so. The prevalent view is the traditional one of their Peruvian counterparts: that the rebels could be finished off were the military to be granted the necessary freedom to act.

While the Brazilian police accused Shining Path of trafficking cocaine in exchange for food, clothes, arms, and munitions in its border zone east of Pucallpa, prior to transporting the goods to the upper Huallaga valley, the Argentinian government claimed in April 1989 that Shining Path had participated in a clandestine meeting in its province of Tucamán. Meanwhile, Argentina's National Security Council, which had been set up after an attack on an army barracks, claimed the Maoists were escaping into national territory through Bolivia. One respected newspaper made the improbable assertion that Shining Path had been paid $100,000 for training the guerrillas of the All for the Fatherland Movement, which was responsible for the barracks assault. Forty people had died in the onslaught.

After the election of President Patricio Aylwin ended sixteen and a half years of dictatorship in Chile, the only rebel groups believed actively to be continuing the armed struggle were a branch of the Manuel Rodriguez Patriotic Front and two apparently linked movements named after Lautaro, an Araucunian Indian chieftain who had heroically resisted the Spaniards. Of anarchistic repute and apparently rooted in secondary schools, Lautaro occupied radio stations, raided shops, and robbed and bombed banks. In 1990 the rebels gunned down two policemen, severely wounding a third. That October Alberto Espina, a right-wing Congress deputy who denounced the group's use of church premises for meetings, said it had "connections with Latin American terrorist movements, among them Shining Path." The following March a prominent police officer was killed and his father, his chauffeur, and another policeman injured in an attack by Lautaro in Concepción; the same day, the group wounded six policemen in a dynamite blast. In April a senator regarded as General Pinochet's ideologist, Jaime Guzmán, died after being machine-gunned in a ruthlessly planned assassination. Few acts could have been so deliberately designed to trigger a backlash by the military (still controlled by Pinochet) and, as the army declared, "threaten democracy in its fundamentals." The killing was accompanied by a dynamite attack on a police station, wounding six people.

Amid further bomb attacks, an assistant police chief, Mario Mengozzi, claimed Peruvians had been involved in the Jaime Guzmán assassination and that Shining Path had provided technical and theoretical aid to extremist Chilean groups. Suspicion turned to Peruvian students, of whom there had been a heavy influx. According to the Chilean embassy in Lima, Peruvians were seeking visas for university studies at the rate of ten a day in the wake of President Fujimori's economic austerity measures the previous year. Jamie Guzmán was shot as he left the Catholic University in Santiago.

The emergence of Shining Path's name in connection with rebel movements and violence elsewhere in Latin America became ever more frequent at the end of the 1980s. Whether or not there were any substantial links, Shining Path set an example for revolutionary violence while at the same time providing a useful scapegoat for governments eager to use the threat to curtail protests by raising fears of destabilization and military intervention.

Mexico and the Dominican Republic also harbored Shining Path support groups. While the Dominican Republic boasts a Committee to Support the Revolution in Peru, Mexico hosts another kind of organization: a Peru People's Movement (MPP). While Shining Path's CSRPs usually maintain a public profile, devote themselves to pacific cultural and political propaganda, are self-generated, and are not subject to party orders, groups of the latter breed, which exist in at least seven countries, are founded by the party, obey the party leadership, are semi-clandestine, and may use violence.

According to Peruvian police, an MPP was formed in Mexico in May 1988 on the anniversary of the prison massacres. Its cover organization was the José Carlos Mariátegui Cultural Center–Civil Association, within which a human rights committee and media group also operated. Peruvian news and human rights cases were publicized and economic aid secured from sympathetic Mexican unions, universities, and institutes. The MPP's objective was to spread Shining Path's political ideology, defend its war, and, according to Peruvian police documents, "bind together people and organizations who identify with the interests of the Peruvian oppressed and with their revolution and the world revolution." The MPP comprised Peruvians, Mexicans, foreign residents, and refugees. It published documents and, under the guise of its umbrella organization, conducted conferences, seminars, and exhibitions. The MPP's chairman, "Guillermo," went to Canada in November 1988 in order to gather funds for its activities in Mexico and to carry out political work among Peruvian residents. Traveling as the coordinator of the human rights committee, he undertook similar activities in what Shining Path is fond of labeling the belly of the beast: the United States.

In 1975, a white union activist in Chicago founded the Revolutionary Communist Party (RCP) of the United States. In its weekly newspaper, which is published in Spanish and English, Bob Avakian outlines its call to arms: "Many groups will protest and rebel against what this system does, and it is essential to support and strengthen those protests and rebellions. However, only those who have nothing to lose but their chains are they who can be the backbone of the fight to smash this system and create a new one that will do away with exploitation and prepare the ground for a totally new world." The party capable of directing the struggle, says Avakian, is the RCP. All those who dream of a new world are enjoined to enroll in its ranks and "prepare the ground for a revolutionary uprising." In its May Day Manifesto the RCP proclaims: "We have to be building up our strength and our conscious organized force to battle them in a new way—all out and all the way—when the time comes."

The RCP, which in 1991 was disseminating Communist and especially Maoist literature through bookstores and other outlets in seventeen cities in the United States, from Honolulu to Atlanta, is Shining Path's biggest overseas ally. Shining Path party members were informed in early 1990 that the RCP had organically accepted Maoism as the third stage of Marxism. The absence of a joint declaration by the middle of 1991 was said to have been for lack of a suitable political opportunity. The RCP's adoption of the universal validity of Maoism was a major ideological triumph for Abimael Guzmán and was likely to trigger off similar conversions by fractional Communist groups elsewhere in the world. However, the triumph was not only stimulated by the progress of Shining Path's revolution in Peru. The hardening of the RCP's Maoist line during the 1980s was a growing response to Chinese and Soviet "revisionism." Maoism offered a foothold out of the ideological and political void into which Marxist-Leninists were tumbling. With the collapse of the Berlin Wall, that foothold became a step.

Most of the RCP's work is devoted to peaceful protest and propaganda. According to a Peruvian source close to Shining Path, it also makes a point of helping refugees. May Day, 1991, was celebrated with, among acts of a similar ilk, the hanging of red flags from an office building on Wall Street and in place of the Stars and Stripes on a military monument in Cleveland, Ohio. Pro–Shining Path slogans were daubed on the Peruvian consulate in Paterson, New Jersey. Mao's portrait flies during rallies, and murals are painted. "Racists, Rambo-Americans, Rulers of America, it's all going to fall on you," clamor banners that summon to rebellion "Outcasts, Downcasts, Slaves, Illegals and Rebels." There are occasional street clashes with police. Mixed in with the railing against U.S. intervention abroad, foreign-policy hypocrisy in the Gulf or Central America, and persecution by the police and FBI are the RCP's panegyrics to the "People's War in the Andes."

There is a hard, racial edge to the RCP. Although there is a white presence, the party mainly attracts the ethnically under-privileged of U.S. society, particularly legal and illegal Latin American migrants and their descendants and, it seems, Texan-Mexicans. There is also a significant black African and Asian component. One of the RCP's martyrs is Damián García, who was killed in Los Angeles in April 1980, allegedly by police. García was accused of recruiting Latin Americans for the RCP. The shooting occurred a few weeks after he had switched the

Texan for the Communist flag at the Alamo, where the Mexican defeat of the Texans preceded Texan independence and the eventual forced cession by Mexico of half its territory (Texas, California, and the entire present-day Southwest were bought for a paltry $15 million). The 1991 anniversary of García's death was celebrated by the RCP in a Latino district of Los Angeles with rallies and barricades of burning garbage and tires. Police did not intervene. A local RCP communiqué said García had been assassinated because he "dared to raise the red flag over El Alamo, the grand symbol of the US domination of Mexico and of people of Mexican descent."

According to government figures, the Hispanic population of the United States increased by 34.5 percent during the 1980s. This compared with an overall rise of 9.9 percent. In 1990 Hispanics accounted for 7.9 percent of the population, and together with blacks they made up a fifth of the total. Projections suggest that by the year 2010 that figure will rise to a quarter. At the end of a decade dominated by free-market economic policies and cuts in government services, the gap between the rich and poor was nowhere more evident than in New York itself, pressurized by the arrival of nearly a million immigrants from the Caribbean, Latin America, and Asia, whom it was unable to absorb. The squalor of filthy streets, gutted tenements, and smoldering fires was no longer restricted to the inner city. Block by block its advance guard was moving up Fifth Avenue. Street vendors of trinkets, ties, and shish kebabs were snuffing out the daylight of jewelers and exclusive clothing stores—where beggars had not already beaten them to it. *The New York Times* called the city Calcutta-on-the-Hudson. Homelessness, crime, and crack addiction soared. And the city was a tinderbox of racial tensions.

The San Francisco Bay Area branch of the RCP formed the U.S. Committee to Support the Revolution in Peru (CSRP) in 1985. The CSRP's national spokesman, Heriberto Ocasio, a middle-aged Puerto Rican, Vietnam protest veteran, and paramedical volunteer in Palestinian refugee camps in Beirut, claimed thirty people worked for it full time in chapters in Berkeley, New York, and Chicago. Ocasio, who said the group had "hundreds" of supporters, planned to open a permanent office in San Francisco's Latino district, the Mission; meanwhile, its venue locally was a Protestant church. The CSRP's goals were to fuel opposition to U.S. intervention in Peru; defend Peru's "political prisoners," contribute to the international publication of *El Diario*; help to translate, publish, and distribute Shining Path literature; and oppose the "disinformation campaign" on Peru by the U.S. media. It also sought to recruit activists, mobilize popular, political, and academic support for Shining Path, and raise funds for its own costs. "We do not send money to Peru because it would be illegal," said Ocasio. "We do not do anything illegal because we know that we are under permanent surveillance."

CSRP activists engage in street and university rallies and materialize at any event that involves Peru. Like the RCP, the CSRP helps refugees and illegal immigrants and includes a high proportion of people from ethnic minorities. CSRP members view Shining Path as the exemplar of world revolution; their primary campaign slogan is "Yankee go home." All formal contacts with Shining Path are conducted by the RCP. An unsympathetic observer said in 1991, "The CSRP is definitely getting bigger. People are really involved in it. You feel there is a core. When I came here in 1986 you did not feel that. The very extent of the organization shows that it is growing. The white Americans involved have no political sense in their lives: They are looking for a cause." Avakian himself fled to France in 1980.

Of all European countries, it is Sweden in particular that has been seen as a paradise for political refugees. Generous social security payments, free education and medical attention, and cheap housing combined with a traditionally liberal attitude toward the harboring of exiles converted it into a magnet for those escaping their countries for political or humanitarian reasons, mainly left-wingers. Iranians, Palestinians, Lebanese, and Somalians are among the largest groups making up the 150,000 such exiles who were there in 1990. However, in a country that for all its egalitarianism is oddly xenophobic, they stand out strongly. They tend not to become incorporated into Swedish society and live a ghetto-ish, if comfortable, existence. As Sweden moved to liberalize its welfare state amid a fundamental shift toward the political right in 1991, popular patience with its radical exiles—who were treated increasingly warily in the aftermath of the 1986 assassination of the prime minister, Olof Palme, and the Lockerbie jet bombing in 1988—started to wear thin. Immigrants as a whole came to incur something of their stigma, which was aggravated by economic decline. Xenophobia evolved into racism.

From the outset of Shining Path's war until late 1990 more than 360 Peruvians were granted residence permits by Sweden for political or humanitarian reasons. About the same number again were accepted because of family links. According to the Peruvian embassy in Stockholm, the exiles' lives revolve around Shining Path, although it claims only 120 are politically active and another 40 are truly dedicated. The kernel of the community is the family of Augusta La Torre; its gray eminence is "Enrique," a handsome, soft-spoken man who generates obedience like a respected senior schoolmaster. Peruvian police documents show that he arrived in Sweden with his family in November 1982 following an apparent split with Abimael Guzmán. After writing a letter of repentance, he created the Ayacucho Studies Group, which won Guzmán's blessing in March 1986. Enrique received orders to reorganize it and select the favored militants, who had to send letters of party loyalty. They became the leaders of what metamorphosed into a Peru People's Movement (MPP). In May 1987 Enrique was appointed by Guzmán to generate MPPs throughout Europe. These were specifically to work with immigrants as well as Peruvians and nationals; their degree of clandestineness was to depend on local circumstances. They were instructed to conduct propaganda work and link themselves to workers and strikers. Where feasible, they were to generate public apparatuses, which henceforth were to be called Sun-Peru Committees instead of CSRPs (presumably in order to broaden their appeal by distancing them from the revolution). And they were to stimulate the reconstitution of Communist parties.

Meanwhile, in late 1986 Enrique and his crowd had their first clash with the Swedish government. They came out on top. Eleven Peruvians were denied asylum for being linked to a criminal organization fighting a democratically elected government. While they went into hiding, police in bulletproof vests and gas masks raided a flat and arrested an eighteen-month-old baby girl in the care of a friend of her parents. Other militants went on a hunger strike in central Stockholm; thousands of people signed a petition rejecting the expulsion order, and the Peruvians were reported to have the backing of the United Nations High Commissioner for Refugees. A series of massacres by the Peruvian security forces, police requests to Lima to the Swedish embassy for the details of the exiles' flight home—and the disappearance in Lima the following day of a lawyer who had done the same—helped to force the Swedish government into a humiliating submission, apparently on the grounds that Shining Path was not a terrorist organization because it did not carry out terrorist actions abroad.

In June and July 1987 a publicity campaign based around the prison massacres was carried out in several European countries with the participation of party delegates from Peru. Meanwhile, the activists in Sweden continued to stage rallies, lobby Latin American events, distribute literature in Spanish, English, and Swedish, and recruit refugees by overseeing their residency applications. They allegedly altered the names in Peruvian newspaper cuttings to "prove" they were being persecuted in their country. After the 1990 Peruvian general elections, when only half the twelve hundred Peruvians in Sweden voted—jostled and jeered at as they arrived to complete their ballot papers—a senior Peruvian diplomat admitted he was scared, partly for himself but mostly for his family back home.


Luis Arce, the editor of *El Diario* who had fled to Belgium to escape the persecution of the Peruvian police, had been hauled in by the Brussels undercover antiterrorist squad in the wake of several nights of race riots in May 1991. Police questioning of a youth, apparently on suspicion of stealing his own motorcycle, had provoked violence that spread rapidly to other districts, leading to the arrests of two hundred North Africans. Later a protest against a planned demonstration by a racist, right-wing Flemish party, Vlaams Blok, had erupted into an attack on a police station, the looting of shops, and the hurling of fire-bombs. The government blamed the violence on high youth unemployment, overcrowding, and the failure of immigration policies (immigrants make up about a quarter of Brussels's population of one million). However, one government minister had claimed the rioting was aggravated by extremists. "There was clear evidence . . . of external elements coming to join the demonstrators," said a regional minister, Charles Picque. A spokeswoman for the Movement Against Racism, Anti-Semitism, and Xenophobia said that the riots were inevitable and that "you only need a small spark to set things off."

"The police thought I was involved in stirring it up," said Arce. "They are as corrupt here as in Peru. I am worried they will try to assassinate me. I am just a journalist and member of the support group to the Peruvian people. The party has not generated an MPP here, probably because it considers there are not enough people sufficiently advanced to form a Communist committee. Living in Europe reinforces my conviction that the revolution as directed by the Communist Party of Peru is the only viable form of liberating the oppressed masses of my country and that it is at the vanguard of the world revolution."

In July 1990 Arce brought out the first international edition of *El Diario*. He receives one dollar for each of the two thousand copies, distributed mostly in Europe and the United States, and the money enables him to cover his costs and live reasonably well. The previous year he had published a book of party documents, *People's War in Peru—Gonzalo Thought*. Arce was forthright about the ethnic, Indian character of Shining Path's struggle, which the party officially underplays: "The Peruvian people have always fought," he said. "The Spanish almost destroyed the Peruvian people and the Incas but that was when the fight started. Chairman Gonzalo is the accumulation of that defiance."

As is done elsewhere, Arce concentrates the local group's effort on propaganda, the attending of Latin American events, and attracting workers and migrants. He claimed that support for Shining Path in Europe was increasing: "A more favorable current of opinion is beginning. The Gulf War helped because it showed the nature of U.S. aggression and how people can no

longer trust the media. Seeing how the media were manipulated made people realize that official Peruvian news should
also be distrusted." Arce boasted that while only a handful of
people attended talks given by visiting members of Peru's "revisionist" left to the Belgian Workers Party, scores attended his.
Nevertheless, he won poor press when he defended the guerrillas' killing of two French aid workers—and threatened an ex-
asperated journalist with becoming a "target of the revolution"
if he ventured to Peru.

Italy, Spain, Germany, France, Greece, and Switzerland are
each host to a Peru People's Movement directly generated by
Shining Path. Assorted, "self-generated" support committees
are present in those countries as well as in the Canary Islands,
Denmark, Finland, the Netherlands, and Great Britain; it is
probable they also exist in Estonia. Apart from Peruvians and
nationals, wherever there is a significant population of immigrants they are strongly represented. The MPPs, under orders
to seek out immigrants, do their best to cater to their needs. In
Madrid, a Peruvian resident reported that an office festooned
with Shining Path posters operated a telephone exchange with
stolen lines where people could call anywhere in the world for
$18 per half hour. Clients were offered party literature; forged
passports were available at $240 each.

The involvement of Shining Path's support groups with non-
Peruvian immigrants is particularly strong in Italy, Germany,
France, and Spain, where migration and racial tensions pose a
growing problem. The day before Luis Arce spoke in Brussels,
police baton-charged 350 demonstrating Arab and African
workers in Rome, and gasoline bombs were tossed into an immigrants' camp in Milan; both incidents were sparked by attempts to move immigrants to different locations. Also on that
day, Spain announced that visas would be required for North
African immigrants; earlier in the month, two hundred had
rioted while awaiting repatriation. A European Community
visa regime that would probably require Latin Americans to
hold visas threatened to provoke similar confrontations with
them. In 1989 illegal immigrants in Spain were estimated to
number 300,000.

The surging tide of African migrants in the late 1980s was

swelled in France and Germany by those from Turkey. In May 1991 two hundred foreigners, mostly Turks or Turkish Kurds, went on hunger strikes in several French cities in protest at the government's refusal to grant them political asylum on the grounds that they were really economic refugees. The French government had speeded up investigations of asylum demands, which nearly doubled in 1989, and about 100,000 unsuccessful applicants were due for deportation. In the month of the hunger strikes, up to 244,000 illegal immigrants were estimated to live in the Paris area alone. Gathering social strife in the Paris suburbs, plagued by poverty and unemployment, assumed racial overtones because of the high proportion of non-Caucasian people involved. Throughout Europe, economic as well as social alienation was stirring up unrest that provoked racist backlashes because "colored" people were a striking common factor. Racism had returned with a vengeance to post–Berlin Wall Germany. A member of an élite "dueling fraternity" at Heidelberg University said to the *Daily Telegraph* magazine, "Le Pen got fifteen percent of the vote in France. Britain has the National Front. A big official of the Ku Klux Klan got forty-nine percent of the vote in Louisiana. There are three million Turks in Germany. What should we do? Have thirty million Turks in Germany?" Another observed, "There is no anti-Semitism in Germany. There are only 30,000 Jews left."

Migration was no more than the world's poor on the move. They were searching for the work and food denied them at home, and escaping war brought about mostly for the same reasons. Africans were escaping famine of horrendous proportions. Speaking in the context of the Kurdish flight from Iraq in the wake of the Gulf War, the head of the United Nations relief operation in Iraq and former head of the office of the U.N. High Commissioner for Refugees, Sadruddin Aga Khan, warned of the need to close the gap between the rich North and the poor South, the First World and the Third World. He said in *The Independent:* "Unless you have some kind of new economic order, people will continue to move north. All the barbed wire, laws and immigration controls in the world— nothing will prevent that. The Kurds are just the tip of the iceberg."

It is among the Turks and Turkish Kurds that Shining Path has encountered its second main overseas ally: the Communist Party of Turkey/Marxist-Leninist (TKP/ML). The group, whose members are mostly Kurds, is one of the three factions of a party that was strong during the 1970s but was crushed in the aftermath of a military coup in 1980. Its militants were tortured, jailed, and killed; many fled abroad. However, although small, it is still active in Turkey. It kills the occasional policeman and has operative links with the guerrillas of the powerful Workers Party of Kurdistan (PKK), by which it has been supplanted. According to a source close to Shining Path in Lima, a concert in Istanbul in support of the guerrillas' war in Peru was attended by thousands of people. Abroad, the TKP/ML is active in France, Germany, and Britain, but possibly in other countries too. As early as 1983 it linked up with Shining Path sympathizers at a workers' May Day parade in Paris. The previous year a Peruvian physicist and former professional colleague of Guzmán, Maximiliano Durand, had arrived in Paris to establish, at his own initiative, a beachhead for the party in Europe. Despite Durand's constant supplications, Guzmán never granted him authorization. However, amid years of internecine rivalry that finally saw him elbowed aside at Guzmán's behest, Durand generated a militant support group that made a name for itself in the Latino and immigrant community. The four leaders of the Sun-Peru Committee he founded with forty members in May 1984 were Peruvian, French, Turkish, and American. A delegate of the TKP/ML, as well as the RCP–USA, was already on the tiny leadership committee of an ambitious, global organization that had come into existence just a couple of months earlier: the Revolutionary Internationalist Movement (RIM).

In response to what was deemed to be communism's worldwide ideological disarray, thirteen Communist parties and groups had joined forces in 1980 to reconstitute international communism and declare their unity on the platform of Marxism-Leninism. "Mao Zedong Thought" was upheld but not considered a third stage. The organizations called themselves the International Communist Movement (ICM). According to Peruvian police documents based on papers confiscated from

Shining Path, the party was visited in Lima in 1983 by two RCP–USA members of its coordinating committee in a fruitless attempt to persuade the Peruvians to sign the movement's declaration. Shining Path refused because Maoism was not enthroned as the third stage of communism. Guzmán also spurned an invitation to the movement's second conference, but he did set out his ideological demands. The conference, which was officially attended by at least fifteen Communist organizations, ceded ground.

At a press conference in London on March 12, 1984, the movement announced it had changed its name to the Revolutionary Internationalist Movement and adopted "Mao Zedong Thought." Both developments were due to Guzmán. Calling it the International Communist Movement was, for him, to jump the gun: Still failing to accept Maoism (a word granting universal validity to the ideas of Mao and his closest associates) and preferring instead "Mao Zedong Thought" (merely granting the ideas local validity), the movement was not yet equipped with the ideological basis Guzmán sought. Without the existence of Shining Path, the ICM/RIM would have been like a boat becalmed; lacking any real direction, it might even have capsized. The movement had no choice but partially to accede to the Peruvians. Shining Path had breathed new life into its sails and Chairman Gonzalo was starting to take the helm.

The obscure signatories of the RIM declaration, which was translated into more than twenty languages, came from Third World countries, with the exception of the RCP–USA, the Communist Collective of Agit/Prop (Italy), and the New Zealand Red Flag Group.* It declared: "In the midst of profound

---

* RIM declaration signatories (1990): Central Reorganization Committee, Communist Party of India (Marxist-Leninist); Ceylon Communist party; Communist Collective of Agit/Prop (Italy); Communist Party of Bangladesh (Marxist-Leninist); Communist Party of Peru; Communist Party of Turkey/Marxist-Leninist; Haitian Revolutionary Internationalist Group; Nepal Communist Party (Mashall); New Zealand Red Flag Group; Organization of Marxists-Leninists of Tunisia; Organization of the Revolutionary Communists of Afghanistan; Proletarian Party of Purba Bangla (Bangladesh); Revolutionary Communist Group of Colombia; Revolutionary Communist Party, USA; Revolutionary Communist Union (Dominican Republic); Union of Iranian Communists (Sarbedaran).

crisis in the ranks of Marxist-Leninists . . . the international proletariat has to take up the challenge of forming its own organization, an International of a new type based on Marxism–Leninism–Mao Zedong Thought, assimilating the valuable experience of the past. And this goal must be boldly proclaimed before the international proletariat and the oppressed of the world."

One RIM resolution ran:

> The Communist Party of Peru, which is continuing on the shining path charted by its founder, José Carlos Mariátegui, has dealt a mighty blow against revisionists of all shades, in particular against the revisionist usurpers in China who have attempted to force the proletariat and oppressed peoples to capitulate to imperialism and its servants. The advance of the People's War in Peru inspires and strengthens the Marxist-Leninist forces the world over who are struggling against modern revisionism. In the absence of a correct Marxist-Leninist line most of the anti-imperialist struggles of the oppressed peoples and nations that are being waged today are being utilized by the two imperialist blocs in their rivalry. But the revolutionary war in Peru concretely shows that a correct line can enable even the people of a small country to initiate and develop their just war against all imperialists and their reactionary puppets.

Two days after RIM's formation, a delegate arrived in Lima in order to persuade Shining Path to sign its declaration. Guzmán is said initially to have refused. However, despite several discrepancies between Guzmán's and RIM's ideology, by September that year Shining Path was among the signatories. The following year, Guzmán's most trusted European militant, Enrique, and a party delegate from Peru, worked alongside the RIM managing committee in Paris. Their task included the launching of a RIM campaign in support of Shining Path. By February 1986 Enrique had visited twenty-six cities in Europe, the United States, and the Caribbean in a bid to popularize the Peruvian revolution. In July the campaign reached Faribad, New Delhi, Ahmedabad, Bombay, Madras, and Calcutta.

Meanwhile, another party delegate from Lima had come to Europe in order to observe the RIM and to hand it over $5,000. That October Shining Path declared it was worried by "hegemonic trends" within the RIM but would work as a faction fighting to enshrine Maoism. A central-committee document stated, "We are for the reconstitution of the Communist International and we regard the RIM as a step in that direction. The RIM will only serve for that purpose if it bases itself on an ideologically correct and just line."

The RIM–Shining Path meetings appear mostly to have taken place in Paris, where the local militants busied themselves not only with graffiti painting, rallies, study meetings, and, according to the Peruvian embassy, helping refugees. They also left a small dynamite charge outside the embassy, which was deactivated, and tossed a lit firework into a chapel of Nôtre Dame as Peruvian embassy officials and residents attended an Independence Day mass; there was a brief panic, nobody was hurt, and the mass went on. Andean music floats through the Métro as Peruvian folk groups sing about freedom in America, accompanied by harps, drums, panpipes, and guitars. If they are asked about Shining Path, their eyes glaze over as if they were scared either of police or rebel persecution in France or Peru. Some admit they are supporters, but hardly any confess that they are not. Militants are active in the universities, allegedly among staff as well as students, and particularly at the international student center near the Porte d'Orléans. According to both the Peruvian embassy and the rebels' documents, Turks have a consistently high profile in Shining Path actions, including during the picketing of the Peruvian residents who voted in Peru's 1990 presidential elections.

Although Paris is said to be the base of RIM's managing committee, the committee's periodical is published in Britain. *A World to Win* is a smart, glossy magazine that comes out two or three times a year and is printed in Nottingham. Its correspondence is received by a fax and mailing service in London. Most issues are available in English, Spanish, Farsi (Persian), and Turkish. In the 1985 premiere issue, the magazine's opening article was entitled "Peru: When the Andes Roar." Most of the articles are contributed by RIM's member organizations and deal with their particular countries; others are by the RIM committee and tend to adopt an overall, international perspective. The greatest attention is paid to Peru and "revisionism" in the Soviet Union and China. The breakup of the Soviet empire was gleefully monitored and the Tiananmen Square protests were seen as a reaction against government corruption associated with capitalist restoration.

A 1990 article headlined "Unleashing the Masses, Unlocking the Future—Mao is the Key!" welcomed the collapse of the Eastern bloc regimes and claimed they were "monstrosities" and travesties of socialism that had debased the Communist cause worldwide. It accused their top Communist party officials of having turned "public ownership into a mere façade hiding their own private expropriation, whose essence was the same as that of all other capitalist exploiters" and added, "The working class and the masses of people in the Eastern European countries have long recognized that a special stratum of privileged people concentrated in the Communist Parties have been appropriating the fruits produced by the labouring people. . . . [W]e should not be surprised that the masses in these countries are hoisting anti-communist banners when the word 'communism' has been used to justify all of the exploitation, inequality and reaction of those regimes. . . . [T]hese people must be challenged, and boldly, with the truth of Marxism–Leninism–Mao Zedong Thought."

Mao, whose teachings are described as the "greatest weapon to understand the current situation and to battle the enemy," is cited principally within the context of socialism being a revolutionary transition period "leading from capitalism and other reactionary forms of class society to the achievement of communism throughout the world." Stalin's purges against "opportunistic elements" are deemed to have struck the symptom and not the cause: "Mao, on the other hand, was able to analyse how a bourgeoisie is inevitably generated under socialism and that, therefore, it is necessary to repeatedly *arouse the masses from below* [sic] to strike down the bourgeoisie within the Communist Party itself and, step by step, dig away at the capitalist economic and ideological soil that was generating new bourgeois elements batch after batch. . . . Mao knew that the proletariat could not simply 'delegate' their dictatorship to the Communist Party."

Mao is praised for placing greater emphasis on "the continuation of the class struggle under the dictatorship of the proletariat" during the socialist phase than on the development of "the productive forces." The article affirms, "Mao also understood the question of centralized planning in a very dialectical way, that is, he understood the unity and struggle of opposites —between balance and imbalance, agriculture and industry, heavy and light industry, and between the centre and the regions." Warming to his theme, the theory underlying the Cultural Revolution, the writer adds, "Seizure of power *only opens the door* [*sic*] to the struggle to transform the ways in which people interact with each other in all aspects of social life. The ideas and practices which have grown up on the basis of thousands of years of class society will not go away without a bitter struggle, and these ideas and practices will continually have a tendency to corrupt and ultimately transform even socialist society."

Spurning Khrushchev, who allowed the possibility of socialist revolution via parliamentary democracy and initiated the policy of "peaceful coexistence" with the West, the writer holds that the Soviet bloc collapsed because it tried and failed to beat the West at its own game. "A genuine socialist country would never enter the race for neo-colonies and Third World feasting grounds," says the magazine, stressing again that the raising of living standards should initially be subordinate to the advance of communism. "It is easy to show, for example, that revolutionary China under Mao or the Soviet Union under Lenin and Stalin were poor compared with the West. But what about the countries the West exploits? The imperialist system has two 'poles'—those who live in the citadels and benefit to varying degrees from the privileged position of those countries *and* [*sic*] those who live in the vast reaches of Asia, Africa and Latin America where whole countries have been deformed and put at the service of the imperialist countries."

The article concludes bitterly but optimistically: "It is true that the imperialist exploiting machine is a powerful motor for 'economic development.' It can chew up people by the millions and spit out tons of broken bones and, in the process, it can build modern cities usually surrounded, in the Third World at least, with equally 'modern' slums. Imperialism can only develop a country by creating in miniature what it does in the world as a whole—increasing wealth at one 'pole' while increasing misery and desperation at the other 'pole.' . . . The masses of people in the oppressed countries, in the East bloc and increasingly in the Western imperialist states as well, are being propelled into struggle against the ruling classes. This is because, as Mao put it, 'Wherever there is oppression, there is resistance.' And where there is resistance people inevitably seek an ideology that will teach them whom and how to fight."

The organizations making up RIM, whose management committee is very clandestine, are minuscule in statistical terms. Nevertheless, from a doctrinaire Marxist-Leninist perspective their analysis of "revisionism" is compelling. And the pseudoscientific emphasis on the "bitter struggle" required to stamp out incipient capitalistic tendencies inherited from thousands of years of "class society" and to "transform the ways in which people interact" is as cold, ugly, and inhumane as ever it was. "Now, gods, stand up for bastards!" shouts Edmund, with legitimate cause, in Shakespeare's *King Lear*. But, as in Guzmán's invocation and obedience to a "universal law" of contradiction, Edmund has to expropriate "Nature" in order to legitimize his actions. All actions are sanctioned by service of Nature's laws.

Human nature in all its love and all its greed is not so mutable or so easily vanquished. The tens of millions of people who died under the purges of Stalin and Mao in the name of dialectical materialism were not merely of an insufficient numerical value to consolidate their leaders' power; they and the internal, ideological weakening of the subsequent regimes were proof that, to take Mao's own words, "wherever there is repression, there is resistance." And the more repression, the more resistance. Yet the ease with which Hitler united his people under a totalitarian regime not only in order to wage an expansionist international war but to exterminate a people also bears witness to man's infinite volatility. (Repression, resistance: Without the genocide there would not be a modern state of Israel.)

Shining Path's banner in Britain is held aloft by a member of one of Peru's richest and most traditional oligarchic families. Adolfo Olaechea, who is not a party member, maintains occasional contact with RIM but does not act as a party delegate. The only British groups to have been involved directly with RIM identified themselves as Communist groups from Nottingham and Stockport and, later, the Revolutionary Internationalist Contingent; however, in 1990 neither appeared among the RIM's list of signatories.

Olaechea, tall, lucid, and lively, was a Marxist militant in student organizations at the National University of San Marcos in the early 1960s before moving to Britain, where he runs an eleven-language translation service in central London. He started propaganda work in support of Shining Path at his own initiative in the early 1980s and won its backing following a visit from Enrique in 1985. He and other sympathizers of Shining Path, among whom Iranians and Palestinians were particularly visible, disrupted Latin American conferences, rallied outside the Peruvian embassy, attended May Day parades, and organized talks by militants in venues such as the Central London Polytechnic. The Peru Support Group, a well-respected body that concerns itself with Peruvian affairs generally, tended to have its activities hijacked by Olaechea and others. Miguel Azcueta, a prominent left-wing politician from Peru who faces death threats from the rebels, was heckled at one of its conferences.

In January 1991 Olaechea formed a Sun-Peru Committee, London, in what he hoped would prove to be the embryo of a Peru People's Movement once the "political will" had been generated. The Left's May Day rally in Islington saw him—carrying a red flag bearing a gold hammer and sickle—at the head of about a hundred Maoists; about one third were Latin Americans and the rest were Turks or Kurds. There was a small group belonging to the Revolutionary Vanguard, U.K., which although inspired by Mao and sympathetic to RIM was dismissed by Olaechea for confusing the "nothing-to-lose" class, or the "lumpen," with the proletariat. Apart from the Mao portraits and slogans, the dominating banner was of the Communist Party of Turkey/Marxist-Leninist. The Maoists were prevented by police from leading off the march. "I have been a lonely man in this country for many years," said Olaechea, "but it is changing—look at the fact that so many of us are here today, and they are only the very committed. People are more radical again. Latin Americans used to hate Sendero Luminoso because it was considered as spoiling the transition to democracy, but that has been shown to be a folly, an illusion. Look at Chile—Pinochet's the minister of war. It is a matter of pride for Latin Americans that Peru has not given up on the struggle for liberation, that the revolution, instead of going downhill, is climbing."

That night was the debut of the Musical Guerrilla Army, which Olaechea characterized as the Sun-Peru Committee's "central means of work" to raise funds for Shining Path's support group in Peru, People's Aid, and to bring about political awareness. A Spanish tapas bar in Richmond was serenaded with Andean folk tunes played on flutes, panpipes, guitar, drum, *charango*, and *clave* as the twelve musicians—Peruvians, Bolivians, and a Colombian—stomped and clapped in their ethnic hats, ponchos, and vests. A rattle made of llamas' toenails was shaken up and down. The music was traditional, but many of the lyrics were not. To the blissful ignorance of most people in the restaurant, they sang in Spanish, "The people's blood has a beautiful aroma, it smells like jasmine, violets, geraniums, and daisies . . . and gunpowder and dynamite, ay *carajo*, gunpowder and dynamite." The group, which was accompanied by several British hangers-on, finished off by singing, "Chairman Gonzalo, Light of the Masses . . . The blood of the people nourishes the armed struggle. . . . Victory is ours, the dawn is already rising, the rickety walls of the old order are already crashing down."

A few weeks later, the Musical Guerrilla Army, billing itself as "the new democratic music from Peru," packed out the Old White Horse in Brixton. Hundreds of people came and many were turned away at the door. Other Latin American folk artists participated; there was dancing, Peruvian food, and an exhibition of "revolutionary art." The following month, a six-hour extravaganza was organized at the Emerald Centre, Hammersmith, in homage to the "people's war" and the memory of the prison massacres. The Musical Guerrilla Army was supported

A World to Win    253

by Turkish, Kurdish, and American musicians and was filmed
by a German director. An award-winning Peruvian film, about
Shining Path and a village massacre by the army, was screened.
There was more art, more literature. An attempt by the Peruvian embassy to intervene against the show ended in ignomini-
ous failure as Olaechea lobbied the media and threatened to
bring a lawsuit. The doors were finally opened and about four
hundred people attended. Later that year, a Sun-Peru Committee was spawned in Bath.


Shining Path's potential to stimulate physical violence not only
in the poorer countries of the world but also in the rich should
not be underestimated. In seizing the ideological initiative in
what was a globally defunct Communist movement in the wake
of Mao, and in conducting a hitherto successful revolutionary
war, Abimael Guzmán has rekindled its flame. He has established a model that both bolsters the legacy of his immediate
ideological progenitor and incorporates ideas of his own that
are coherent developments within a Marxist-Leninist perspective. In the same way that the return of democracy in Peru
converted the rest of the left into "parliamentary revolutionaries," leaving the radical ground clear for Shining Path, so too
has Shining Path been strengthened internationally by perestroika itself. Pro-Soviet Communist parties have been destroyed and moderates undermined, generating a political
vacuum which Maoism, with Shining Path as its lead advocate,
is on hand to fill. Bill Tupman, a Marxist scholar, China expert,
occasional lecturer at the Junior Division of the Staff College
at the Royal School of Infantry and director of the Centre for
Police and Criminal Justice Studies at Exeter University, said
of Maoism in May 1991, "Sendero Luminoso is quite right. The
young revolutionary has only the one place to run to. And
Maoism gives people something to do: Trotskyism was about
waiting around and selling newspapers. I see it coming back in
a big way. It has all the bits of popular appeal: a step-by-step
guide to action, a sophisticated model for the study of revolutionary struggle in your own country—Mao gets into the different sorts of classes, the ways in which they interrelate, and the

contradictions within them—it is simply put over, and it is an easy way to justify being violent. Unlike the anarchists, Maoism gives you different ways of being violent against different targets. It permits compromise and pragmatism—you can make alliances."

Confessing to being "impressed and intrigued" by Abimael Guzmán's Communist scholarship, some sophisticated ideological originalities, and the overall internal coherence shown in his interview with *El Diario*, but wary of Guzmán's belief in the central importance of violence and of his apparent lack of compassion, Tupman added, "Guzmán is demonstrating it is possible to conduct a revolution without being the agent of another power. [What is dangerous abroad] is not Sendero Luminoso in practice but what it offers as an image. There are many young people out there looking for some way to channel their anger. There has been an upsurge in anarchism. I think the wheel is turning and people are getting fed up with pacifism and green issues. We are due a period of 'direct action' again. If there is large-scale social dislocation and many people end up living in shantytowns in the world, with inadequate facilities, someone who can focus revolutionary activity in those areas and give those people a sense of identity through revolutionary activity has a head start."

One year previously, an article in the *Guardian* noted that "the catalysts for violence in several of the poll tax protests" had been anarchist and Maoist groups. It said that because their crowd-incitement potential was out of proportion to their size, they were feared "both by that segment of the Left which reckons they will seize the running, and by the authorities, who do not always seem fully prepared for the action they precipitate." Their supporters were described as mostly young, often bright, disaffected college students whose message was aimed at the young homeless and jobless. "While anarchist formations such as Class War have been around since the early 1980s," the article declared, "one of the strangest ideological revivals in Britain is of Maoism."

Britain, as elsewhere in Europe, faces growing racial tensions. In May 1991 a Jewish newspaper editor was sent a pig's head through the mail. Reported anti-Semitic incidents rose fifty percent in the first half of 1990, when they had increased by forty percent over the previous year amid a general escalation in racial harassment. Also in May, the visiting New York preacher Al Sharpton called on blacks to "build a nation within a nation" and there were skirmishes after a smoke bomb was hurled into the building where he was due to speak. Meanwhile, it was reported that the Home Office estimated thirty thousand people sought political asylum in Britain in 1990, a five-hundred-percent increase in two years. Most were said by the government to be economic refugees. Police had identified forty gangs helping immigrants to steal into the country unnoticed. One case described as typical involved five Turkish nationals, themselves seeking asylum in Britain, who had arranged for more than sixty people to enter the country illegally in the past two years. The country's employment, education, and housing were already under strain. Nearly three million people were unemployed. A United Nations report, also in May 1991, showed that nearly half of British adults had not received upper secondary education (compared with the average for industrialized countries of thirty-six percent)—and that there were at least 400,000 people homeless. The report, which was cited by *The Independent on Sunday*, said there was "growing distress" in rich countries and pointed to Britain's "cardboard cities" as an example of deprivation amid affluence. It warned that life in rich countries was increasingly threatened by their consumption patterns and a "weakening" social fabric, resulting in rising crime, drug-related offenses, murder, suicide, and family breakup.

Deteriorating social and economic conditions coupled with racial tensions are the eternal breeding ground for violence. A smoke bomb in London or a firework in Nôtre Dame is, in its way, the equivalent to a car bomb in Lima, and the pig's head is analogous to the hanged dogs. Such anger is easily fueled by nationalist and liberationist political ideologies, especially if the ideology offers a hot line to universal truths as a spur toward achieving an earthly utopia, in whose pursuit all means are thereby justified and violence borders on becoming an end in itself, a spiritually quickening exercise of scientific purity in whose name personal sacrifice assumes all the ecstasy of the

Passion. Such fury, on whatever scale in whatever country, may easily be ignited by a leader with his finger on the popular pulse of a given group. Communism, particularly as preached by Mao and in the actual climate of profound political and ideological turbulence, could continue to appeal to the world's oppressed and dispossessed as a tool with which to smash the systems that condemn them to hardship and starvation. The Third World is not growing richer: Between 1979 and 1987, growth per capita in the "developing" countries shrunk by 1.7 percent, according to U.S. government figures. The World Bank's 1991 development report said that more than a billion people—a fifth of the global population—earned less than a dollar a day. Neither is it more tranquil: Business Risks International reported that there were more "terrorist" attacks in July 1991 than in any month since 1970, when the firm began tracking them. The vast majority were in the Third World; Peru was the leader, accounting for one fifth of "terrorist" attacks globally the previous year. Apart from El Salvador, the five runners-up to Peru all host members of RIM.

While Shining Path has rescued the flag of Communist revolution, the popularity of Mao Zedong has revived in China itself. Amid chronic corruption, economic corrosion, and the political and intellectual paralysis embodied by the geriatric core leadership, where the balance of power will probably only be altered by whoever dies first, Mao has come to represent clean government, a sense of purpose, and even national tradition for those who associate the present ills with the government's flirtation in the 1980s with Western culture and liberalism. Up to a tenth of the protestors at Tiananmen Square in 1989, when inflation was between thirty and forty percent, were waving Mao banners.

A *Time* magazine article in February 1991 said, "The old Chairman is more popular than at any time in the past decade. Mao badges and portraits are selling fast in some shops and stalls. Last year 900,000 people visited his birthplace in Hunan province, a record since the late 1970s when Deng Xiaoping started to initiate the economic reforms that shattered Mao's legacy. On the ninety-seventh anniversary of the Great Helmsman's birth, more than 10,000 tourists trooped to his mausoleum in Tiananmen Square to honor his memory. Recent years had only seen a trickle of visitors. . . ." Mao is beginning to be treated both as a god and as a person who lived simply. A film was planned depicting his lighter side, including his fondness for ballroom dancing. Popular feeling, forgetful of the purges during the Cultural Revolution and of the twenty million people who died during the establishing of agricultural communes in the "Great Leap Forward" of 1958–1961, could help tip the balance in favor of those in the Politburo hostile to liberal Westernization.

Shining Path has already brought about the adoption of "Maoism" by the Revolutionary Communist Party in the United States, thereby leading to greater radicalization within RIM, of which the RCP–USA is the prime organizer. A resurrection of Mao in China, even if more in name than in political and economic practice, would serve inevitably to boost Shining Path's cause internationally and to edge it toward the global ideological legitimacy for which it hankers. Although Abimael Guzmán is not believed to have met Mao Zedong, he is said by militants to have been among an élite of foreigners on a party-to-party visit who were invited to stay in China by Chu Teh, a veteran leader of the Long March and the army's Commander in Chief, in order to participate in the second wave of the Cultural Revolution. Guzmán, who reportedly refused because he was needed by the party in Peru, can claim to be a Communist of good political pedigree. And in siring the Communist Party of Peru, he has quickened the blood of what looked like a tottering beast on the edge of extinction.

If Peru is unable to secure the economic and military resources it so desperately needs, and fails to develop a well-administered, coherent, multitiered, and long-term counterinsurgency strategy that seeks to bolster its democracy and win the active support of the population, at the same time as conducting structural economic reforms to make itself a more authentically liberal and just society with which the millions of culturally alienated Indians and poor, marginalized mestizos can identify, the chances are that the state will continue to implode before Shining Path's advance. Clumsy U.S. intervention could help the rebels prosper, while a military coup or heavily stepped-up counterterror campaign would play straight into the guerrillas' hands. A 1990 report by the Rand Corporation for the State Department said, "To succeed, the army would have to kill or incarcerate Sendero Luminoso members and sympathizers faster than they could form. Such a campaign, whatever its ethical objections, is probably beyond the army's ability to carry out. . . . If the military's counter-terror campaign were pushed to its logical conclusion and Sendero proves to be as resilient and adapted as suggested . . . it could also end in a guerrilla victory."

However, cocaine may prove to be a wild card that corrodes Shining Path from within or confronts it with equally ruthless and more powerfully armed Peruvian drug barons. It might also be undermined by the government's arming of peasant militia, or *rondas*, in certain areas, although the policy could equally well backfire on the state, either because the guerrillas might obtain the weapons or because the peasants could, as is already starting to happen, use them among themselves to settle disputes and thereby generate still greater lawlessness. Nevertheless, in late 1991, there were signs that the *rondas* in parts of Ayacucho and Junín, whether armed or simply organized by the army, were posing Shining Path a significant threat, despite its reprisal massacres amid the failure of the military to offer the *rondas* consistent protection.

The bitterest blow to the rebels would be the premature death of Abimael Guzmán, who in 1994 will be sixty years old. But the circumstances could turn him into a martyr and there may be someone equally capable waiting in the wings. Meanwhile, the rebels are building patiently toward a moment when their armed forces might openly take on, infiltrate, and subvert those of the state at the same time as there is a general, popular insurrection in Lima. That exceedingly difficult moment, if there were no economic turnaround, might only be a few years away.

Perhaps the greatest service the rest of the world could offer the Peruvian state would be to forgive its public debts. If the government were released of a burden that prohibits it paying even the most meager of wages to the public sector, sapping its will and self-respect—in June 1991 the average teacher was taking home about $85 per month and an army general $250 amid soaring costs of living—the state would be helped to carry through far-reaching liberal reforms, recover its support, and finance the development of its pitiful infrastructure as well as the all-embracing counterinsurgency strategy it requires.

The United States saw fit to cancel seventy percent of official U.S.-Polish debt as a signal of its commitment to Poland's national security and not just its economy. Egypt was forgiven its $8.4 billion military-hardware debt in repayment for its support in the Gulf War. Peru merits similar treatment. It may seem a far corner of the world whose governments in the last few decades have shunned the United States and the developed countries of the Western bloc as well as rough-handling international creditors. However, not only are those problems very much of the West's own making—through exploitative policies, bad lending, and protectionist practices—but Peru's economic torment has already generated a cholera epidemic that has spread across the Latin American continent and could easily advance elsewhere. That same economic suffering propels Shining Path, whose existence is a threat not just to the rest of the continent but to the Third World as a whole and even, in terms of the potential that its example has to whip up physical and material violence, the richer countries themselves. The Soviet empire may have collapsed but, while hundreds of millions of people are starving, the Communists of the Revolutionary Internationalist Movement may not be dreaming when they declare: "To paraphrase the writer Mark Twain, 'The rumors of my death have been greatly exaggerated.' "

# Epilogue

It was a Sunday morning in early spring. As the dogs rolled with their legs in the air on the dusty, baked brown earth, and cockerels shrieked intermittently from among the neatly aligned adobe brick huts, every eighty yards across the compound little groups of men, women, and children were intently digging holes. In some of them, electricity poles had already been erected and their bases filled in with cement. The community of Raucana, a settlement of about twelve hundred people on the eastern edge of Lima, was engaged in an *ayni*, an ancient Indian tradition of communal work.

At the same time, and with an equally convivial and shared sense of purpose, families were drawing water in buckets from the seventy-five-foot wells they had dug in each of the community's seven sectors and which took pride of place in the center of each sector's patterned pebble square. As they did every Sunday, they were sweeping and cleaning everything, including the public lavatories they had constructed, and irrigating their communally organized gardens of bananas, sweet potatoes, onions, peas, and flowers. Meanwhile, men without any income were hard at work for themselves in Raucana's quarries. Hundreds of adobe bricks, molded in wooden boxes, were drying in the sun; four thousand bricks, enough for a typical dwelling on a 950-square-foot lot, could be bought for just $45.

Unusual for a shantytown, whose inhabitants invaded the land on Independence Day in July 1989, no land was being set aside for a chapel. And although the central clearing had a flagpole in the center, no flag was flying. Inhabitants talked with pride of how Raucana's discipline and organization, incomparable with other shantytowns, were the keys to its success. The deputy secretary general, Rene Subia, explained that thieves, wife-beaters, prostitutes, drunks, and drug addicts were whipped after "people's trials" in which they were denounced and underwent self-criticism.

"We make them see their errors before punishing them, as an example to others," he said. Sipping *chicha*—a traditional Indian brew containing fermented corn and quinoa—Subia invoked the "Inca laws against thieves, liars, and sluggards" and continued, "After a first offense, a delinquent may be sentenced to forced labor or receive four lashes from each sector; if he continues to offend, he is expelled." Raucana, which is in a zone that used to be known as Little Chicago, is free of crime.

Later, sitting on an adobe bench inside a semi-built, roofless communal kitchen, the acting secretary general, Félix Cóndor, described how each sector contained between sixty and eighty homes and was organized by a committee elected not by votes but by "popular will" because "to vote was to traffic in reality." The sector committees comprised five members: secretaries for organization/discipline, work, and economy, as well as the deputy delegate and delegate to Raucana's central board, which in turn comprised the full delegates and five secretaries, including one for defense, as well as the secretary general and his deputy.

"All our achievements have been made without outside help because that brings with it political obligations," he added. "Also, if development is the fruit of the people's own sacrifice, they care for it better. There is no Christian church presence because we are still in formation and religion is like a drug, it holds you back. Once we are ready, any church can enter— people are free to believe what they want."

As soccer players started to emerge on the field beside the perimeter wall, which had been built before the settlers came, gun bolts clicked and a few moments later, soldiers stomped past, chanting antiterrorist slogans. They came from the army camp that had been set up in Raucana three months earlier. The army's presence had followed a series of clashes with police and hired thugs who had tried unsuccessfully to oust the settlers from the land which its Italian-born owner, Teoldo Isola, was fighting to recover. ("He came after the Second World War and got hold of the land through a swindle," said Cóndor. "The people have regained what is rightfully theirs.")

To protect their land seizure from attack, the community had built watchtowers, dug trenches outside, and fought off their attackers using catapults, *huaraca* slings, burning tires, and Molotov cocktails. Dozens were wounded and one man, Félix Raucana, was shot dead, giving the settlement a martyr after whom to name itself. With the army's arrival, three people were jailed; five more allegedly disappeared after detention. Following the explosion of a car bomb outside his factory, Isola withdrew his eviction demand and Raucana's leaders were finally recognized officially by the local council of Vitarte. "Isola was bribing all the authorities," said Subia. "We are prepared to do anything for this land and this community we have built. We had no choice but to win it with military means and, if forced to, we will defend it again in the same way."

Along with the army came prostitution, theft, and destruction. Girls were brought in at night and paid for their services in a hut beside the soccer field. Soldiers stole windowframes and doors for firewood and trampled on the collective kitchen gardens. In a much-publicized bid to win over the "hearts and minds" of the settlers through "civil action," the army had once distributed rice—which proved to be rotten. Meanwhile, the secretary general, Valentin Cachas, a fruit seller, had been arrested by the army while carrying dynamite and a walkie-talkie; he alleged that he had found it beside his hut and was getting rid of it before he was accused of being a terrorist.

Later that same Sunday, a fifteen-year-old boy, whose brother had been among those jailed, was forcefully invited by some soldiers to have a drink with them. When he returned, he told his friends that they believed he was a terrorist and were pressuring him to name others. A few days later his body was found less than a mile away on a garbage dump, with three bullets in the head and the fingernails missing. Soldiers fired in the air to quell the ensuing disorder on the streets of the town as the maddened settlers hurled stones and accused them of his murder.

At Jhonny Rafael's burial, there was no blessing or reading from the Bible. Instead, after leading a funeral procession of several hundred people to the municipal cemetery, Félix Cóndor proclaimed at the top of his voice before the flower-strewn coffin, "They say we are terrorists because, in this land, he who has the most economic power is he who rules, because he who does not have anything is worth nothing. The law, the political constitution of the state, serves only for those who have money, but for those who do not have money, the justice is not justice, it is a tremendous injustice. The terrorists are those who kill us with hunger every day. The terrorists are those who give us a minimum wage that is not even enough to pay for a grave or the most miserable of food; those are the terrorists."

Raising his voice still higher, Cóndor shouted, "Jhonny Rafael Veliz, who-oo killed him?"

"The genocidal army!" roared the crowd.

"Who-oo killed him?"

"The genocidal army!"

"Who-oo will revenge him?"

"The peo-ple of Peru!"

"Who-oo will revenge him?"

"The peo-ple of Peru!"

A note was distributed by Raucana's leaders. It concluded, "This is the so-called 'civil action,' more repression and genocide for the people. Those responsible are the Fujimori government and its armed forces and police who, in collusion with all the Reaction, are executing the sinister plans of Yankee imperialism in order to detain the uncontrollable advance which is displaying its brilliant development in broad daylight."

Orchestrated with great subtlety and even anonymity, Raucana is Shining Path's first "liberated area" in the Peruvian capital. The party has directed the settlers' land struggle and created a model community while keeping its banner discreet. Existing under the very noses of the army in late 1991, Raucana is an embryo of the People's Republic of New Democracy.

# Afterword

Nineteen ninety-two was a watershed year in the Peruvian war. On April 5, President Alberto Fujimori seized dictatorial powers in dissolving Congress and suspending the constitution. The judiciary was "reorganized" in order to enable the president to insert his own appointees. Fujimori claimed that Congress was blocking his economic reforms as well as his counterinsurgency policy when, in fact, Congress had mostly supported his free-market reforms and had given him extraordinary legislative powers to achieve them. And far from just rejecting the president's ill-considered counterinsurgency measures, a remarkable all-party consensus in Congress had remolded the measures into the most coherent counterinsurgency package ever passed.

The seizure of dictatorial powers by Fujimori, who promised to restore democracy within eighteen months, came with the full backing of the armed forces. While it united the political establishment against him—many leading politicians were initially placed under house arrest for their "protection," and former president Alan García eventually fled the country after spending two days hiding in an empty water tank—the move was welcomed by the huge majority of Peruvians. They had no love for the corrupt Congress and seemed forever ready to pin their hopes on an authoritarian figure promising short-term miracles. Thus, the president's legitimacy came to rest solely on opinion polls.

Amid international credit sanctions, widening discontent

with the ever bleaker state of the economy, and the draconian application of the free-market reforms, and in the wake of futile, clandestine attempts by the former Congress to swear in two other presidents in his place, Fujimori needed to keep pulling rabbits out of a hat to maintain his momentum. At a time when Shining Path had finally brought about the demise of democracy and Peru's political parties were in complete disarray, the Maoists were jostling to present themselves as the only effective opposition to the dictatorial regime. As Fujimori's opinion poll ratings started to falter, events moved fast.

In late April, the *El Diario* newspaper was closed down and twenty-four workers arrested. In early May, some of those workers were among the approximately fifty Shining Path prisoners massacred in Miguel Castro Castro after resisting their transfer to other jails. Among the dead were important party members as well as Janet Talavera and Elvia Zanábria, my main contacts with Shining Path's organization. (Another acquaintance, Jorge Cartagena, a pro–Shining Path lawyer, was machine-gunned in his office in Lima.) In June, the leader of the MRTA guerrillas, Víctor Polay, was rearrested.

Prior to Fujimori's *autogolpe* or "self-coup," Shining Path had been stepping up its campaign in the capital's shantytown for several months. One killing that captured international attention was that of María Elena Moyano, a charismatic *morena* or mulatto who, as deputy mayor in the district of Villa El Salvador, had taken a very public stand against Shining Path. During an "armed strike" ordered by the rebels and that paralyzed much of Lima, she led a few hundred people out of the half a million residents of Villa El Salvador in a peace march defying the Maoists. The following day she was shot dead in front of her children, and her corpse was blown up with dynamite. Considering local custom and the size of the municipality, the attendance at her funeral of approximately six thousand people was alarmingly low.

The crescendo of rebel violence in Lima that began in early May, which coincided with a resurgence of reports throughout the country of suspected guerrillas being taken away by the security forces, came to a head in July when Sendero unleashed another ferocious campaign in the build-up to Independence Day. An armed strike, the most violent and effective yet, paralyzed much of Lima for two days. Few police and military patrols were visible on the streets, and in spite of the night curfew and the greater freedom Fujimori had given the security forces, the guerrillas were able to coordinate sustained and serious bomb attacks. Working in platoons of fifty to a hundred, the rebels targeted police stations in the shantytowns and, in one instance, it was reported that police reinforcements approaching a police station under attack were fired upon and driven back. Lima was witnessing Shining Path's military preparations for full-scale insurrection.

Powerful car bombs were deployed with increasing regularity. One car bomb that exploded in the rich, residential district of Miraflores killed 25 people and wounded more than 140, destroying some apartment buildings. Together with the curfew and the now almost nightly electricity blackouts, it finally made Lima's upper classes realize that they had a war on their hands. When President Fujimori, looking increasingly isolated, unexpectedly failed to attend either the principal diplomatic ceremony of the year or the Cathedral mass on Independence Day, rumors that he was about to be cast aside by the military reached a fever pitch.

An apocalyptic scenario seemed ready to unfold. Enrique Obando, the security analyst at the Peruvian Center for International Studies, said: "You could suddenly see businesses preparing to close, and people leaving the country and taking their money with them. If the pressure had been maintained, it would have led to the collapse of banks and government revenue, with no money to pay the army or other state workers, a massive loss of jobs, and a collapse in services as well as law and order. The state would have been at the mercy of Shining Path."

Meanwhile, the rebels announced that they were preparing to move into the third phase of its war, the "strategic offensive." As its strength in the shantytowns became more and more manifest, with uncooperative community leaders being killed regularly, the rebels began to plan a major offensive against national elections in November for what was to be called the Democratic Constituent Congress. The Constituent Congress's task would be to draw up a new constitution prior to fresh congressional elections at an unspecified date; the municipal and regional elections in November had been postponed. The political parties protested bitterly but vainly as the president sought to lay ground rules for the Constituent Congress that they feared would become nothing but a rubber-stamp body for his dictatorship. Fujimori, in turn, feared it might throw him out of power.

Then, on the night of Saturday, September 12, Abimael Guzmán was arrested by police in Lima. Detectives of the antiterrorist unit, DINCOTE (formerly DIRCOTE), had moved in on a modern, two-story building in the middle-class district of Surco, which borders Miraflores, after discovering medicine for psoriasis, the skin disease from which Guzmán suffers, and cigarette stubs of a brand known to be favored by him in the house's rubbish: It was a breathtaking victory following weeks of painstaking, poorly paid surveillance work.

The house was rented by Maritza Garrido-Lecca, a ballerina and the niece of Nelly Evans, the former nun who had been arrested in January. While Maritza Garrido-Lecca and her husband, Carlos Incháustegui, an architect, lived on the ground floor, where they had a dance studio and office, Guzmán lived upstairs with his lover, Elena Iparraguirre. The police, who fired into the air as they entered the house—one of them shooting himself in the foot—met with no resistance. Along with Guzmán and Iparraguirre, Laura Zembrano, a leader of the Lima metropolitan committee, and María Pantoja, who was believed to be Guzmán's secretary and in charge of his computer, were also arrested. Zembrano and Pantoja had bedrooms on the roof terrace. Two visitors, Celso Garrido-Lecca, Maritza's uncle and a prominent Peruvian composer acquainted with Mario Vargas Llosa, and a girlfriend of Garrido-Lecca's, Patricia Awapara, were detained as well: They were innocent.

Guzmán was working at his desk when the officers entered. Iparraguirre and Zembrano reportedly threw themselves in front of him, the former grabbing Shining Path's flag and singing "The International," the Communist anthem. Centrally placed on top of a nearby bookcase was a human skull. The head of DINCOTE, General Antonio Vidal, came in shortly afterward. Despite a video recording of their meeting, it was instantly mythologized. Guzmán was reported to have said: "Sometimes you win, sometimes you lose. This time I lose." His actual words were, pointing a finger at his head: "You can take anything away from a man, except what he has here. This cannot be removed [from a man] even if he is killed. And even if they do kill him, the rest [of his followers] will remain." In one of his pockets there was a badge featuring Mao Zedong. He was permitted to keep it. No weapons were found in the house.

Guzmán was taken to the police headquarters in Lima, where an army colonel from military intelligence arrived to request that he be handed over to the armed forces. According to colleagues of General Vidal, the general refused, for fear that Guzmán might be shot out of hand and made into a martyr. One supporter of Shining Path described Vidal as behaving "like a gentleman."

On Sunday night, President Fujimori went on television to present selected video images of a tubby, fifty-seven-year-old Guzmán without his shirt and fumbling with his trouser buttons. Despite the attempt at public humiliation by the president —unwise in a country where people are inclined to sympathize with the victim of such treatment, whatever his crimes—Guzmán displayed considerable poise and dignity. The bespectacled "Red Sun," sporting a roughly trimmed gray beard and looking around him a little quizzically, like a mole emerging from the ground and blinking in the sunlight, appeared perfectly relaxed.

The country was swept by euphoria. Shares leaped on the stock exchange, national flags were hung and, in Miraflores, spontaneous celebrations broke out in the streets. Meanwhile, President Fujimori called for Guzmán to receive the death penalty, which was technically only applicable in cases of treason during an external war. He went on to suggest that the government would abide by the will of "the people" as to whether it be carried out. While graffiti appeared in Lima's shantytowns, universities, and poorer districts throughout the country calling for the life of "Chairman Gonzalo" to be defended, it was announced that Guzmán would face a military tribunal. The verdict was handed down on October 7; the date for an appeal and sentencing by the Supreme Military Justice Council was set for three weeks later. Guzmán's likely fate would be lifetime imprisonment at the naval base on the island of San Lorenzo off the Lima coast.

Guzmán's capture will probably mean that Shining Path will never take power. He has been both the head and body of the revolution and has been given a semi-divine status by many of his followers. His arrest will be a massive blow to morale. It is unlikely that anybody else can inspire the same level of self-sacrifice or command the same fanatical and self-purifying ideological discipline. Without these, Shining Path's remarkable organic unity will suffer. It is also difficult to imagine a new leadership possessing Guzmán's awesome capacity for political, military, strategic, and tactical planning.

However, insofar as it has demythologized Guzmán, his arrest has also converted the Communist Party of Peru into a more tangible, public force. His physical presence brings it onto the center stage both within Peru and internationally. Were he, for instance, to be condemned to death, the world's leading human rights groups would wage a campaign clamoring against the sentence and Shining Path would be granted a propaganda coup; the fairness of the military tribunal is already in public dispute in Peru and abroad although nobody disputes Guzmán's guilt. It is as though the veil of myth and mystery surrounding Shining Path's origins and objectives has somehow been lifted, thereby exposing it as a radical but arguably orthodox Communist organization instead of a messianic Andean movement with almost supernatural overtones. Through his pro–Shining Path defense lawyer, Alfredo Crespo, Guzmán will enjoy a public platform for his statements.

Ironically, a few months prior to Guzmán's capture, an internal, draft party document entitled "Between Two Hills" was circulated that indicated that a big defeat for the party might be a painful prerequisite for stronger growth. One Shining Path activist said: "The party's controlled response to the arrest of Chairman Gonzalo, its issuing of the correct slogans afterward, and refusal to be provoked into a wild backlash proves the party is well built and can take the most severe punishment. The chairman's arrest will make no difference to the conquest of power. All the guidelines are already laid."

The violence is likely to continue for a long time. Shining Path's plans are laid out months, if not years, in advance, and have the active support of tens of thousands of people. Even if the organization's discipline breaks down, the violence may become more random, as well as desperate. Factions may develop, too—particularly in the coca-growing areas where allegiance to Chairman Gonzalo could rapidly switch to the more earthly god of Mammon. The evolving of different factions would finish off Shining Path as a strategic threat to the Peruvian state, but as a multiheaded beast it could still inflict considerable social, political, and economic damage.

Meanwhile, despite President Fujimori's efforts to turn Peru into a model of free-market virtue, the majority of Peruvians remain as poor and as ethnically discriminated against as always while the state remains corrupt. With Fujimori's candidate list for the Democratic Constituent Congress now looking invincible he is granting this body greater autonomy in the knowledge that it will support him. Whether it succeeds in drawing up a modern constitution that brings about true democracy in the Western sense, seeking to incorporate the millions of Peruvians alienated from the state, is another story.

London
September 23, 1992

*Post Scriptum*

Guzmán was condemned to life imprisonment by hooded judges on October 7, 1992, although the threat of execution still hung over him. Meanwhile, before his trial, he had been presented to journalists in a cage. Dressed in a black-and-white-striped "convict's" suit, he declared that Shining Path was to go ahead as planned with its sixth military campaign.

November 18, 1992

# Bibliography

## Books

Adrianzén, Alberto (ed.). *Pensamiento Político Peruano 1930–1968.* Centro de Estudios y Promoción del Desarrollo, Lima, 1990.

Anderson, James. *Terrorism in Peru. Sendero Luminoso: A New Revolutionary Model?* Institute for the Study of Terrorism, U.K., 1987.

Ansion, Jean-Marie. *Desde el Rincón de los Muertos, El Pensamiento Mítico en Ayacucho.* Grupo de Estudios para el Desarrollo, Lima, 1987.

Arce Borja, Luis (ed.). *Guerra Popular an El Perú: El Pensamiento Gonzalo.* Brussels, 1989.

Ayala, José Luis. *Pacha Mama.* Editorial Juan Mejía Baca, Lima, 1986.

Belden, Jack. *China Shakes the World.* Penguin/Pelican Books, London, 1973.

Blanco, Hugo. *Land or Death: The Peasant Struggle in Peru.* Pathfinder Press, New York, 1977.

Burga, Manuel. *Los Profetas de la Rebelión (1919–1923).* In *Estados y Regiones en los Andes.* Instituto Frances de Estudios Andinos, Lima, 1986.

———. *Nacimiento de una Utopía, Muerte y Resurrección de los Incas.* Instituto de Apoyo Agrario, Lima, 1988.

*The Cambridge Encyclopedia of Latin America and the Caribbean*. Cambridge University Press, U.K., 1965.

Centro de Estudios y Promoción del Desarrollo. *Violencia Política en el Perú, 1980–1988*, vols. I and II. DESCO Publicaciones, Lima, 1989.

Congreso de la República. *La Barbarie no se Combate con la Barbarie: Dictamen en Mayoría de la Comisión Investigadora del Congreso del Perú sobre los Sucesos Acaecidos el 18 y 19 de Junio de 1986 en los Penales de Lurigancho, El Frontón y Santa Bárbara*. Atlantida S.A., Lima, 1987.

Degregori, Carlos Iván. *Ayacucho 1969–1979: El Surgimiento de Sendero Luminoso*. Instituto de Estudios Peruanos, Lima, 1990.

————. *Que Difícil es Ser Dios: Ideología y Violencia Política en Sendero Luminoso*. El Zorro de Abajo Ediciones, Lima, 1990.

Díaz Martinez, Antonio. *Ayacucho: Hambre ye Esperanza*. Mosca Azul Editores, Lima, 1985.

Duviols, Pierre. *Cultura Andina y Represión: Procesos y Visitas de Idolatrías y Hechicerías Cajatambo Siglo XVII*. Centro Bartolomé de Las Casas, Cuzco, 1986.

Fernández Salvatteci, José. *¡Que No lo Sepa Nadie!* Editorial Patria Libre, Lima, 1979.

Flores Galindo, Alberto. *Buscando un Inca*. Instituto de Apoyo Agrario, Editorial Horizonte, Lima, 1988.

García Sayín, Diego (ed.). *Coca, Cocaína y Narcotráfico: Laberinto en los Andes*. Comisión Andina de Juristas, Lima, 1989.

Gorriti Ellenbogen, Gustavo. *Sendero: Historia de la Guerra Milenaria en el Perú*, Vol. I. Apoyo S.A., Lima, 1990.

Gott, Richard. *Rural Guerrillas in Latin America*. Penguin/Pelican Books, London, 1973.

Gutierrez, Gustavo. *Teología de la Liberación: Perspectivas*. Centro de Estudios y Publicaciones, Lima, 1990.

Gutierrez, Miguel. *La Generación del 50: Un Mundo Dividido*. Ediciones Setimo Ensayo 1, Lima, 1988.

Hemming, John. *The Conquest of the Incas*. Harvest/HBJ, New York, 1970.

*The Holy Bible* (New International Version). Hodder and Stoughton, London, 1978.

*The Holy Bible for the Family.* Longmans, Green and Co., London, 1958.

Loayza, Francisco. *Juan Santos, el Invencible.* Asociación Editora Los Pequeños Grandes Libros de Historia Americana, Lima, 1942.

Mariátegui, José Carlos. *Siete Ensayos de Interpretación de la Realidad Peruana.* Empresa Editora Amauta, Lima, 1989.

Marzal, Manuel. *La Transformación Religiosa Peruana.* Fondo Editorial de la Pontificia Universidad Católica del Perú, Lima, 1988.

McCormick, Gordon. *The Shining Path and the Future of Peru.* Rand Corporation, Santa Monica, Calif., 1990.

Mejía, Feliciano. *Kantuta Negra: Poesía para la Liberación.* Amaro Ediciones, Lima, 1990.

Mercado, Roger. *El APRA, el PCP y Sendero Luminoso.* Fondo de Cultura, Lima, 1985.

———. *El Partido Comunista del Perú: Sendero Luminoso.* Librerias Studium–La Universidad, Lima, 1986.

Morote Best, Efraín. *Aldeas Sumergidas: Cultura Popular y Sociedad en los Andes.* Centro de Estudios Rurales Andinos Bartolomé de las Casas, Cuzco, 1988.

Ossio, Juan (ed.). *Ideología Mesiánica del Mundo Andino.* Edición de Ignacio Prado Pastor, Lima, 1973.

Ossio, Juan. *Violencia Estructural en el Perú: Antropología.* Asociación Peruana de Estudios e Investigación para la Paz, Lima, 1990.

Palomino, Salvador. *El Sistema de Oposiciones en la Comunidad de Sarhua.* Consejo Indio de Sud América, Lima, 1988.

Pease, Franklin. *El Dios Creador Andino.* Mosca Azul Editores, Lima, 1973.

Pedraglio, Santiago. *Seguridad Democratica Integral: Armas para la Paz.* Instituto de Defensa Legal, Lima, 1990.

Poma, Huamán. *Nueva Crónica y Buen Gobierno.* Instituto de Apoyo Agrario y Ediciones Rikchay Perú, Lima, 1990.

Roldán, Julio. *Gonzalo El Mito.* Consejo Nacional de Ciencia y Tecnología, Lima, 1990.

Rowe, John. *El Movimiento Nacional Inca del Siglo XVIII.* In *Túpac Amaru II: 1780.* Lima, 1976.

Testimonios Evangélicos. *Entre el Dolor y la Esperanza.* Concilio Nacional Evangélico del Perú, Lima, 1989.

Tse Tung, Mao. *Cinco Tésis Filosóficas.* Imprenta Editores Tipo-Offset, Lima, 1987.

## Newspaper and Magazine Articles

Arce Borja, Luis, and Talavera, Janet. "Presidente Gonzalo Rompe el Silencio." *El Diario* (Lima), July 24, 1988.

Cunningham, John. "Poll Tax (The Riot Aftermath): Shadowy Source of Violent Revolt." *Guardian*, April 2, 1990.

Curátola, M. "Mito y Milenarismo en los Andes: Del Taki Onqoy a Inkarri, la Visión del Pueblo Invicto." *Allpanchis* (Cuzco), 10 (1977), 65–92.

Gellhorn, Martha. "Future Leaders of Deutschland." *Telegraph* magazine, May, 11, 1991.

González, Raúl. "MRTA: La Historia Desconocida." *Que Hacer* (Lima), 51 (1988).

Gorriti Ellenbogen, Gustavo. "Terror in the Andes: The Flight of the Asháninkas." *The New York Times Magazine*, December 2, 1990.

Nicholson-Lord, David. "UN Raps Britain's Quality of Life." *The Independent on Sunday*, May 19, 1991.

Shakespeare, Nicholas. "In Pursuit of Guzmán." *Granta*, Spring 1985.

Ascherson, Neal. "The Prince and the Paupers." *The Independent*, May 5, 1991.

FlorCruz, Jaime, and Turner, Mia. "How Now, Old Mao? He's Back." *Time*, February 18, 1991.

## Reports and Unpublished Studies

Ames, Rolando (ed.). *Informe al Congreso sobre los Sucesos de los Penales, Comisión Investigadora.* Talleres Gráficos OCISA, Lima, 1988.

Ansion, Jean-Marie. *Le Sentier Lumineux et la Pensée Andine.* Lovaina, 1984.

González, Raúl. *Abimael Guzmán: Datos Bibliográficos, la Teoría del Espacio, el Derecho a la Rebelión.* DESCO, Lima, 1984.

Portocarrero, Gonzalo. *La Dominación Total.* Universidad Católica, Lima, 1978.

Senado de la Republica. *Diez Años de Violencia en el Perú, Informe 1990.* Senado, Lima, 1991.

————. *Violencia y Pacificación, Informe General.* Senado, Lima, 1988.

Servicio de Inteligencia Nacional. *Abimael Guzmán: Una Aproximación a Su Vida y Pensamiento Político.* Lima, 1984.

# Index

277